One Party
Country

One Party Country

The Republican Plan for Dominance in the 21st Century

TOM HAMBURGER
AND
PETER WALLSTEN

WILEY

John Wiley & Sons, Inc.

Published by John Wiley & Sons, Inc., Hoboken, New Jersey
Published simultaneously in Canada

Design and composition by Navta Associates, Inc.

For general information about our other products and services, please contact our Customer Care Department within the United States at (800) 762-2974, outside the United States at (317) 572-3993 or fax (317) 572-4002.

Wiley also publishes its books in a variety of electronic formats. Some content that appears in print may not be available in electronic books. For more information about Wiley products, visit our web site at www.wiley.com.

Library of Congress Cataloging-in-Publication Data:

Hamburger, Tom, date.
  One party country : the Republican plan for dominance in the 21st country /
Tom Hamburger and Peter Wallsten.
    p. cm.
  Includes bibliographical references and index.
  ISBN: 978-0-470-12858-9

  1. Republican Party (U.S. : 1854–   ) 2.   Political parties—United States. 3.   Politics, Practical—United States. 4.   United States—Politics and government—2001–
I. Wallsten, Peter, date. II. Title.
  JK2356.H35 2006
  324.2734—dc22

                                                                            2005036100

Printed in the United States of America

10 9 8 7 6 5 4 3 2 1

CONTENTS

ACKNOWLEDGMENTS

This book, by two reporters at one newspaper, would not have been possible without the generous support, encouragement, and sacrifice from multiple corners of that newspaper, the *Los Angeles Times*.

We offer thanks first to our coworkers in the *Times*'s Washington bureau who covered for us and counseled us through the past year.

This effort started with words of guidance—and a grant of time—from our bureau chief, Doyle McManus. His deputy, Tom McCarthy, worked the levers of the bureau and the paper to make the project possible.

At a critical moment they suggested we consult with Richard Cooper, a senior editor at the *Times*, who is both a critical thinker and a gifted wordsmith. Dick worked his magic on our rough prose, and his efforts, often on weekends and squeezed in between other projects and out-of-town hockey games, made this a far better book.

Aaron Zitner and Don Woutat, our Washington desk editors, dramatically improved several initial stories that formed the basis for key parts of this book. Colleagues on the White House beat, Ed Chen, Warren Vieth, and Jim Gerstenzang, paid a steep price for our distraction—and they did so with generosity and class.

Those reporters, along with several others at the *Times* and other news organizations, helped us understand how to write about this administration and its operation. In addition to the White House team, the other reporters who worked with us on individual stories cited in this volume include Alan C. Miller, who helped reveal the role that GOP corporate backers played in making and influencing policy. In addition, the authors wish to thank Nicholas Riccardi, Julie Cart, Maura Reynolds, Janet Hook, Sonni Efron, and Henry Weinstein. The Washington bureau's former office manager, Alison McIntyre, provided logistical and psychological support throughout the year, as did the paper's technology experts, Phil Ruiz and Jim Robinson.

This largeness of spirit—and the consistent interest in diving deep into the stories of our time—reflects the priorities at the helm of a great newspaper. Our thanks to those at the top—Dean Baquet, John Carroll, Scott Kraft, and Doug Frantz.

We are indebted to several readers, commentators, other holders of strong opinions whose feedback and support proved crucial: Bill Adair; Ellie Hamburger; Eric Black; Lawrence Jacobs; Bruce Freed; Mike Hamburger; Tom, Sharon, and Scott Wallsten; Jen Sermoneta; Tania Ralli; and an executive branch official who examined our manuscript in great detail yet asked to be unnamed. Mike Wakeford weighed in from Chicago with crucial impressions and opinions that could only come from a Chapel Hill native and blog aficionado. Stacey Bosshardt offered keen and witty insights into the evolving fortunes of the conservative movement and baked the occasional tasty brisket. Thanks to Brad Snyder for his legal expertise and author commiseration and Leora Kahn for advice on book promotion and Web design.

Researching a book about Republicans in power demands a lot from Republicans in power, particularly at a time when openness and transparency are not valued in that world. We wish to think those who helped us, particularly those public-spirited staffers who took our calls, arranged interviews (or tried to arrange them), and provided documents, PowerPoint presentations, and inside perspectives.

The senior staff of the Bush White House did not cooperate in the preparation of this book, but the staff in the press office was, as always, friendly, good-natured, and professional. We owe a special debt to some present and former administration and party officials who took time to explain the intricacies of the executive branch, the White House, the Republican Party, the Bush family, or just politics in general. In addition, there were those who were frequent visitors to that world or who have studied it closely. We include in this broad category: Stanton Anderson, Michael Baroody, Sally Bradshaw, Deborah Burstion-Donbraye, Chris Butler, Mike Casey, John Milton Cooper Jr., Valerie Ervin, Ben Ginsberg, Todd Harris, David Johnson (the one in Tallahassee), Brian Jones, Larry Kanter, Adam Levine, Paul Light, Bill Patterson, the Reverend Eugene Rivers, Justin Sayfie, Eric Schaeffer, Tracey Schmitt, Darrell Shull, Beth Solomon, Andrew Stern, Cory Tilley, Dirk Van Dongen, Patricia Westwater, and Adrian Wooldridge. Several former colleagues and current friends deserve credit for providing us entrée into the rarified realm of the Bush family operations in Washington, Texas, and Florida, and working with us on many of the stories that filtered their way into the thinking behind this book. Others have served as important sounding boards for ideas. We thank John Harwood, Jerry Seib, Alan Murray, Glenn Simpson, and Phil Kuntz at the *Wall Street Journal*, along with Lesley Clark at the *Miami Herald* and Lucy Morgan and Tim Nickens at the *St. Petersburg Times*, Diane Roberts of many affiliations, Manuel Roig-Franzia at the *Washington Post*, Brian Crowley at the *Palm Beach Post*, and Johanna Neuman, Deborah Nelson, Mark Mazzetti, and Bob Drogin at the *Los Angeles Times*.

The authors believe that their work on this project was split evenly. But we cannot overstate the role of a third reporter, Benjamin Weyl, a Grinnell College student and former research intern at the *Los Angeles Times*. Ben helped investigate several initial stories and fact-checked the entire manuscript. Another former intern, Emma Schwartz, provided research assistance for an initial story on the White House faith-based initiative. Our understanding of this area was aided greatly by conversations with Representative Chet Edwards and his staff, Robert Wineburg, and Anne Farris and the staff of the Roundtable on Religion and Social Welfare Policy. Steven Hill provided an important private tutorial on the Republican edge in winner-take-all electoral politics.

Joe Garcia and Noam Neusner offered thoughtful insights into the increasingly complicated worlds of Latino and Jewish politics, respectively.

This book was launched, literally, by our literary agent, Sandra Dijkstra, who also emerged as an editor, a provocateur, and a friend. We were helped throughout by Sandy and her colleagues, including Elise Capron and Kevan Lyon.

Our editor at Wiley, Eric Nelson, has our deep gratitude. He believed in this project from the outset, shaped it in its early days, and continued to guide us in important ways throughout the process. Thanks, as well, to Kimberly Monroe-Hill, the production editor at Wiley, who was both rigorous and flexible in her zeal to publish this work in a timely fashion, despite several revisions requested by the authors.

Our deepest debt is to our families and friends, who endured our wildly changing moods and around-the-clock working—but did so with humor and only occasional expressions of regret. It must be said that Ellie was somehow always upbeat, willing to read and reread manuscript drafts, even while practicing medicine, cooking gourmet meals, and keeping an often disheveled half of this author team on track.

This book is dedicated to Tom's children, Lily and Ben, a continual source of inspiration for their dad, and to Peter's parents, Tom and Sharon, and brother Scott, who nurtured and enabled a political junkie's addiction from early on and later never doubted success in the face of life's obstacles.

Introduction

One night a few months after President George W. Bush and the Republican Party declared a euphoric victory in the 2004 elections, the new chairman of the GOP drove to the Washington suburb of Largo, Maryland, for his first public speech as party leader. He could have picked any venue for this appearance, and it was not happenstance that on this February night he chose a Black History Month celebration in predominantly black Prince George's County. As recently as the 1970s, PG County, as it's called, had been mostly white and rural, a backwater still marked by the attitudes and customs of the Old South. By the turn of the century, however, it had turned overwhelmingly black, and was home to a large and upwardly ambitious black middle class. Fresh, well-groomed subdivisions had sprung up, more than a few with their own McMansions and stylish shopping plazas. Moreover, one of the county's residents, Michael Steele, had been elected the Republican lieutenant governor of Maryland, making him the highest-ranking elected African American Republican in the country and a favorite to win election to the U.S. Senate in 2006.

All of this was what attracted Chairman Ken Mehlman that night. It was also what led him to talk about President Bush's ideas to help workers invest their money and get rich. One aspect of the Bush plan, letting people put a portion of their social security taxes into investment accounts, would prove a hard sell to Congress and the broader public. But Mehlman had his reasons for focusing on it before this audience, which was predominantly Democratic but eager to hear a new pitch.

"These accounts are the key to the American dream," he said. "If you can't save money, if you can't build wealth, if you're living paycheck to paycheck, for the first time ever you are going to have a nest egg." The audience burst into applause. "Give us a chance," Mehlman said, standing on stage with Steele, "and we'll give you a choice."

A few days later, the equally new chairman of the Democratic National Committee, former Vermont governor Howard Dean, also gave a speech. Appearing in a downtown Washington hotel before an audience that included many African Americans, the head of the Democratic Party all but jeered at the idea of a Republican Party official trying to draw in blacks. "You think the Republican National Committee could get this many people of color in a single room?" he asked. "Only if they had the hotel staff in here." The Democrats responded with laughter and applause.[1]

Considered objectively, it was hard to see what the Democrats had to laugh about. Tears might have been more appropriate. Only a few months before, on Election Day 2004, a seven-percentage-point rise in black support for Bush in Ohio had created the cushion he needed to carry that pivotal state and secure reelection.[2] Bush had gained ground among black voters in other states as well—due in part to the work of his so-called faith-based initiative that directed millions of dollars to African American church groups and to appeals like the one delivered by Mehlman during that 2005 speech in Maryland.

Bush had also improved his showing among Latinos, Jews, young people, and blue-collar workers. The Democrats had increased their overall turnout in 2004, but Republicans had increased their turnout by much more. Even in Florida, where Al Gore four years earlier had come within 537 votes and a split decision in the Supreme Court of winning the White House, Republicans stretched their margin to a relative landslide, winning the state by more than 300,000 votes.

How could this have happened? Was it just a fluke? After all, by the spring of 2006, Republicans seemed to be teetering on the precipice. American troops were stuck in a military quagmire in Iraq years after an invasion sold to the public with arguments that ultimately proved false. Government officials bungled the response to a hurricane so devastating it wiped out an entire city. Icons of the ruling Republican Party, such as ousted GOP strongman Tom DeLay, faced criminal investigation, perhaps even jail. Poll ratings plummeted. And, in a perfect metaphor for the GOP's troubles, the vice president, who was once the rock of stability and unflappable competence in the Bush White House, accidentally shot a hunting companion in the face.

Things looked so grim for Republicans that a 1994-style political revolution seemed like a real possibility—this time returning long-suffering Democrats to power in a city dominated for more than a decade by conservatives. Suddenly, Howard Dean's confidence that his party could maintain its old coalitions and build a dominant majority for the future didn't seem so far-fetched. Democrats might well benefit from Republican woes in the immediate future, perhaps taking one or both Houses of Congress in 2006.

But as this book explains, such immediate success will not erase the years of accrued deficiencies that pushed Democrats into backbench marginalization. Instead, Democrats at the start of a new century face steep odds that could well prevent them from turning potential short-term gains into a political revolution that would restore their status as the country's leading political party.

The Republican drive for long-term dominance in national politics was never designed to rest on the short-term fortunes of George W. Bush, Dick Cheney, or Tom DeLay alone. Rather, the conservative vision reached back more than forty years. It had arisen from the ruins of Senator Barry Goldwater's crushing defeat at the hands of

President Lyndon B. Johnson. And in the years that followed Goldwater's loss, conservatives had built a political comeback on foundations so fundamental and strong that many believed no short-term success by Democrats could crack them.

The Republican Party of the early twenty-first century may perform poorly in individual elections, but it remains firmly in the lead when it comes to the science and strategy of attaining power—and keeping it. That advantage has been constructed painstakingly over decades and then, using taxpayer dollars and unprecedented politicization of government bureaucracies, strengthened dramatically under the presidency of George W. Bush.

The GOP controls every part of every element of the federal government, from the White House and the executive branch through the Senate and the House of Representatives. Seven of the nine Supreme Court justices were appointed by Republican presidents, and the court is trending increasingly conservative. A majority of governors are Republicans as well, including in the country's four biggest states of California, Texas, Florida, and New York. Conservatives can no longer credibly claim the news media are liberal. As the traditional television networks lose ground to cable, the dependably conservative Fox News routinely tops the cable ratings. And the Democrats have no one to match the likes of Rush Limbaugh, Sean Hannity, Laura Ingraham, Matt Drudge, and other conservative commentators and bloggers who define the issues of the day.

While the numbers of voters who label themselves Democrats and Republicans have remained roughly equal, the results of national elections have told a different story. Since 1994, when Republicans took over the House and the Senate, their control of Congress has rarely been seriously challenged. And by the time George W. Bush's second term ends on January 20, 2009, Republicans will have occupied the White House for twenty of the past twenty-eight years.

So pervasive and durable is the Republicans' strength, it is time to ask: is the United States becoming a one-party country?

Will Democrats slip into the status of a permanent, carping minority? Will conservatives achieve their dream of building a lasting majority?

The fortress that has put Republicans within reach of long-term dominance is not made of smoke and mirrors. It is real, built with shrewd design, mountains of money, and decades of hard work and self-discipline. The most important but least understood tenet of the GOP strategy is that its success was never predicated on a utopian notion of converting millions of voters to conservatism in some giant feat of political evangelism. Rather, it rested on structural changes and application of proven techniques that, taken together, subtly tilted the political playing field in their favor. In tangible present-day terms, this means not attempting to win the majority of, say, black voters. Instead, it means wooing enough conservative blacks, like the crowd that applauded Mehlman, to sap Democratic strength and build the conservative majority.

The GOP renaissance began with the traditional Republican base in the business community. Even in the mid-1960s, it was clear that what conservatives hoped to achieve would require money on a scale that had not been seen before—not just for campaigns but for the construction of organizations and machinery necessary to assure long-term success. Such funding could only come from the leaders of corporate America, who would fill the party's coffers on an unprecedented scale in return for national leadership that was prepared to place federal policy and decision making at their service.

Big businesses supplied more than votes and money. They supplied organizational skills and manpower accustomed to the teamwork and discipline of the corporate world. They also provided a kind of dual citizenship for individuals who wanted to work for the party but also pursue lucrative careers. On a far larger scale than their Democratic counterparts, GOP operatives could count on corporate clients for their private consulting activities or jobs with sympathetic businesses when needed—a career path, in other words, that did not require talented individuals to choose between politics and affluence.

The business world was linked to another factor that spurred the successful rise of modern conservatism: the latest knowledge, techniques, and technology from marketing, advertising, demographics, and other such fields. Republicans have generally stayed years ahead of the Democrats in harnessing computers to manage information, including the masses of data necessary for successful get-out-the-vote campaigns. In 2004, the GOP mastered the art of niche marketing: identifying and communicating with small groups of potentially sympathetic voters, then tailoring messages to fit each microconstituency down to the level of individual precincts and households.

At the same time, dating back decades, far-sighted conservatives invested in the creation of think tanks and policy institutes, and they endowed university chairs to develop new ideas, foster supportive research, and nurture the scholarly expertise necessary to compete in the intellectual marketplace. These investments ensured that conservative proposals would gain legitimacy in the expert communities that increasingly set the terms of serious policy debates. They also made conservative ideas competitive in the news media. No longer were the "experts" quoted in news reports reliably centrist or liberal. And the outpouring of conservative ideas and analyses from organizations such as the American Enterprise Institute and the Heritage Foundation infused the political right with an intellectual freshness and excitement that the left was eventually hard-pressed to match, even though liberals still dominated the faculties at the country's most prestigious universities.

The rise of an influential conservative intellectualism was an ominous development for a Democratic Party that had drawn political strength from the world of ideas. During the early years of their quest for realignment, Republican strategists leaned heavily on the so-called Southern strategy to register gains. This not-so-subtle appeal to racism and to the backlash against the Democrats' championing of civil rights turned the once-solid Democratic South into a bastion of Republicanism.

But by the 1990s, George W. Bush and others began to turn away from that approach and try to improve their party's appeal to blacks, Latinos, and other minorities using the power of ideas centered on moral values and wealth creation.

Beginning in the mid-1990s, the Republican Party also began to draw into its ranks the bulk of the nation's evangelical Christians, who had decided to enter the political arena out of concern for the excesses of popular culture and an apparent decline in traditional values. Like the business community, religious conservatives—evangelical Protestants but also tradition-minded Catholics—provided both financial support and thousands of dedicated voters. The evangelicals gave the GOP a burgeoning network of grassroots organizations and volunteers already accustomed to working together. It was much like the network that labor unions had once provided for Democrats, but the evangelicals were imbued with a level of commitment and zeal that labor leaders could no longer even dream about.

If Ronald Reagan was the father figure of the conservative revival, the presidencies of George H. W. Bush and George W. Bush were the laboratories in which the movement as it exists today was developed, even if what conservative strategists learned from the elder Bush fell mostly into the category of mistakes not to be repeated. Reagan advanced the movement by winning traditionally Democratic households based on moral issues and the need to rein in government. He inspired a new generation of conservatives, many of whom occupy important positions in Washington today. But while Reagan won landslide victories and showed Republicans how to put a human face on their cause, he and his White House staff never attempted to engineer the kind of pervasive, long-term dominance sought under George W. Bush, the man conservative organizer Grover Norquist calls "Reagan's son."

The younger president Bush and his political guru Karl Rove carried the one-party vision to a higher level. They broke new ground in strengthening majorities by building the base rather than going after centrists. Besides campaigning in the kinds of black community centers visited by Mehlman on that winter night in 2005, Republicans have trolled for potentially responsive voters in urban Hispanic barrios, suburban synagogues, and even Japanese tea rooms outside Seattle. With stunning audacity, they have capitalized on government power and policy to advance the interests of a host of different constituencies, small and large. They hammered together the parts of the conservative universe into a machine designed not only to win elections but also to undercut the foundations of Democratic strength and reduce the Democrats' chances of regaining power. Under Rove, for instance, Republicans have pressed for legislation designed to hamstring the trial lawyers and union leaders who have bankrolled the Democrats. They have designed the faith-based initiative to both reshape the way government helps the poor and win new converts to the conservative cause. They have rewritten government regulations to favor supportive industries. They have instructed federal bureaucrats to consider the impact of their decisions on Republican incumbents. And they have relentlessly remade the face of the federal judiciary.

Franklin Roosevelt's top aide, Harry Hopkins, once said that Democrats would "tax and tax and spend and spend and elect and elect." But Rove, with a portfolio as broad as Hopkins's and influence far greater, introduced a new political doctrine, effectively putting the federal bureaucracy and the bully pulpit of the White House in service of long- and short-term GOP political ends.

During this Republican rise, Democrats unwittingly lent a helping hand. Incumbent Democratic members of Congress, along with African American and Hispanic politicians at the local level, put their personal interests ahead of their party by cooperating in the early 1990s with Republican efforts to redraw the boundaries of electoral districts across the country. Individual Democrats and black and Hispanic politicians benefited by winning elections, but the overall result was a stronger Republican grip on legislative seats at all levels. With Democratic voters packed into urban minority districts, adjacent suburban and exurban districts sent more white conservatives to Washington. These changes, along with gerrymandering by both parties on the state level, was so pervasive that it left only about two dozen of the 435 seats in the House close enough to be competitive in a typical election. That makes it harder for Democrats to reverse their minority status, even during a period of Republican scandal and upheaval.

And Democrats in the early twenty-first century have not proven themselves capable of the sustained discipline that has fueled Republican success. In picking candidates, in developing campaign messages and staying on them, and in executing electoral strategies, the Republicans are the New York Yankees of American politics—the team that, at the start of every season, has the tools in place to win it all.

None of this is to say Republicans will win every election in the years ahead. The Rove strategy has depended, after all, on cobbling together narrow majorities in a divided country. John Kerry was just one state away from denying Bush reelection in 2004. And unpredictable factors such as candidates' personalities, the economy, or a domestic terrorist attack could sway voters in any particular election.

But like a dominant sports franchise, the Republican Party has put in place a series of structural and operational advantages that give the GOP a political edge for the foreseeable future. The chapters that follow describe how this advantage came into existence, traced out in the evolving political journeys of the Bush family and modern-day conservative visionaries as they set the stage for what could become, at least for a time, a one-party country.

CHAPTER 1

The Real Center
of Power

Republicans have now won 7 of the last 10 presidential elections. We hold 55 Senate seats, 232 House seats, and 28 governorships. These facts underscore how much progress we have enjoyed in the last four decades, and it has been a remarkable rise for our party and our movement. But it is also a cautionary tale of what happens to a dominant party when its thinking becomes ossified, when its energy begins to drain, when an entitlement mentality takes over, and when political power becomes an end in itself rather than a means to achieve the greater good.

— KARL ROVE, ADDRESS TO THE CONSERVATIVE POLITICAL ACTION CONFERENCE, RONALD REAGAN BUILDING, WASHINGTON, D.C., FEBRUARY 17, 2005

The security guard nodded as the stream of visitors trooped through the wood-paneled lobby at 1920 L Street in downtown Washington. It was Wednesday, and the guard was accustomed to the weekly influx of dark suits—150 or more—making their way to the elevators and up to the spacious conference room on the second floor. The guard recognized some of the faces, the regulars as they trooped through on a balmy day in October 2005.

David Keene, chairman of the American Conservative Union, was a familiar face. So were staff members of the Bush White House and senior advisers to Senate majority leader Bill Frist and House Ways and Means Committee chairman Bill Thomas, along with a blue-chip sampling of the capital's most influential conservatives outside government. The others comprised a continually shifting collection of individuals—all of them more than willing to be labeled conservatives, yet representing a surprising diversity of backgrounds, viewpoints, and priorities. This diversity lifted the "Wednesday meeting," as attendees called it, above the ordinary, and freighted it with the potential to change history.

As they entered the conference room on this particular Wednesday, most visitors hurried to find places among the rows of metal folding chairs. But most also took a moment to survey the large conference table in the center of the room. That's where the day's special guests would sit: a visiting cabinet secretary, a prominent Republican governor, the chairman of an important congressional committee, perhaps even Karl Rove, who made it a point to come several times each year. As the assemblage settled itself, advocates for causes ranging from sexual abstinence to criminalizing abortion and privatizing education passed among the rows, distributing petitions and invitations to rallies and other upcoming events.

The buzz of conversation faded as a diminutive, ruddy-faced man entered and took a seat at the center of the big table. "We have a fun-filled, star-studded agenda today," he said. And with those words, one of the most important weekly conversations in the United States got under way again.

Though most Americans have never heard of it, the Wednesday meeting has come to play a unique role in the complex mechanism that conservative Republicans have assembled to further their dream of the "one-party country." There are many power centers—in the White House, on Capitol Hill, and elsewhere—that are more important than this one, many places where conservative leaders meet and make decisions that shape the news of the day and even the future of the country. What makes the Wednesday meeting so important is that it is a place where nearly all the leaders meet, where the diverse and sometimes uneasy bedfellows who form the conservative political movement in the early twenty-first century regularly come together. Catholic conservatives share space with Orthodox Jews. Gay members of the Log Cabin Republicans may sit beside Christians who believe homosexuality is a sin and, with God's help, can be cured. African American conservatives attend, as do their sometime-rivals, the Hispanic conservatives. There are also Pakistani Americans, Indian Americans, Iranian Americans, and Arab Americans. Libertarians mingle with conservative religious activists who are more than willing to use the coercive power of government to reshape American mores.

Lobbyists for Microsoft and Verizon are there, too, along with advocates for some of the rest of the Fortune 500. Their attitudes toward the government also vary—though their shifting positions on the issues of the day are more situational than abstract, tending to favor federal intervention when it furthers their interests and opposing it when they think it does not.

The meetings also include a generous sampling of policy wonks from the Heritage Foundation, the Cato Institute, and other think tanks, each reflecting a different hue in the conservative rainbow. Visiting politicians from around the globe drop in. And political hopefuls join frumpy job seekers working the crowd.

This diversity, reflected in the Wednesday meetings, has given twenty-first-century conservatism the breadth it would need to dominate American politics for the foreseeable future. But it is the complex interactions among the diverse groups and, more important, the strategies of leadership on display here that make such a vision more than a pipe dream.

The host, creator, and guiding hand behind the Wednesday meetings—and the state-level clones that have begun to pop up around the country in recent years—is a conservative activist named Grover Norquist, who heads a little-known organization called Americans for Tax Reform. The weekly meeting is held in the Americans for Tax Reform conference room, but the organization, like the meeting and Norquist himself, does not confine itself to the issue of tax policy. Like many of the operatives who form the heart of today's conservative political network, Norquist got his start as a member of the College Republicans in the 1970s. It was there that his relationship with Rove began, but while Rove went on to focus on domestic politics, especially in the West and the Southwest, Norquist turned toward foreign policy. For several years, he traveled the globe advocating for anti-Communist rebels in Afghanistan, Latin America, and Africa. Norquist worked as a staff aide in Ronald Reagan's presidential campaigns in the 1980s. As the Cold War ebbed, he began to see domestic policy as the key to future conservative power, and his eye for the promising issue proved to be both keen and farsighted. In 1985, he founded Americans for Tax Reform, which pioneered the antitax movement that has become a central tenet of the conservative creed. Americans for Tax Reform was started, he says, at the suggestion of Ronald Reagan himself. It expanded and by 2004 had sprouted affiliates in nearly every state. Norquist also emerged as a behind-the-scenes architect of Newt Gingrich's Contract with America while helping to guide legislative and political campaigns on the state and national level into the 1990s. He drafted the no-new-taxes pledge that quickly became the conservative seal of approval for any would-be Republican politician. Dishonoring that pledge contributed to the defeat in 1992 of the first President Bush: he angered the movement by making a deal with congressional Democrats that brought fiscal restraint to the federal budget process—a traditional GOP goal—but also embraced higher taxes.

Norquist was, by his own description, an uncompromising conservative, a "market Leninist" who had declared war on the "bad guys" (Democrats) and anyone who sympathized with them. A decade later, his basic beliefs had not changed, much less his goals, but the secret of his increasing success was how he had modified his tactics. In the early days of the conservative resurgence, when the unflinching spirit of the GOP's 1964 standard-bearer, Senator Barry Goldwater of Arizona, defined the movement, its energizing principle was a refusal to compromise. Norquist came to embrace a different approach, perhaps equally inflexible in its ultimate goals, but more pragmatic in its daily operations. As embodied by Norquist of the Wednesday meeting, it is an attempt to bring to twenty-first-century conservatism the practical, big-tent principles of traditional American politics.

The change did not begin with Norquist and his weekly meetings, of course. In two terms as president, Ronald Reagan had carried the conservative creed into the White House and broadcast it to every region of the country. At the same time, he had been an eminently practical politician, too. Rhetorically, he embraced the conservative cause in its entirety, and he pursued many conservative policies. But he also took care never to endanger the real foundation of his political success—the great personal affection that millions of mainstream Americans felt for him. It was the fiercely anti-Communist Reagan, he of the "evil empire," who held summit meetings with a leader of the Soviet Union that later helped bring about a peaceful end to the Cold War. It was Reagan, the right-to-life champion, who declined to appear in person at the massive antiabortion marches that annually looped their way around his White House, instead addressing the crowd by telephone. And it was Reagan who, in defiance of every Republican principle of fiscal responsibility, presided over a surge in deficit spending that doubled the national debt during eight years of uninterrupted peace. Reagan was a true conservative in his heart, in his words, and—when practicable—in his deeds. But the wellspring of his political career was his extraordinary personal gifts.

As conservatives such as Norquist and Rove understood, those gifts were nontransferable. It was useful to remind Americans of Reagan and his legacy, as Norquist did with his Ronald Reagan Legacy Project to name buildings, roads, and airports after the fortieth president. But nostalgia for Reagan would not serve as the foundation for lasting political strength. For such a foundation, for conservatives to think realistically about a one-party country, they would need institutions and mechanisms and organizations, resources that transcended a single individual. It was to this end that conservative strategists bent their energies. They tapped old sources of money not just to support candidates and campaigns but to create conservative think tanks that would nuture conservative scholars, writers, and commentators. They linked up with Christian evangelical activists. They persuaded their traditional allies in corporate America to increase support for all this. Most important of all, they began to foster a powerful, if often tacit, alliance between business-oriented Republicans and social conservatives, persuading each to support the other's agenda even if it sometimes meant swallowing hard.

One example of the movement's strategic expansion was the K Street Project, named after the high-rent boulevard in downtown Washington that is home to many of the major lobbying shops, law firms, and trade associations. Historically, K Street had tended to be amoral in politics, filling its ranks with insiders from both political parties as insurance against shifts in the electoral winds. Norquist and other movement chieftains, including Representative Tom DeLay of Texas, the iron-fisted Republican leader in the House, set out to change that. They began to pressure the K Street firms, often successfully, to tilt sharply to the right in hiring. The labor unions, Norquist would say, hire ideologically compatible lobbying staff; business ought to do the same thing, bringing on board people who favor lower taxes, reduced government, and reining in lawsuits.

By 2000, the movement was on its way to building a political machine that would knit together the scattered resources of political power and influence in a single, well-coordinated network. The arrival of George W. Bush in the White House gave the network new power. During the Clinton years, Norquist and his comrades had operated as contemptuous outsiders. Now they became part of the capital's power structure. Conservatives extended their influence over all three branches of government, into the mainstream media, and into the states. At every level, they preached the necessity of staying on message and staying united, even when doing so necessitated compromises that might go against the grain of some conservative ideologues, or even against past commitments. As part of his efforts to unify the movement and the White House, Norquist worked closely with the Republican National Committee and Karl Rove as the administration pushed for passage of Bush priorities that some of the faithful might dislike but the leaders considered beneficial to the larger cause. Some fellow conservatives criticized Norquist, for example, for not opposing a Bush-backed plan to add the costly prescription drug benefit to Medicare. The program was the first large-scale expansion of the government's health-care program for elderly Americans in decades. Budget hawks deplored the tens of billions of dollars it would add to a federal budget already soaring into the red. Small-government conservatives railed against the heresy of Republicans creating another big government program. But Rove and other strategists believed the drug benefit could help make senior voters a long-term part of the GOP's ruling coalition.

At the same time, Norquist and his organization—which by now had spawned counterparts in forty-eight cities from Seattle to Minneapolis to New York[1]—served the immediate needs of the coalition. They threw themselves into the fights for tax cuts and private investment accounts in Social Security. And Norquist pushed pet causes such as outsourcing government jobs to private contractors and reducing the influence of government labor unions, both of which tended to strengthen the GOP's hold on power. Unions, after all, had been stalwarts of the Democratic coalition dating back to the days of Franklin D. Roosevelt. Unions of government workers were among the few healthy survivors of that long-ago time. They were now prime targets. As for outsourcing, which paid private firms to do work otherwise done by government employees, it emerged as a modern-day system of spoils and patronage.

Beyond all this, however, Norquist's biggest contribution to the conservative movement was establishing the Wednesday meeting. No greater testament to its importance can be found than the envy of Democratic strategists and liberal activists across the country who have thus far labored in vain to create a mechanism with such reach and unity of purpose and action.

The meetings bring together nearly every conservative interest in Washington: big-business lobbyists advocating deregulation, home-schoolers opposing the public education "monopoly," libertarians decrying big government, and evangelicals eager to keep the courts from endorsing gay marriages or prohibiting classroom instruction in Intelligent Design. The unifying concern for most of these disparate groups, Norquist says, is keeping the government off their backs.

Through the strength of this connecting thread of philosophy and Norquist's hyperactive, peripatetic personality, the groups represented at his meetings remain together most of the time, though the centrifugal force that threatens any such diverse coalition is plain to see, and may ultimately prove stronger than anything Norquist and his friends can do to keep it together. That's why, each week, they take pains to remind their guests of what they have in common, of the movement's long-term goals and short-term priorities—and of what might happen if the movement flies apart and the liberals take charge once more.

The meetings are, to a significant degree, a vital nerve center for conservative Republicans' continued unity and success. Understand what goes on in the room each week and you can see why conservatives—despite scandals, sliding presidential approval ratings, and party infighting—still have a chance to bury for good the Democratic coalition and reign dominant for decades to come.

The room also provides historical context. The list of attendees often includes such longtime leaders of the conservative movement as Phyllis Schlafly of the Eagle Forum, David Keene of the American Conservative Union, and Morton Blackwell, president of the Leadership Institute that has trained young conservatives since 1979. Doughy and aging, they represent the mid-twentieth-century visionaries who waged the early fight from the fringes. They endured scorn from many in the press and their own party, but they helped shape the positions and sharpen the rhetoric that would later become party doctrine. Keene's American Conservative Union, for instance, hosted an annual conference for thirty years that for the most part drew lonely conservative college kids and far-right academics. His efforts gained respectability and power during the Reagan years; Reagan himself was a regular speaker at the conference. By 2005, the annual gathering had grown into a sellout event, attended by thousands of students from major universities who give rock-star treatment to presenters such as Rove and Vice President Dick Cheney. Norquist likes to say that Schlafly, Keene, and Blackwell "were far-right conservatives before it was cool."[2]

Aspiring collegiate politicos from major universities also seek admission to Norquist's meetings and compete for internships with the myriad organizations represented there. Lobbyists seek his counsel and support but must wait in line behind members of Congress, White House staff, and a national press corps that attentively seeks Norquist's opinions even though he views many of its members with contempt.

The Wednesday meetings routinely feature appearances by researchers from the conservative foundations that provide intellectual heft and respectability to the movement. Their upcoming conferences and seminars are announced at the Wednesday gatherings, and their handsomely published research papers are distributed.

Some of those in attendance—former House Speaker Newt Gingrich, pollster Kellyanne Conway, and former Republican representative Bob Barr of Georgia—are recognizable as news analysts on cable television, especially on the Fox News Channel. As a general rule, working journalists are admitted only after they have been screened by Norquist and his staff and have agreed to strict ground rules governing what can be later published or broadcast.[3] But some are always welcome, such as John Fund of the *Wall Street Journal*'s online opinion page, who once described Norquist as "the grand central station" of modern conservatism.[4] So are Robert George, a conservative editorial writer for the *New York Post* and *National Review*, and Ralph Z. Hallow of the *Washington Times*, along with an editorial assistant for columnist Robert Novak.

As the parade of candidates that shows up each week knows, the gathering is more than just a gab fest and idea exchange. It provides the Bush White House with a link to the Washington offices of the wide array of groups that make up the conservative movement, from the National Rifle Association and the National Right to Life organization to the Property Rights Coalition and the U.S. Chamber of Commerce. The meetings also provide a forum for testing ideas. It is at this gathering that conservatives are likely to learn first about an administration initiative, such as the controversial push for steel tariffs in 2002 or the more recent Medicare drug program. And it is here that the White House can sound the trumpet for grassroots support for its initiatives and its nominees. Only at the Wednesday meeting can one so readily and efficiently reach millions of conservative activists with a common message.

The Wednesday meeting performs a wide array of services for the conservative cause, but its continued importance on the Washington calendar rests primarily on the fact that Norquist has demonstrated an extraordinary capacity to bridge ideological and cultural gaps. Time and again—to the despair and secret envy of his opponents on the left—he has persuaded disparate interest groups to look past their differences and see their shared goals. When the auto industry needed help in its fight against federal fuel efficiency standards in the mid-1990s, for example, Norquist convinced social conservatives preoccupied with teen pregnancy and prayer in school that the energy standards were their fight, too. He talked Phyllis Schlafly into seeing fuel standards as a form of "back-door family planning."

"You can't have a whole lot of kids in a tiny fuel-efficient car," Norquist says he told her. And, he says, Schlafly agreed, telling him, "I hate those cars."[5]

Norquist has even bridged divides between the most mortal of all enemies, Muslims and Jews. A handful of his fellow conservatives have accused him of associating with terrorist sympathizers, but he has rejected the criticism and persisted, drawing to the Wednesday meetings Near Eastern and other Muslims who partner with Orthodox Jews and pro-Israel activists in pursuit of the one-party cause. Working with lobbyist Jack Abramoff, an Orthodox Jew, Norquist encouraged Jewish Republican activism, even allowing the Orthodox organization Toward Tradition to use Americans for Tax Reform headquarters as its Washington office. At the same time, Norquist helped found the Islamic Free Market Institute, which raised money and sponsored conferences to promote conservative ideas in the United States and the Muslim world. In 2005, Norquist's outreach took a personal turn when he wed a young Muslim woman, Samah Alrayyes, who once worked as communications director for the Islamic institute he helped create.

A few members of the conservative alliance, notably former Reagan defense official Frank Gaffney, complained that Norquist was providing terrorist sympathizers with creditability and access to the

White House.[6] One of the Muslims who drew special attention from Gaffney's campaign was Suhail Khan, a Transportation Department official formerly in the White House outreach office. Khan's late father was affiliated with a mosque once visited by a top Al Qaeda leader traveling under an assumed identity to raise funds in the United States. There was no indication that Khan's father was personally aware of the visit by Dr. Ayman al-Zwahiri, but Gaffney and his allies continued to raise questions about the younger Khan and other Muslim Americans working in the administration. In 2003, Rove was asked about Gaffney's concerns with Norquist and his Muslim associates. The presidential adviser rejected the charges as having no substance. "There's no there there," Rove said.[7]

Norquist angrily slammed Gaffney as racist and unfair and banned him from attending the Wednesday meetings. Meanwhile, Norquist has remained close to Khan, soliciting advice from the young lawyer and asking Khan to chair the meetings in his absence. Khan continued to be active in movement and presidential politics, organizing Indian Americans of all faiths into a formidable new Republican group that helped raise more than $1 million for the Bush campaign in 2004. During this period, Norquist also continued to encourage the GOP as a whole to court Muslim voters, a traditionally Democratic voting group.

An equally striking example of Norquist's impulse to probe for conservative toeholds in seemingly unpromising quarters occurred in the late 1990s. The recording industry was fighting rampant piracy of CDs and pressing for passage of the Digital Millennium Copyright Act, a controversial law to criminalize black-market technology that could copy music and movies. The industry's problem was that Republicans ruled Congress, and the industry was led by Hollywood liberals, who were not exactly insiders to the burgeoning one-party movement. Norquist viewed the law as an idea consistent with conservative principles, and he saw an opportunity to make new friends. So he enlisted another element of his center-right coalition, the rural activists who were asserting the primacy of private property rights over government efforts to take over western lands. He made the case— successfully—that the blue-state recording industry and the red-state ranchers and farmers had a common desire to protect ownership. The law was passed with the support of western lawmakers such as Senator Conrad Burns of Montana and Senator Orrin Hatch of Utah and then House majority leader Dick Armey. And the bread that Norquist had cast upon the waters came back cake. The recording industry was motivated to hire Republican lobbyists, and GOP candidates suddenly won greater financial support from a traditionally Democratic industry.

Hilary Rosen, who ran the Recording Industry Association of America until 2003, called Norquist "central" to winning support in the Republican-controlled Congress. The industry itself had been able to muster strong support among representatives of such media-savvy urban centers as New York, Los Angeles, and Nashville, she recalled. But that was not enough; victory was assured only when Norquist brought western and Southern lawmakers to the fight.

Rosen, a Democrat and gay rights advocate, directed her organization to pay a $10,000 fee to join Americans for Tax Reform, and she subsequently met with Norquist at his Capitol Hill town house for a series of dinner seminars. She also sent Republican staffers to his Wednesday meetings. Norquist subsequently helped organize a formal property rights alliance that would go on to meet regularly and plan future cooperation on policy proposals. Rosen lamented that the Democrats "don't have a Norquist or a Wednesday meeting."[8]

Other liberals have attended and addressed the Wednesday group, including billionaire philanthropist George Soros, Al Gore, and Gore's 2000 campaign manager, Donna Brazile. Brazile won applause at a meeting in early 2005 acknowledging the gains of Republicans in getting out the vote in the 2004 election, particularly in reaching African American voters. Norquist found common ground with Brazile: her Washington lobbying practice includes developers pushing to end the District of Columbia's nineteenth-century restrictions on constructing buildings taller than the Capitol, a restriction any free-market capitalist or libertarian would love to hate. "We found we had a lot in common," Norquist said after meeting Brazile. "She's religious, from a military family, believes in hard work. She's a natural Republican; she just doesn't know it yet." Brazile laughed at Norquist's suggestion but acknowledged envy. "Grover and Rove and those guys have so much going for them. They are unified in their opposition to Democrats and they are organized," she said.[9]

Norquist and his meetings are not without their detractors. Some GOP stalwarts question the value of the eclectic crowd. One well-placed administration official once likened the gathering to a "*Star Wars* bar." And in hindsight, some Wednesday meeting veterans are disturbed by the memory of sessions in the 1990s when Norquist focused, however briefly, on a peculiarly remote topic: the tiny Marianna Islands in the South Pacific. Marshall Wittman, an attendee during that period, says he wondered why the islands deserved the movement's support because their leaders were struggling to establish free-market capitalism against a backdrop of restrictive U.S. regulations. What Norquist did not mention then is that officials in the Mariannas had hired his old friend Abramoff as their lobbyist.[10]

Norquist says that Wittman, who has gone on to work for the Democratic Leadership Council, exaggerated the attention the Wednesday meeting gave to the Mariannas. But Abramoff has pled guilty to federal fraud charges in 2006, and e-mails reveal he directed his Indian gambling clients to contribute substantial sums to Norquist's antitax organization. This may not be illegal, but the episodes have brought a whiff of scandal to the meetings. Norquist protests that the negative associations are unfair and that no investigator has yet suggested he or his organization has done anything wrong. His very predicament illustrates the dangers that lurk beneath the surface of an operation that brings together the world of high-stakes lobbying, interest group politics, elections, and legislation.

Norquist waves away such unpleasantness, keeping his eyes on the one-party prize. In his pocket calendar, he keeps a scrap of paper with his long-term goals: ending tax increases, privatizing Social Security, shrinking the federal government, privatizing the postal service. The thread tying together every goal is a belief in market-based approaches, and the conviction that those approaches will attract legions of voters to the GOP for years to come.

"The more independent people you have, the more Republicans you've created," Norquist said. "The more savers and investors and owners of homes and shares—the more Republicans. The more gun owners, the more Republicans. The more self-employed people—the more Republicans. On the other hand, the more government workers, the more trial lawyers, the more Democrats. So it is a virtuous cycle, where sound policy from a Reagan Republican standpoint is sound politics."[11]

Norquist elaborated on that point in an opinion article in 2004: "Big-city Democratic political machines thrive on federal grants and state-granted powers." And the coercive utopians—the radical environmentalists, animal-rights activists, feminists, and others who would use state power to force on us tiny non-flushable toilets and cars too small to hold families, take away the circus and our pet cats, and otherwise impose more fussbudget impositions on our lives than Leviticus—all depend on government grants to use and misuse federal and state power. But outside state power, the Democratic coalition withers and dies. Without effective control of the government, the Democratic Party is like a fish out of water, a vampire in the sun, Antaeus held aloft, an appliance unplugged."[12]

Thus, as Norquist sees it, the Republicans' present political power springs from successful attacks on government over the past three decades. And continuing those attacks is what will keep Republicans in power. With Democrats lacking an effective beachhead in Congress, and the GOP still in charge, Republicans can continue to harness the power of policy making to pursue their goals while obstructing the other side. Norquist ticks off enemy targets: trial lawyers, labor unions, government employees. All will be damaged as the conservative agenda moves forward. In a way, the strategy sounds obvious. But imagine a Democrat speaking in similar terms. Is there a liberal idea—like raising the minimum wage or creating health care for all—specifically designed to advance a policy goal but also to undermine the Republican Party and its ability to function?

Norquist believes that private enterprise has become the people's champion. Government, he hopes, will be seen increasingly as antithetical to the general welfare.

"My goal is to shrink the size of government in half over the next twenty-five years," Norquist said, cutting it from 33 percent of GDP in

2005 to 16 percent or less in a quarter century. Speaking hyperboli-
cally, he said, "I don't want to abolish government. I simply want to
reduce it to the size where I can drag it into the bathroom and drown
it in the bathtub."[13]

If the image seems a bit rough, Norquist has a reputation for
playing rough with those who cross him, his organization, or their
conservative principles. The first President Bush felt the sting when
he broke the tax pledge and then suffered a humiliating defeat in
1992, due at least in part to the anger of Norquist and other disaffected conservatives. That election contained many lessons for
Republicans, not least for the defeated president's son, George W.
Bush. But in Washington at least, it taught ambitious Republicans to
respect the network and to ignore its power at their peril.

Certainly that lesson was not lost on those who gathered in Norquist's
big conference room that day in October 2005. They all shared
Norquist's dream of building a conservative movement so strong that
for all practical purposes the United States would become a one-party
country. And they shared their host's specific goal of dismantling
the half-century-old pillars of the Democratic party: the social welfare
programs that began in the New Deal and blossomed under Lyndon
Baines Johnson, the labor movement that provided money and manpower for Democratic campaigns, the loyalty of minority and immigrant voters, and the underlying public faith that government was a
force for good.

And the men and women sitting around the conference table and
occupying the ranks of folding chairs had reason to be hopeful that
day. Their president had scored a reelection victory. He did not owe
that victory to compromises aimed at winning over moderate and
independent voters, the usual formula for winning a presidential election. Instead, Bush's triumph came from the extraordinary ability of
the conservative movement to turn out the base. The conservative
network had not only reelected Bush, it had expanded the GOP
majority in Congress and maintained the majority of governorships—
twenty-eight—in the hands of Republicans.

Yet, for all of those achievements, there was an undercurrent of anxiety as Norquist called the weekly session to order on October 19, 2005. That very morning, a Texas court was issuing an arrest warrant for House majority leader Tom DeLay on charges of money laundering and conspiracy. In Washington, a federal prosecutor had already indicted a senior aide to Vice President Cheney in the long-running investigation over the leak of a covert CIA officer's identity; the prosecutor was still weighing whether to bring charges against Karl Rove as well. Moreover, Norquist and fellow conservative strategist Ralph Reed, founder of the Christian Coalition and a key idea man in the GOP leadership, were being mentioned in press reports about a separate corruption investigation of Jack Abramoff.

Tension was high in the room for other reasons, too. Just two weeks earlier, participants had savaged Ed Gillespie, the former Republican National Committee chairman and loyal movement soldier. Gillespie had come before the Wednesday meeting as an envoy from the White House seeking support for the president's latest Supreme Court nominee, Harriet Miers. Angry objections voiced during that meeting helped fuel a rebellion over the fact that Bush had nominated his friend Miers rather than the kind of well-known conservative jurist these activists believed he had promised to appoint. Miers ultimately withdrew to quell the revolt, but the episode had left bruises. It had also demonstrated the challenge of maintaining unity in an increasingly large and diverse coalition.

The Miers dispute had come at a time when the movement was already showing signs of trouble: Hurricane Katrina had just devastated New Orleans and other Gulf Coast communities. Everyone shared the Gulf Coast's pain, of course. But small-government fiscal conservatives, already upset about pork-barrel spending under the GOP, were unhappy with others in the party who wanted the government to play a central—and costly—role in rebuilding the region. And the spectacle of the federal government bumbling its initial response to the massive natural disaster did no one in the Republican Party any good.

Those tensions were on display now. The audience heard first from Paul Teller, a senior House staffer representing conservative members who had been sounding the alarms on post-Katrina spending plans. Next was Tom Schatz of Citizens Against Government

Waste, publisher of the annual *Congressional Pig Book*, with another warning about excessive spending.

As the presenters continued with their reports, a buzz rose across the room. Heads turned toward the door. A surprise guest had arrived. Tom DeLay himself—under indictment and derided by Democrats as the poster boy for Republican hubris and overreach—had come to the pulsing heart of the conservative movement he had helped to build. DeLay and Norquist had never been particularly close, and the former House majority leader had recently irritated others in the room when he tried to argue that government excess had been tamed despite an explosion of spending on bridges, roads, community centers, and other hometown projects. Still, everyone knew DeLay was a critical cog in their machine. And they knew the party line on his legal troubles: the Texas prosecutor who brought the charges was nothing but a Democratic Party attack dog.

Apparently undaunted, DeLay strode to the center of the room grinning broadly. Standing in front of the conference table, he glanced around where he could see a former colleague from the House whom he had helped elect, aides to the president with whom he had plotted strategy, and lobbyists whose jobs he had helped secure.

"So," DeLay said, "how has your month been?"

The crowd erupted in laughter and cheers.

DeLay did not directly address the charges against him, speaking instead that day about the importance of curbing federal largesse, even apologizing at one point for his earlier suggestion that spending was in check. The House would get the job done, he said. The Senate, he implied, might benefit from some pressure from the assembled group.

The message was clear: even when one of the movement's leaders was in trouble, the crusade must still focus on conservative ideals and the ultimate goal: building a one-party country. DeLay's legal foibles were potentially embarrassing. But the modern conservative movement, once so reliant on the fate of individual leaders like Speaker Newt Gingrich in the mid-1990s, had matured. It had built a firm foundation that transcended individuals.

"It is larger now than any one man," Norquist said.

CHAPTER 2

Stacking the Electoral Deck

I knew that Lee Atwater and his team were quietly cutting deals as part of a redistricting scheme that was going to hurt us in the future. But the Democrats were doing nothing in the nineties to build a fortress around our majority status.

—Donna Brazile, recalling her efforts to sound a warning about Republican redistricting efforts, in an interview in Washington, D.C., September 2005

L ong before Washington's conservative power players began clamoring to fill Grover Norquist's boardroom every Wednesday morning or dreamed their dreams of perpetual dominance, back when George W. Bush was a high school student at Andover, his father was struggling to find his way through a turbulent transition period in American politics. At some stages of his long career, George Herbert Walker Bush represented the GOP's sometimes ugly transitions—as it moved from Yankee Republicanism to the party of the Southern white man. At other stages, he reflected a morally beclouded party as it evolved toward something new.

Eventually, he became a mournful victim of what the party of his fore-bears had become. But whether the elder Bush was riding the wave or drowning in it, the story of the father is the story not only of the making of two presidents but also the making of the political system that the younger George W. Bush came to embody. After all, it was during George H. W. Bush's one term as president that the strategists he put in charge of the GOP's national political apparatus devised a cunning plan for advancing the cause of one-party goverment. That plan was the redrawing of congressional and state legislative district maps to give them an enduring tilt toward the Republican Party.

Looking back, one might say that in the decades immediately after World War II, the Democrats fought the civil rights war and the Republicans fought the Cold War. For Democrats, the point of no return came at their national convention in 1948. President Harry S. Truman and northern Democrats let South Carolina senator Strom Thurmond and his fellow "Dixiecrats" walk out of the party rather than continue their unholy bargain of accepting de jure Southern racism in exchange for the votes of the "Solid South." The schism deepened through the presidency of John F. Kennedy, who tried to sidestep the issue but had it thrust upon him. And it grew deeper still under Lyndon B. Johnson, who understood what supporting civil rights was doing to his party but nonetheless pushed through the greatest federal commitment to equal rights since the passage of the Fifteenth Amendment to the Constitution in 1870 that guaranteed the right to vote regardless of "race, color, or previous condition of servitude."

The Republican Party, meanwhile, did its best to avoid the issue of race during the decades immediately after the war. President Dwight D. Eisenhower sent federal troops to Little Rock, Arkansas, to enforce a federal court order on school desegregation, but he did so with a visible lack of enthusiasm. And the developing attitude of the ultraconservative wing of the GOP was reflected in the ineffectual but symbolically revealing campaign to remove Chief Justice Earl Warren after he presided over the landmark *Brown v. Board of Education* decision that declared racially segregated "separate but equal" schools unconstitutional. In this period, instead of emphasizing civil rights, the Republican Party emphasized the struggle against the Soviet Union, China, and the threat of Communism. Against a background of nuclear apocalypse, the GOP made itself the emblem of hard-line resistance to Communist expansionism and unquestioning support for huge defense budgets.

As the 1950s and 1960s gave way to the 1970s and 1980s, however, the Republican approach to racial politics began to change. The Democrats were becoming ever more closely tied to the civil rights movement, and the movement's increasing militancy made it ever more disturbing to white voters, especially in the South. That presented a historic opportunity for Republican politicians who were not too squeamish to seize it. In Texas and all across the South, Republican politicians began to pursue a "Southern strategy" made famous at the national level by Richard M. Nixon. It combined a theoretical opposition to racism with concrete opposition to virtually all the demands and proposals of the civil rights movement. It was a nudge-nudge, wink-wink strategy that grew increasingly effective with Southern voters—and with many northern blue-collar and lower-middle-class voters as well. George H. W. Bush embraced the new Republicanism as it helped carry him to Congress, the vice presidency, and the Oval Office, though he never seemed entirely comfortable with the man he had become, and many of his new conservative soul mates never quite believed in his conversion to their cause.

Just after World War II, in the heady days of the Permian Basin oil boom, the first George Bush moved from Connecticut to Texas. A child of privilege, raised and educated in the moderate, internationalist Republican traditions of Wall Street and its New England enclaves, this Bush represented all that the party of Lincoln, out of the House of Morgan, had come to represent: a morally upright if no longer rigorous antipathy toward racism, an old-school sense of noblesse oblige, and a conviction that a man who was also making his fortune could honorably turn to politics as an outlet for unceasing ambition.

As an envoy of East Coast capital to the "oil patch," Bush had no trouble becoming wealthy in his own right. As for politics, the first step was his election in 1962 as chairman of the Republican Party for Harris County, Houston. From that beginning, as Bush clambered upward, moving by fits and starts, he struggled to convince his Texas neighbors that he was truly one of them. Old-style Texas conservatives derided the Yale-educated Bush as a tool of the Eastern establishment, a "Rockefeller plant." At one point, advisers suggested he wear a cowboy hat to prove his Texas bona fides. But it would take more than new costuming to win over the skeptics, and Bush began to embrace their values and positions on issues as well. Old family friends back east grumbled to his wife, Barbara, that her husband had moved too far to the right. "What a world: George was too conservative for the East and too liberal for Texas," Barbara wrote in her memoir. "If I had to label George, I would say he was a fiscal conservative and a social liberal."[1]

Despite his trouble fitting in, Bush decided to mount a dark horse campaign for the United States Senate in 1964, challenging the liberal incumbent Ralph Yarborough. With support for then vice president Lyndon Johnson plummeting in his native Texas, many—including Bush—thought Yarborough was beatable. And in the campaign that ensued, Bush the "social liberal" was nowhere to be seen. He embraced the Republicans' presidential candidate, Senator Barry Goldwater of Arizona, and the Goldwater brand of conservatism that included opposition to the 1964 Civil Rights Act. Yarborough had supported the legislation, and Bush believed the vote meant "sure defeat"[2] for his opponent.

Privately, Bush fretted that he was on the wrong side of history. "My heart is heavy," he confided to one supporter."[3] While he knew that race could bring down Yarborough, Bush conceded, "I am not sure that a fair and moderated debate on civil rights can do it." Writing to a friend in Houston less than a month after then president Johnson signed the Voting Rights Act into law, Bush worried about how to straddle the issue in his campaign. "We must develop this position reasonably, prudently, sensitively—we must be sure we don't inflame the passions of unthinking men to garner a vote; yet it is essential that the position I believe in be explained," he wrote. "I believe I am right—I know we must have restraint, yet I don't want this restraint to prevent right from prevailing. . . . What shall I do? How will I do it? I want to win, but not at the expense of justice, not at the expense of the dignity of any man—not at the expense of hurting a friend nor teaching my children a prejudice which I do not feel."[4]

That was in private. In public, Bush invoked the code words and carefully drawn positions of the Republican Southern strategy to send sympathetic signals to segregationist whites while not appearing overtly racist. Bush argued that the new civil rights law was unconstitutional, a violation of "states' rights." He blasted Yarborough for having voted to end a grueling, seventy-four-day Senate filibuster that had blocked passage of the law. "I oppose the Civil Rights Bill on the grounds that it transcends civil rights and violates many other rights of all people," Bush said in campaign materials. "Job opportunities, education and fair play will help alleviate inequities and should be encouraged. Sweeping federal legislation will fail. . . . Texas has a responsible record in this field, and Texas is capable of solving its own problems in this difficult area."[5]

Lee Atwater, the possibly unscrupulous but unquestionably brilliant young Republican strategist, explained the subtleties of the Republicans' racial game years later in an interview with political scientist Alexander P. Lamis: "You start out in 1954 by saying, 'Nigger, nigger, nigger.' By 1968 you can't say 'nigger'—that hurts you. Backfires. So you say stuff like forced busing, states' rights and all that stuff."[6]

Bush lost the 1964 Senate election; Lyndon Johnson's landslide victory over Barry Goldwater was too much for Texas Republicans to withstand. Yet Bush's dilemma—whether to stay with his old principles or pursue his political ambitions at their expense—remained with him for the rest of his public life. His party was changing and he was caught on the cusp, torn between his inherited principles and his emerging opportunities.

He escaped the dilemma in part by moving to the unelected side of public service, as ambassador to the United Nations and chairman of the Republican National Committee under President Nixon, for example, and then as chief of the U.S. liaison office in China and later director of the Central Intelligence Agency under President Ford. But the problem reemerged when he became Ronald Reagan's running mate in 1980 and served two terms as Reagan's vice president. And the tension between personal values and political expediency was there with a vengeance in Bush's 1988 campaign for the presidency against Democratic nominee Michael Dukakis of Massachusetts. As he had in the 1964 race against Yarborough, Bush set aside whatever inner twinges he may have felt and did the pragmatic thing.

Reagan's second term had ended badly, clouded by scandal and hobbled by a president whose mind had begun to fail. As a result, the vice president entered the battle trailing his Democratic opponent by almost twenty points in public opinion polls. As the campaign developed, the vulnerabilities that the Democratic Party still carried from the 1970s took a toll. Dukakis, seeking to show he was not soft on national security, allowed himself to be photographed in a tank. The image, the diminutive governor's helmeted head rising turtlelike above the rim of the turret, turned out to be unconvincing and — worse — comic. During a televised debate, Dukakis was judged to have bobbled the answer when a reporter asked, hypothetically, whether he would oppose the death penalty even for a man who had raped his wife; Dukakis's difficulty with the question seemed to epitomize the moral paralysis that conservatives ascribed to liberals. But what would linger longest in political memory was an anti-Dukakis television commercial featuring a Massachusetts convicted murderer named Willie Horton.

Horton, a black man, had been released from prison under a state furlough program. Dukakis had no direct role in running the program, but when Horton assaulted a man and repeatedly raped a woman while on a weekend furlough, conservatives used the incident to produce and broadcast a racially charged television commercial accusing Dukakis of being soft on crime. The Bush campaign was not directly responsible for the ad, but the vice president's master political strategist, Lee Atwater, who had cut his teeth on the Southern strategy, was quoted predicting, "by the time this election is over Willie Horton will be a household name."[7] Democrats accused Bush of racist tactics. And the racism of the ad was unmistakable. But there was another element as well: just as Republicans had portrayed Democrats as soft on the threat of Communism, now they were portraying Democrats as soft on crime. Willie Horton became an icon of the Republican victory in 1988. As the elder Bush ascended to the Oval Office, the Republican Party had become something quite different from the party of his forebears. It was about to metamorphose again. And, while Bush would play an even more central role in this transformation than he had in the first, in the end this change would destroy his political career.

During Bush's presidency, the Cold War came to an unmistakable end. For a time, hardliners such as Bush's secretary of defense, former Wyoming congressman and Nixon administration wunderkind Dick Cheney, had continued to argue that the Soviets' newfound eagerness for arms control agreements might be a trick. But soon, with the Berlin Wall turning to rubble and the Soviet Union descending into chaos, it became impossible to play the national security card as the ace of trumps. Nor could the GOP go much further with the race issue: the Willie Horton gambit might have been effective, but it had come perilously close to crossing the line. Moreover, minority voters were becoming so numerous—in the South as well as the North—that the old game had to end, at least at the national level.

Taking everything together, the Republican Party had to reinvent itself or risk decline. The Democrats faced a similar challenge. The civil rights movement of Martin Luther King Jr. had been buried alongside the anti–Vietnam War movement. Although black voters remained a crucial element in the Democratic base, the country as a whole had moved on to other issues. So both parties needed to change. As it happened, only the GOP was ready.

The new Republicanism consisted of four principle elements. First, it retained the party's hard-line approach to security, though for a time public fear of crime had to stand in for the old fear of Communism and nuclear war. Second, the Republican leadership held tight to its historic position as the party of business and free-market opportunity; it advocated economic growth and market-based approaches to social problems, favored an end to government "inter-ference" with business, and committed itself to opposing taxes. Third, in part as a natural outgrowth of the Republicans' deepening roots in the South, the national party began to embrace the concerns of evan-gelical Christians and other social conservatives. Finally, the Repub-licans changed the way they approached race. And this may have been the cleverest of all the things GOP strategists did to reinvent themselves: they renounced the Southern strategy and began to reach out to racial and ethnic minorities, including African Americans. This would culminate years later with Bush's son in the White House when Republican National Committee chairman Ken Mehlman offi-cially apologized for the Southern strategy and declared at a meeting of the National Association for the Advancement of Colored People: "We were wrong."

Cynics might suggest that making overtures to the black commu-nity was safer now that racial issues had lost some of their power to move masses of voters. Moreover, the new GOP still calibrated its actions and couched its appeals in language designed to avoid spreading alarm among race-sensitive Southern voters and their northern counterparts. By appealing to blacks through their religious leaders, for example, Republicans could emphasize their commit-ment to the traditional values dear to white conservatives. GOP strategists also focused on successful blacks whose economic interests ran parallel to the business-oriented wing of the party.

Looking beyond the black minority, Republicans also began reaching out to the newer, faster-growing Latino minority, whose reli-gious convictions and emphasis on hard work and family gave them a degree of kinship with the new Republicans. And when it came to wooing both black and brown voters, Republican strategists like Lee Atwater and Karl Rove were content with limited goals. Some might dream of a day when racial and ethnic minorities would flock to the GOP. Pragmatists like Atwater and Rove would be content with diminishing their value to the Democrats.

The increasingly subtle Republican strategy, coupled with the Democrats' weaknesses, combined to put George H. W. Bush in the White House by a wide margin following that 1988 campaign.

In the jubilation of victory, not much importance had been attached to an earlier episode that would both haunt the Bush presidency and serve as a major turning point for the conservative movement. Trying to reassure Reagan conservatives, who were still skeptical of his commitment to their cause, Bush, trailing Dukakis, made a promise in his presidential nomination acceptance speech at the Republican National Convention. "The Congress will push me to raise taxes," he said, "and I'll say no, and they'll push, and I'll say no, and they'll push again, and I'll say to them, 'Read my lips: No new taxes.'" For a Republican, it seemed a routine line, though the language was uncharacteristically vivid for Bush. Down the road, what amounted almost to a throwaway line would take on fateful importance. But that day was four years off. In the meantime, the new president would preside over one of the most important steps the GOP would take to advance its dream of one-party rule.

At the outset of George H. W. Bush's presidential term, the notion that Republicans could win control of the entire federal government seemed far-fetched. Indeed, there was a question whether they could hold the gains Reagan had made. After all, on Inauguration Day, January, 20, 1989, Democrats controlled the House with 260 seats compared with just 175 for the Republicans; the Democrats had gained House seats even as Bush took the presidential vote. The Democrats also controlled the Senate, by a 55–45 margin, and held the majority of state governorships and legislatures. Two factors were not reflected in the numbers, however: Lee Atwater, and the new president's readiness to embrace his ideas.

As Bush settled into the White House, Atwater took over as the chairman of the Republican National Committee. Just thirty-eight, Atwater was already known for bare-knuckled political tactics and political savvy. A native South Carolinian, he had been a hellion as a child and all his life loved to play rhythm and blues on his guitar; James Brown and Otis Redding were among his favorites. A voracious reader and a keen observer, he grew up to have a profound understanding of the contemporary South and its evolving political nuances.[8]

Atwater understood that the campaigns of George H. W. Bush and scores of other Republican politicians had turned the South into a region that could almost be considered Republican territory, especially for GOP presidential candidates. But he also knew that Democrats continued to control congressional seats across the South. That was because, while Democratic presidential candidates tended to toe the party's more liberal line on race and social issues, locally elected white Democrats tended to be more moderate, with deep roots in their communities. Atwater thought he saw a way around that with the help of new provisions in federal election law passed during the Reagan years.

The provisions, upheld and sharpened by subsequent court rulings, required state lawmakers to create more minority districts, that is, districts that would elect more blacks and Latinos to Congress and state legislatures. Contained in amendments to the bill renewing the 1964 Voting Rights Act, the requirements were advocated most vocally by liberal Democrats and civil rights groups as a way to give minorities a greater voice in government. Even when Reagan signed the measure in 1982, many Republicans opposed it on grounds that the minority-district provisions amounted to setting quotas. Atwater, on the other hand, came to see it as a powerful weapon that could be turned against its champions.

Atwater understood that white Democrats had continued to survive in the South despite Republican gains because they positioned themselves as moderate conservatives and had strong local roots, but also because of the rising number of African American voters. Spread across the South, these new voters had become an electoral factor in urban centers and rural areas alike. Though seldom numerous enough to elect black candidates, they helped give solid though not overwhelming margins of victory to white Democrats in elections for Congress and state legislatures. What Atwater and a handful of his fellow Republicans figured out was how the newly amended Voting Rights Act could change that reality—and with it the Democrats' hold on Congress.

The Constitution requires that seats in the U.S. House of Representatives be apportioned on the basis of population, as measured by the census conducted every ten years. The census results are used to determine the relative number of House seats each state gets and the disposition of those seats within each state. The new population figures to be compiled in the 1990 census would have to be followed soon afterward by new district maps, drawn by state officials.

The decennial task of redrawing district maps is one of the most important and politically rancorous jobs a state politician tackles because it is a way of stacking the electoral deck. With the jot of a pen, map drafters can shift the political balance of a district—to make it safe for one party or the other, to assure an incumbent of reelection, or to throw the race wide open. For that reason, maps had traditionally been drawn in secretive meetings that tended to favor powerful incumbents and the status quo. In Georgia, for instance, lines had been drawn in such a way that the Democrats controlled nine of the state's ten congressional seats in 1990, even though the Democratic candidates received just 61 percent of the overall vote. Four years later, the Republicans had turned things around, controlling seven of the state's eleven seats, though they received just 55 percent of the vote.[9] Political gerrymandering was as old as the Constitution, but Atwater and his lieutenants knew that this round of redistricting would be different. The law pushed by liberals and signed by Reagan over conservative objections would see to that.

As Atwater and his legal counsel at the time, Benjamin Ginsberg, saw it, the new legal requirement to concentrate African Americans in certain districts so as to assure election of African Americans would—if artfully managed—rob neighboring white Democrats of their winning margins. The same was true with the Democratic-leaning Latino voters in California. A plan that would help neutralize the Democratic advantage among minorities by turning the liberals' new rules against them to elect more Republicans seemed almost too good to be true. But it was exactly the kind of political jujitsu that appealed to those who dreamed of long-term GOP dominance.

Atwater and his team realized that the approach had another advantage for Republicans. Federal courts were turning increasingly Republican, thanks to eight years of Reagan appointments. By law, judges would decide any districting fights that could not be settled by warring state lawmakers. And it was a Bush-led Justice Department that had to sign off on state redistricting plans, or send them to those courts.[10]

"Lee understood all of this intuitively," said Ginsberg, who was hired by Atwater to oversee the Republicans' below-the-radar redistricting campaign. Ginsberg would go on to be a critical player in the Republican Party's legal battles and the Bush presidential races. "Republicans really felt like a perpetual minority," Ginsberg added. "But one of the first things we did was look at what it would mean if the Voting Rights Act was strictly applied to the congressional map. What was just as obvious as day following night was that if you took districts as they were you could see how minority communities had been completely dissected by the Democrats to provide enough votes for the suburban liberal white guys. That had the effect of depressing the numbers for both the Republicans and the racial minority groups."[11]

During the first year of the first Bush presidency, Atwater and his lieutenants set to work creating an unlikely coalition. GOP strategists began linking up with civil rights leaders who hoped to elect more minorities. As the strategy progressed, Atwater, having set the idea in motion, faded from the forefront; he was battling a brain tumor that would ultimately take his life. Ginsberg and other operatives, though, traversed the country, meeting with civil rights leaders and local activists from Los Angeles to New York and Cleveland to Miami. They forged alliances with black and Latino advocacy groups that quietly agreed to unite with GOP legislators and pursue maps to achieve each side's goals. The effort was aided by the fact that advances in computer technology made it technically possible for many more groups to draw their own maps. The once-arcane process could be taken out of the hands of local political bosses who had dominated it in the past.[12]

In Washington, a thirty-year-old African American Democratic Party activist named Donna Brazile watched the Republican redistricting effort with horror and tried to sound the alarm. Working then for a think tank, Brazile authored a memo that she circulated "as widely as I could" warning of the potential for Republican gains that could last decades. "It was about Lee Atwater and what they were doing—cutting deals with black lawmakers" that would redraw congressional districts in ways that would add minority seats but that, overall, would provide a strong advantage to Republican candidates in the future, she said.

Few picked up on her strongly worded warnings. "I was ignored so bad it hurt my feelings," she later said.[13]

In Tallahassee, Ginsberg and local Republicans met frequently—and quietly—with some of Florida's leading black legislators. Republican operatives remember Corrine Brown, then an outspoken member of the Florida House, stopping by the state GOP headquarters a few blocks from the Capitol. She was all business, with little time for fashion—sometimes, Republicans recall, appearing for hastily arranged late-night meetings with her hair in curlers and big pink slippers on her feet. Her efforts to coordinate with the GOP paid off: Brown was elected to Congress in 1992 from a new district that culled black neighborhoods from Jacksonville to Orlando nearly 150 miles to the south.

In 1990, Ginsberg and the Republican National Committee's field representative for the West, Steve Kinney, met in the cafeteria of the Los Angeles courthouse with Antonia Hernandez, a longtime advocate for Mexican Americans and a supporter of electing more Latinos. As they discussed the GOP strategy with Hernandez, she seemed to agree. "She looked across the table from me and said, 'I'll make a pact with the devil if it will help my people,'" Ginsberg recalled.[14]

Hernandez later described such an encounter with a Republican operative. "GOP strategists know exactly what they're doing in approaching Latinos and African Americans with offers of cooperation," she wrote in the *Los Angeles Times* on April 29, 1990. "Some political analysts believe that cities with large minority populations, and which have traditionally supported white Democrats, could be reapportioned in such a way that minority groups will elect their own representatives. But to do that, many white voters in neighborhoods nearby would have to be shifted into suburban districts, where Republicans do well. That could force white Democrats to compete with Republicans on their turf. Republicans think this bodes well for them, and obviously most Democratic incumbents would prefer to keep districts well-stocked with 'safe' Democratic voters, be they white or minority."

Ultimately, Hernandez declined to cooperate with the Republican National Committee. Her group, the Mexican American Legal Defense and Educational Fund, was suing the Republican-controlled Los Angeles County Board of Supervisors to create more Latino districts on the local level. But, she wrote in the *Times*, "We are cognizant that the political process is one of accommodation, and so we will allow ourselves to be 'used' as long as we also are accommodated. We enter into this 'negotiation' with our eyes open and with a clear understanding of the role we can and should play in the political future of this country."

Across the nation—and particularly in the South—Ginsberg and the Republican National Committee were finding success. Blacks and Republicans joined forces in Florida, Georgia, Mississippi, and Alabama in ways that would add minority and GOP seats in Congress.

At the same time, Republican officials were quietly investing in groups set up to assist minorities in their quest for more districts. One lawyer with GOP ties, Robert E. Freer Jr., created an organization called Lawyers for the Republic—founded in part with a loan from the Republican National Committee—that made redistricting technology available to civil rights groups. "We want to allow the NAACP to play with the big boys," Freer said at the time.[15] Ginsberg saw twin benefits for the party in pushing the redistricting project. First, it would help elect more Republicans to Congress. Second, it could improve the party's image among minority groups. "If somebody thinks that allowing minority groups to gain strength in Congress and state legislatures is perceived as pro-Republican, I think that's great," he said.[16]

An early model for success was Florida, where after 1990 Democrats controlled the governor's mansion, nearly every statewide office, and the legislature. That appeared to give them a strong position for the coming battle over legislative and congressional districts following the 1990 census. The stakes were high, since Florida was gaining four congressional seats, going from nineteen to twenty-three. Democratic leaders in the legislature quickly began pursuing a variety of map designs, all of which would increase their party's share of the congressional delegation. The Democrats' plans included the creation of one district designed to elect the state's first African American congressman since the nineteenth century. But several black lawmakers were angry. The new Voting Rights Act, they said, entitled African Americans to more than just one district out of twenty-three. Several defied their party, offering fiery speeches accusing white Democrats of holding them back.

One black Florida lawmaker, Darryl Reaves of Miami, compared white Democrats to George Wallace and derided fellow blacks who sided with their party's white leadership as "having a leash around their necks."[17] Reaves was heavily lobbied by top GOP leaders, lunching once with President George H. W. Bush and conferring frequently with the president's second-oldest son, Jeb, a Miami resident who was meticulously building his own political machine in the state.[18] Reaves had once envisioned himself as one of Florida's first modern-day black congressmen, but he knew that his party was likely to undermine his candidacy in the wake of his rebellion. Still, he did not regret what he had done. "I am not assigned by my blackness to be a Democrat," he said.[19]

State Republicans, consulting closely with Republican National Committee headquarters in Washington, joined forces with Reaves and other black leaders in the Florida Capitol. One plan they crafted would have created as many as four black-dominated districts, plus an additional Hispanic district in South Florida to elect a Cuban American Republican. The plan drew support from key members of the black caucus and reinvigorated partisan camaraderie with a Cuban American caucus that had been estranged from GOP leaders in Tallahassee. But opposition from white Democrats who held power in the Florida Capitol led to a stalemate and the maps went to the courts, just as Republicans had hoped.

In the end, Republican-appointed judges gave their blessing to a slightly different GOP-backed plan that had black and Hispanic support. It created three black congressional districts—a historic achievement hailed by civil rights groups and black leaders, almost all of whom were Democrats. The outcome highlighted the irony of the Voting Rights Act amendments: pushed by Democrats in 1982, the amendments helped elect more black Democrats but also pushed Republicans closer to their dream of becoming the dominant national party.

In the 1992 election, three black Democrats were sent to the U.S. House from Florida, but packing African Americans into those districts led to GOP gains in the neighboring suburban districts.[20] The Republicans picked up three new congressional seats and made historic gains in the state legislature as well: for the first time in more than a century, Republicans effectively prevented the Democrats from having a majority in the state Senate. After the 1992 elections, the chamber was deadlocked 20–20, largely due to the creation of a black seat drawn to connect minority neighborhoods stretching the length of the sprawling Tampa Bay area. Creating that seat required adding Democrats from surrounding districts and replacing them with Republicans, thus dooming several Democratic candidates and making four neighboring districts more GOP-friendly.[21] For Republicans, this was a major victory in one of the country's biggest states, where rapid growth was creating a battleground for future presidential elections.

In all, eight Southern states created new black districts, sending twelve first-term African Americans to the U.S. House after the 1992 elections—helping to increase the total number of blacks in the House from twenty-five to a historic thirty-eight.[22] At the same time, those eight states sent nine new Republicans to the House.[23] The Republican gains that year were not enough to take control, but GOP strategists began to believe that a takeover was possible, perhaps within one or two election cycles—largely because new district boundaries were increasing pressure on white Democratic incumbents across the South and the Sunbelt.

The results "showed that the Democratic Party was intentionally diluting the voting strength of African Americans in a kind of patronizing way," said Miguel de Grandy, a Miami lawyer who, as a state legislator in 1991 and 1992, helped guide GOP redistricting strategy. "They were saying it's okay to have a Democratic majority (with white Democrats), because we'll take care of you."[24] Such sentiments were echoed by senior Republicans, who declared the post-1990 redistricting a smashing success that foreshadowed gains into the future. "We have won the redistricting war," said Richard N. Bond, who took over the Republican National Committee in 1991 after Atwater's death, in an interview with the *Washington Post*. "It is our assertion that we have made 80 [previously Democratic] seats competitive for the '90s . . . [and] minority representation is going to be dramatically increased because of the Republican Party."[25]

Democrats who considered themselves the party of racial progress suddenly faced an uncomfortable reality. If they objected to the new minority seats, they risked being denounced as racists by minority activists. If they allowed the changes to go through unopposed, they risked losing four decades of political control of the House of Representatives. Democratic Party strategists ended up supporting the creation of more black and Hispanic seats, though not as aggressively as the Republicans did. "For the most part, we acquiesced to it," said Mark Gersh, the director of the National Committee for an Effective Congress, a Democratic group that helped coordinate redistricting strategy. Still, while Democrats knew they were likely to lose some seats as a result of the Voting Rights Act changes, few saw cause for panic. "There was a feeling of inviolability about permanent Democratic control of Congress," Gersh recalled. "Erosion might be sustained as a result, but there was a disbelief or incredulity that what we were talking about could lead to losing control of the House. It was not taken as seriously as it should have been." He said there was a "complete lack of understanding" of what the Republicans were accomplishing.[26]

As for the African American and Hispanic communities, the Republican strategy had helped them increase their numbers in Congress. It had created new opportunities for individual black and Hispanic politicians—and for the local political organizations beneath them. Whether the change had helped them achieve larger goals is less clear. In the U.S. House of Representatives, for example, the Black Caucus grew to a record size over the next two decades. But its influence on legislation evaporated with the ebbing fortunes of the Democratic Party as a whole. In the following decades, Republicans opposed much of what African American Democratic lawmakers stood for. And instead of getting greater consideration for their views, these representatives would find themselves fighting rearguard actions as conservatives sought to roll back the liberal gains of earlier years, from the social safety net and affirmative action to traditional urban aid and housing programs.

By 1994, Democratic Party activists understood the brilliance of the GOP scheme. In just four years, Republicans—aided by President Clinton's unpopularity in his first term and GOP success in "nationalizing" congressional races around Newt Gingrich's Contract with America—achieved the seemingly impossible: control of the House for the first time in four decades. Many pundits saw the 1994 congressional elections as a sign that the country had swung hard to the right. But the reality may have had less to do with an ideological shift than with underlying political mechanics. A wave of Democratic retirements meant an unusually high number of seats were open. And the fact that many of those seats ended up in GOP hands owed at least as much to the new, pro-Republican tilt of many congressional district maps as to popular enthusiasm for the Contract with America.

In retrospect, Gersh said there was no doubt that the new maps paved the way for the takeover, with dramatic shifts in the delegations from Florida, North Carolina, Georgia, and elsewhere. California added two new Democratic Hispanic seats, but Republicans secured five of the seven districts that had been added as a result of population growth.[27] In Florida, as in other states, Republicans took control of the State Senate in 1994. In 1996, they took the State House—a victory that paved the way for Jeb Bush to win the governor's office in 1998 and for a distinct GOP advantage in the battle for the state's twenty-five electoral votes when the governor's older brother, George W. Bush, ran for president in 2000. By the mid-1990s, Republicans were drawing more votes all across the once solidly Democratic South, but it was the redrawn district lines that produced a Republican revolution in congressional power.

The benefits of redistricting were not confined to the South. Across the country, the strategy contributed to incremental gains from Minnesota to Ohio, Wisconsin to New York. GOP advances in many state legislative races depleted the Democrats' influence over drawing maps. In 2006, despite the sagging fortunes of President George W. Bush and the meager achievements of the scandal-plagued Republican Congress, many pundits and Democratic strategists have failed to comprehend the strength of the barrier protecting the GOP from losing its grip on power in Washington.

As the president who set all this in motion, George Herbert Walker Bush might have felt entitled to the admiration and undying support of conservative Republicans. That's not the way the story ended, however. Instead, for the elder Bush it ended in a humiliating defeat — and one more lesson in how hard riding waves of tectonic change could be. Even though Lee Atwater and his troops had engineered major advances toward the conservative goal of lasting dominance, conservatives had grown narrower and more doctrinaire in their attitudes during Bush's rise to the White House.

Where that new reality caught up with him was in the realm of fiscal policy. Historically, conservative Republicans had opposed both high taxes and high deficits. They had resisted new taxes and what they called fiscal irresponsibility with equal fervor. But in the Reagan years, that had begun to change: Reagan cut taxes, but he also doubled the national debt, pumping up federal spending — especially on defense — with little regard for revenues. Without anyone quite coming out and saying so, concern for deficits all but disappeared, while opposing taxes rose almost to the level of religious doctrine.

President Bush seemed not to have noticed. Fearing rising deficits and a potential recession heading into his 1992 reelection campaign, Bush struggled to negotiate solutions with the Democrats who had not yet lost control of Congress. Democrats were arguing for tax increases. Just two years earlier, with his first presidential campaign teetering on the edge, the then vice president had made his famous "read my lips" promise. But by 1992 circumstances had changed. It looked like political suicide to accept a stalemate on federal spending,

with the prospect that the resulting growth in red ink could undermine investors' confidence in the economy and increase the chances
of an election-eve downturn. Bush decided he had to act.

On June 26, 1990, with Washington consumed by a much-
anticipated appearance by Nelson Mandela, recently freed after
twenty-seven years in captivity by South Africa's apartheid government, President Bush quietly issued a written statement that White
House officials hoped would be overshadowed by the day's other
news. Just three paragraphs long, the statement began: "I met this
morning with the bipartisan leadership—the Speaker, the Senate
majority leader, the Senate Republican leader, the House majority
leader and the House Republican leader—to review the status of the
deficit-reduction negotiations."

"It is clear to me," the president's statement said, "that both the
size of the deficit problem and the need for a package that can be
enacted require all of the following: entitlement and mandatory program reform, tax revenue increases, growth incentives, discretionary
spending reductions, orderly reductions in defense expenditures and
budget process reform."

Buried in a lengthy, dull-sounding list of proposals issued by
Bush that day were three critical words: tax revenue increases. Bush
had officially reneged on his pledge. In no time, conservatives who
had read his lips and rallied to his 1988 campaign turned against
Bush. David Keene, chairman of the American Conservative
Union, accused the president of "selling out."[28] Republican lawmakers and candidates moved quickly to distance themselves from
Bush, some pledging to confront the commander-in-chief personally. Senator Malcolm Wallop, who was chairman of a conservative
group of senators called the Republican Steering Committee,
offered a devastating assessment at a luncheon meeting: "I don't
want to use the word 'betrayed,'" Wallop said. "But people feel they
are victims of some ill-conceived actions. Politically, this has been
really badly handled. Whatever their intentions, this has been
touted as 'Bush's big lie.'"[29]

Bush had given his base many reasons to be angry. Not only did
his deal increase taxes, it also added a new bracket for high-income

earners—a direct retreat, conservatives felt, from trickle-down Reaganomics that fulfilled a GOP tenet of encouraging wealth. Grover Norquist was particularly incensed because Bush's actions violated the no-new-taxes pledge that had put his Americans for Tax Reform on the map. Years later, Norquist continued to display prominently in his office hallway a reminder of that moment: an enlarged framed copy of the October 2, 1990, *Wall Street Journal* editorial headlined "Honor Thy Pledge." The editorial listed the names of Republicans who had taken the Norquist oath and urged them to vote against the Bush tax increase.

Bush made scant public appearances on the day of his fateful statement. He ducked the only question he was asked during a brief Rose Garden event. The next day, on the eve of leaving Washington for a much-needed July 4 holiday, the president faced a press corps salivating over one of the most striking flip-flops in modern political history. "Mr. President," came the first question from the assemblage gathered in the cramped West Wing briefing room, "I'd like to ask you about your reversal on 'no new taxes.' Do you consider that a betrayal of your promise, and what do you say to Republicans who complain that you've robbed them of the same campaign issue that helped get you elected?" The president seemed to stammer. He called his decision a "necessary step" to get budget talks moving. But the questions kept coming. Had he misled the voters? Was politics really that cynical?

"The arrows have been flying, front, back, sideways, but that's what I get paid for," he said defiantly. "And I think—I think we're on the right track now. And I think we'll have strong support from both sides of the aisle." At times, the exchange with reporters was downright uncomfortable. One journalist even commented during a question, "I know it's hard for you. I can tell it is somewhat difficult." Another journalist cited the *New York Post*'s screaming headline on the day following his statement: "Read My Lips: I Lied." Bush's political career essentially ended that week. His popularity among the general public still soared near 70 percent at the time, a vestige of his success in ousting Saddam Hussein from Kuwait in the Persian Gulf War. But many conservatives knew they would not enthusiastically support the president's reelection. Conservatives such as Norquist viewed the elder Bush as part of the old Nixon-Rockefeller GOP that compromised with Democrats instead of standing firm on conservative principles. Wholehearted support for Bush in the November election was now out of the question.

On election night, the extent of the damage was visible almost immediately. Early on, the networks called three traditionally Republican states—Vermont, New Hampshire, and Georgia—for Democrat Bill Clinton, whose campaign had its own problems but nonetheless succeeded in positioning Clinton as a centrist Democrat. After Vermont, New Hampshire, and Georgia, the industrial heartland—the land of Reagan Democrats—fell to Clinton as well. The blue-collar voters who had defected to Reagan returned home that night. The pain did not end there. Clinton also scored impressive gains in the South, which had emerged since Richard Nixon's presidency as a Republican stronghold. With heavy turnout from minorities, city dwellers, and what remained of the union vote, Clinton surged ahead in every region.

As the president appeared before a crowd of supporters in the ballroom of the Westin Galleria Hotel in Houston to issue a concession statement, he turned to Barbara and whispered "It's over."[30]

In the weeks that followed, Republican leaders engaged in a vicious postmortem. Richard Bond, the outgoing Republican National Committee chairman, blamed the party's right wing for dividing the party and presenting an extremist image of Republicanism, especially on abortion. "An image of intolerance threatens to drive millions of people away from voting Republican in the future," he said. "Our job is to win elections and not to cling to intolerances that zealots call principles."[31]

Among Republicans, however, that was a minority view. Karl Rove, then working as a political consultant in Austin, did not see it that way. Neither did Jeb Bush, whose strategy for becoming governor of Florida rested on an unwavering commitment to the new tenets of conservative ideology. Most important of all, it would turn out, George W. Bush also rejected Bond's analysis and his advice for the future. George W. emerged from election night 1992 bitter about the humiliation his father had suffered. But turning against his party's conservative base was the last thing he intended to do. Instead, he would commit himself wholeheartedly to the right's agenda — and to the goal of reshaping the American political landscape in its image.

CHAPTER 3

The End of the Southern Strategy

I want it to be known that a conservative candidate can carry the Hispanic vote.

—GOVERNOR GEORGE W. BUSH IN A CONVERSATION WITH REPORTERS DURING
HIS REELECTION CAMPAIGN, EL PASO, TEXAS, OCTOBER 1998

In the days that followed the 1992 election, members of the extended Bush family dispersed unhappily to their separate homes. The president, nursing a deeply bruised ego, repaired to the ancestral compound at Kennebunkport on the coast of Maine. He tended to his ailing mother and saw few visitors. Jeb and George, the most politically engaged of the president's children, went home to Florida and Texas, respectively. They seethed over the fact that Bill Clinton, a self-indulgent draft dodger already dogged by sexual scandal, had somehow triumphed over their big-hearted, war hero father. But there was something extraordinary about the way the two brothers responded to the humiliation of 1992, something almost chilling in what it suggested about the steel core of ambition at the political heart of the outgoing president's oldest sons. Both understood clearly that their father had lost the White House primarily because the conservative wing of his own party had deserted him. In the midnight hour, the conservatives had turned their backs on George Herbert Walker Bush even though he had labored on behalf of their cause for most of his adult life. And they had abandoned the president at the very moment they began to reap the rewards of all he and his lieutenants had done to give Republicans a winning edge in congressional and in state legislative districts across the country. Taken all together, it was hard to see the conservatives' action as anything less than complete betrayal—massive disloyalty to a family that prized loyalty above all.

Yet if Jeb and George W. Bush felt any resentment toward their party's conservative wing, not the slightest trace of it seeped out. Instead, in the decade and more after their father's defeat, the two brothers—pursuing their political goals in different states but on parallel tracks—bound themselves all the more closely to the conservative movement. Quite literally, instead of making their father's enemies their enemies, they paid those enemies the sincerest of compliments: they imitated them. They embraced the doctrine of no new taxes; they would even embrace the godfather of that principle, Grover Norquist. The two brothers also extended their identification with evangelical Christians and other religious conservatives. And they continued to pursue revitalization of the Republican Party's operating structure on lines that conservative political operatives had laid down.

In one area Jeb and George W. Bush broke ground that was not already sacred soil to conservatives: their insistence that the Republican Party renounce the covertly racist Southern strategy that originated with Nixon and still flourished through the Reagan era. Henceforth, the GOP must reach out to racial minorities—both African Americans and the faster-growing population of Hispanic immigrants. Publicly at least, George W. got to that position more quickly than Jeb, but they ended up side by side. And the position they staked out was potentially even more significant for the party's future than their father's role in redistricting.

Grover Norquist and some other conservative strategists had become convinced that the GOP needed to take this step, but neither Norquist nor others like him had the stature to make it happen. No Republican leader in the years after 1992 did more than George and Jeb Bush to turn the GOP around on the issue of race and embrace diversity. There would be exceptions like George W. Bush's 2000 appearance at Bob Jones University, a South Carolina college that banned interracial dating—but in general the brothers rejected strategies that relied on a racist appeal. In a sense, the two brothers redeemed the moral compromise their father had made. It was good politics, a change whose time had come, but it was also risky. As the coming years would show, it could strengthen the Republican Party, but it could also drive a wedge into the strategic alliance on which conservatives pinned their hopes of long-term power.

All that was still a few miles down the road, though. As the Bush brothers licked their wounds and prepared to move on, George W. especially had a few things to get off his chest.

He was openly critical of some Republicans he felt had benefited from his father's generosity and failed to repay it. And he took note of some staff aides he thought had not worked hard enough, or had let their personal priorities and preferences get ahead of the candidate's best interests. The president's oldest son had a thing about that. During 1992 and his father's earlier campaigns, his self-assigned role had been to head up the devotion police. Aides—no matter how senior or important—had felt his wrath if they failed to put the candidate's best interest first, down to the smallest detail. Once, in 1988, George W. had even upbraided Lee Atwater, his close friend and a master strategist, for showing disrespect by conducting a magazine interview about the campaign in his underwear. Afterward, Atwater wrote a letter of apology to Barbara Bush.[1]

There were no such outbursts from Jeb Bush. As the public would come to understand more clearly in the future, the two brothers' lives had some uncanny parallels, but they displayed quite different temperaments and political skills. Those differences, though, were not what most people—including their own parents—thought they were. Jeb is six years younger than George W., but he had always been considered more thoughtful and disciplined. Even before the 1992 campaign, Jeb had the calm, confident, polished air of an experienced politician. He had moved to Miami in 1980 to run the Florida part of his father's first unsuccessful presidential campaign. He remained there after the election, concluding that the cosmopolitan Latin city would be a comfortable home for his Mexican-born wife, Columba, whom he had met during a prep school exchange program. They had married when Jeb was just twenty-one, and had lived in Caracas for a short time.

Soon after the couple settled in Miami, Jeb was hired as a real estate developer by one of his father's supporters, Armando Codina, an emigrant from Cuba who had become a millionaire in the United States. Jeb had no experience in real estate but soon held a large stake in a new partnership, the Codina Bush Group. Jeb pursued other business deals as well, and by the late 1980s, he was rich — traditionally a prerequisite for members of the Bush family interested in political careers. Jeb also had a serious interest in the details of public policy, as his involvement in education reform would later demonstrate. In 1992 he had worked hard to deliver Florida for his father, though some analysts would look back and read the victory margin — less than two percentage points — as an omen.

All in all, at least in the eyes of his parents and members of their inner circle, it was Jeb who seemed destined to carry the family banner in national politics. According to Peter and Rochelle Schweitzer's book, *The Bushes: Portrait of a Dynasty*, when Jeb first told his parents he was considering a run for governor in Florida, his father's response was "Go for it." That reflected the fact that family members and close friends shared the assessment of former White House aide Pete Teeley: "Jeb's got his feet on the ground. He doesn't suffer from the ego problems of George."[2]

What Teeley was referring to was George W. Bush's tendency to call attention to himself, often in what his family considered inappropriate and unflattering ways — a tendency some attributed to an insecure ego, though others dismissed it as simple immaturity. There was the helter-skelter existence of George W.'s early adult years. The difficulty achieving financial success, despite repeated assistance from the family network. The drinking problem. And the continuing tendency to pop off at inopportune moments and in impolitic ways. His mother once said George W. took after her, rather than Poppy Bush, adding tartly, "that is not a compliment."[3] Small wonder that when he told her that he planned to run against incumbent Texas governor Ann Richards in 1994, his mother snapped, "You can't win."[4]

In important ways, however, by the mid-1990s, the negative side of George W. Bush amounted to less than the sum of its parts. He may have been little more than a playboy in his twenties, but when he got married, he chose a wife who would help him confront and lick the drinking problem, support his ambitions, and—though she had to overcome her natural reserve to do it—adjust well to the role of politician's wife. Moreover, the cold-turkey way George W. gave up alcohol when Laura made him see that it threatened their life and family suggested no small amount of inner strength.

And by the end of the 1992 campaign, Bush had extricated himself from a flagging oil business and took with him a handsome profit. He used the money to buy into a syndicate that was taking over the Texas Rangers baseball team. Both moves were facilitated by family contacts, but when Bush sold his interest in the Rangers venture in 1998, it brought him nearly $15 million on an original investment of some $500,000, making him financially secure for life.[5]

Moreover, George had shown what looked like a born campaigner's feel for the personal side of retail politics: he used the baseball franchise of all things to make himself widely known as a can-do business leader with a likeable personality. By 1993, he had led a successful campaign to get $138 million in public funding for a new Rangers ballpark. And somehow, by making himself a fixture at Rangers games, lounging comfortably in shirtsleeves in the owners' box between third base and home plate, bantering with fans, handing out autographed cards, he established himself as a well-known public figure and a regular guy in ways his father never could.

Moreover, the 1992 election, though it ended in defeat, brought George W. a sense of liberation, just as it did Jeb. For the first time in their adult lives, the political siblings did not have to fret over their father's next campaign and their role in it. Henceforth, they could focus on plotting their own careers, with the added impetus of seeking to redeem the family's political honor.

By the spring of 1993, George W. Bush was ready to make his move. He broached the topic of a campaign for governor with his friend and confidant, political consultant Karl Rove. Rove signed on, and together they began making the rounds, meeting with GOP activists and fund-raisers, outlining their plans and drawing in commitments of support. George invited Dallas businessman James Francis, a prominent Republican and a family friend, for a fishing excursion to his vacation home at Rainbo Lake, a private resort in East Texas. Francis agreed to chair the campaign.[6]

"He worked the politics of the situation very quickly—his dad was out of the White House, he got the Rangers deal done—fewer people were saying he was running because of his dad," Rove said at the time.[7]

With campaign funds flowing in and the nucleus of a campaign team assembled, what Bush and Rove needed next was a handful of specific issues and proposals on which to build their appeal to voters, a campaign agenda that would showcase his conservative ideology and still have broad appeal in a politically and ethnically diverse state. "My father let Bill Clinton decide what issues the two of them were going to talk about," George W. once said, "and I wasn't going to let that happen to me."[8] The chief issue he and Rove settled on was education. It was an unusual choice for a Republican, but it met the twin challenges of being acceptable to conservatives while appealing to voters across the ideological spectrum. And it had an added advantage that Texas Republicans had usually paid little attention to: shrewdly managed, the education issue gave Bush a way to reach out to minorities without serious risk of alienating white voters. Bush also put forward initiatives to rein in damage awards in lawsuits and to reform welfare and juvenile justice. But the heart of his campaign for governor in 1994 would be the education plan—and with it, the new outreach to minorities. Soon George W. Bush and his political adviser Karl Rove began showing up in Texas towns and neighborhoods that most other Republican politicians barely knew how to find on a map.

In the spring of 1994, money woes in the Texas public school system dominated the headlines. Student test scores were declining in a
state that already ranked near the bottom. The schools had many
problems, but inadequate funding lay behind many of them, especially for districts serving poor children, which in Texas meant districts in both rural and urban areas. Governor Richards backed a
proposal to help poor, low-performance districts by shifting funds
from affluent districts. Texas voters emphatically rejected the plan in
May. That left a vacuum—and gave Bush his opening. He put forward a plan that offered schools more money and gave local officials
more authority, but also held them accountable for results.

Bush's approach foreshadowed the No Child Left Behind Act,
which would become one of only a few highlights in his domestic
policy record as president. The approach was not entirely new; it also
owed something to a successful education reform plan crafted earlier
by another canny Southern politician, Bill Clinton of Arkansas, and
the idea of setting standards and demanding accountability had been
the mantra that education reformers in both parties had embraced for
years. Also, there were inherent problems in the approach: it threatened to put local officials on the spot by exposing their bad schools,
and accountability almost always meant standardized tests, which
raised a host of controversies.

But those problems would not surface until years after such a
plan had been adopted. For Bush's purposes, it was just about
perfect as a campaign issue. The idea of cutting back the role of
big government—even state government—and giving more control
to local leaders was music to conservative ears; so was making
government—read "bureaucrats"—more accountable. The approach
also had a commonsense quality that appealed to voters across party
lines. Moreover, nothing Bush said threatened the racial status quo.
Nor did it raise the specter of liberal social engineering, as Governor
Richards's plan did, with its almost Marxist notion of taking money
away from successful, predominantly white taxpayers and giving it to
the children of other, less successful, predominantly black and
Hispanic taxpayers.

Beyond the specifics, focusing on education helped Bush, a

neophyte in public service, project himself as a politician who knew how to handle serious issues. Talking about education also reminded voters that they had just repudiated the incumbent governor's approach to a major problem. And it gave the challenger something to talk about with traditionally Democratic black and Latino voters, many of whom saw the chronically poor schools in their neighborhoods as obstacles to a better life for their children. When liberals and their allies in the teachers' unions sought to support Richards by attacking Bush's education plan, Bush deftly accused them of espousing the "soft bigotry of low expectations." The phrase marked almost a full reversal of the old code language of the Southern strategy.

To understand why George W. Bush was so insistent about courting minorities, it is only necessary to look at the numbers: African Americans comprised 11 percent of Texas voters, and 15 percent of the total U.S. population. Hispanics, who had long been part of the social fabric in Texas, made up more than 25 percent of the state's population and their numbers were growing so rapidly that they would represent almost one-third of the Texas population by the year 2000.[9] No political party could continually concede such numbers of voters to the other side, as Republicans normally did, and hope to prevail on a consistent basis.

As he campaigned across Texas, Bush made a bigger pitch for black votes than most Republicans had in the past, but George W. expended far more energy in 1994 trying to win Hispanic votes. He could expect no help from the existing Mexican American advocacy groups; their Democratic leanings were too strong. So he reached out on his own. His communications director at the time, a black woman named Deborah Burstion-Donbraye, was astonished at the candidate's insistence on packing his early 1994 schedule with visits to heavily Democratic Latino cities on the border with Mexico. Bush's speeches in these enclaves always mentioned his education initiative, with added emphasis on how it might help heavily Latino schools. He warmed his audiences with emotional rhetoric describing Latinos' ability to overcome obstacles and become part of the American dream.

The appeal was low-key, calculated to avoid triggering a backlash from resentful whites. Instead of hot-button topics like affirmative action, he talked about his education program, which was supposed to help everyone. And, in speeches and radio commercials, he stressed the common values shared by Latinos and Anglos in America — conservative values of family, freedom, and pride in their heritage.

"Bush has never underestimated the growing importance of the Hispanic vote," wrote Jorge Ramos, an anchor for Univision, the Spanish-language news network. "Bush quickly grasped that his political future in Texas could very well depend on capturing the Latino vote," Ramos wrote. "Since 1994, his strategy has been the same: gain more of the Latino vote. How? Appear on Hispanic television, speak — or try to speak — Spanish, and emphasize the importance of family."[10]

Soothing as it was meant to be, Bush's approach differed from that of most other Republican politicians in one significant way. Often, the GOP had seen the Hispanic population as a vehicle for firing up white voters by inveighing against illegal immigrants. George W. Bush did not rail against immigrants. In fact, he soon began to use his more tolerant position on immigration to distinguish himself from other GOP leaders, not just in Texas but across the country.

Meantime, in Florida, Jeb Bush was pursuing the governorship of another politically important state with a remarkably similar approach. Governor Lawton Chiles, a popular old-line Democrat, was seeking reelection. Jeb Bush sought to unseat him with all the usual conservative lines of attack. Chiles was promoting big government and big spending, Bush charged, while going soft on criminals and welfare recipients. For his part, the challenger talked of limited government, lower taxes, free enterprise, private-sector responses to social problems, and self-reliance and family values. Jeb Bush opposed gun control and special legal protections for gays. He called for speedier application of the death penalty. Like his brother in Texas, Jeb Bush also advocated education reform. But he had moved further to the right than his brother, railing against public schools and calling for abolition of the state's Department of Education.

Such hard-right rhetoric, along with his victory in a hard-fought GOP primary, won the attention of conservatives everywhere. Grover Norquist flew south to meet Jeb in Miami. In some ways, it was a bizarre encounter, the son of the rejected president face-to-face with one of the men who had engineered the rejection. But they huddled for a lengthy conversation in a nearly deserted restaurant after a day of Spanish-language campaigning in Little Havana. In person, Norquist recalled, Jeb was even more impressive than he had expected. Norquist was struck by Jeb's confident manner, and by the evident depth of his conservative convictions. Norquist told Jeb he could scarcely believe he was talking with the son of a man he had hounded from office.

"I said, 'How is it that, when I speak to you, it is as if I am speaking with someone who shares the values of Ronald Reagan and not of a more recent Republican president?' And I can remember that it was awkward. And he said, 'I love my father, but I am a product of my time.' He basically defined it as generational, which I think is accurate."[11] Norquist believed the Bush brothers, like many conservatives of their generation who came of age during Reagan's presidency, had been more deeply influenced by Reagan's robust rhetoric and philosophical conviction than the paler moderation of their father. Of course, Reagan's way had the added appeal of being crowned with political success, while President Bush's moderation had led to embarrassment and defeat.

Norquist didn't seek out George W. Bush in 1994. With limited time, he wanted to get to know the most important political figures. "Jeb was the next president, not his brother," Norquist later explained.[12]

At the time, Norquist was only saying what most people thought about Jeb and George Bush: that it would be the serious-minded, settled-down Jeb who carried the family banner into the next generation of national politics. What almost no one realized was that in some critical respects, Jeb's political maturity lagged behind his older brother's, especially when it came to the hand grenade of race.

Jeb did not lag in his ability to campaign for Latino support. In the heavily Hispanic areas of southern and central Florida, Jeb delighted audiences with his fluent Spanish. His marriage and his time living in Latin America had given him a command of the language and its colloquial idioms that his older brother struggled to match but never attained. Jeb was particularly tight with Miami's influential Cuban American community, long characterized by loyalty to the Republican Party. During Jeb's tenure as chairman of the Dade County GOP in the 1980s, he encouraged Cubans to remain loyal, and, through his frequent appearances on Miami's lively Spanish-language talk radio, Jeb proved an important link between conservatives and the Cuban exiles.

It was with African Americans that Jeb Bush had problems. In 1994, blacks made up about 15 percent of the Florida population. And like his brother in Texas, Jeb was making some effort to reach out to them. He called for education reform, but he had not put forward the kind of concrete package his brother had. As he was to discover, that essentially left him in the position of appearing before black audiences with little more than the basic, white-oriented conservative agenda to talk about. That could be dangerous.

During a summertime GOP primary debate in Tampa, a black woman in the audience rose to ask Jeb Bush and his rivals what they would do for her community. The forty-one-year-old Bush offered a response that was straight-from-the-heart conservative theology and remarkably impolitic. "It's time to strive for a society where there's equality of opportunity, not equality of results," he said. "So I'm going to answer your question by saying: probably nothing."[13] Members of the audience gasped, but the candidate continued: "I think what we ought to do is to have a society where you go out and pursue your dream and you're not punished for working hard and playing by the rules."[14]

"Probably nothing" became the battle cry of the Democrats, who seized on Jeb's words as proof that he was a child of privilege and power who lacked compassion for those without his advantages. Still, the polls showed Jeb maintaining a slight lead over Chiles—until two weeks before the election, when he shot himself in the foot again by demonstrating that he did not quite understand the lesson of the Willie Horton ad. As the gubernatorial race came down to the wire, Jeb Bush's campaign aired a nasty television spot accusing Chiles of being soft on crime and the death penalty. The ad focused on a Florida woman named Wendy Nelson, whose ten-year-old daughter, Elsa, had been kidnapped and murdered while on her way to school. The man convicted of the crime had been sentenced to death. Bush essentially accused Chiles of being "too liberal on crime" to let the execution go forward. The ad was a blunder on more than one level: both the Nelson family and Elsa's killer were white, but the death penalty was a subject inextricably tied to African Americans. So the ad instantly brought back memories of Willie Horton and its tacitly racist appeal to white fear. At a more immediate level, the ad rested on a factual fallacy: Chiles, whatever his personal feelings, did not have the power to execute the killer. The case was still on appeal.

Chiles pointed out that the case was still in the courts. He ran his own counteradvertisements in which judges and prosecutors confirmed his assertion. And Chiles himself drew the line to Willie Horton.[15] In a subsequent televised debate, Chiles ferociously attacked the ad and Bush's personal decision to run it. "You knew it was false. You admitted it was false. And I am ashamed that you would use the loss of a mother in an ad like this." Bush responded lamely, "The symbol of crime needs to have a human face on it."[16] The controversy over the ad bumped up negative perceptions of Bush, reinforcing Chiles's charge that the Republican candidate was taking instructions from pollsters and consultants. A week before the election, public opinion polls showed Chiles taking the lead.

On Election Day 1994, Republicans scored a historic national victory. They captured several key governorships, made important gains in state legislatures, and took control of the United States Senate. Best of all for conservatives, they took control of the House of Representatives for the first time in more that forty years—thanks in large part to the redistricting strategy begun under George H. W. Bush. Representative Newt Gingrich of Georgia, who had rallied the GOP around his Contract with America, became Speaker of the

House and prepared to launch the "Republican Revolution." For the first time, there was serious talk of a realignment that could give Republicans the kind of long-term dominance in national politics that Democrats enjoyed after the New Deal.

In terms of presidential politics, however, the off-year elections of 1994 required conservatives to rethink the situation: while his brother scored an unexpectedly solid win in Texas, Jeb Bush went down to defeat in Florida. The death penalty ad was a factor in the Florida outcome. So was Chiles's hard-swinging campaign, which benefited from a late infusion of public campaign financing; the money enabled the Democratic governor to nearly match Bush on the airwaves.[17] There was also a series of anonymous phone calls to senior citizens suggesting that Jeb Bush would take away Medicare. Together, these and other factors gave Chiles a 75,000-vote victory, the narrowest victory margin in a Florida gubernatorial race since 1876. In Texas, George W. Bush won 53 percent of the total vote and captured nearly a third of the ballots cast by Hispanics.

How the family felt about the outcome was expressed by its patriarch, with more candor than he may have intended. "The joy is in Texas, but our hearts are in Florida," said the former president from his office in Houston. Chiles had won by "going negative personally, not on the issues," the elder Bush said. "I am very upset about it."[18]

Nonetheless, Jeb's loss and George W.'s victory meant that the new governor of Texas had taken over the lead position to restore the family name. He wasted no time nailing that position down. And the fallout from a relatively little-noticed episode that occurred shortly after the election provided an ideal vehicle for Bush to begin defining his place in the firmament of Republican presidential hopefuls—and to give new importance to one element in the conservative strategy for achieving long-term power.

One of the Republican hopefuls was Governor Pete Wilson of California. Wilson was up for reelection in 1994, and as the year began, he found himself trailing his Democratic opponent by twenty percentage points in the polls.[19] Wilson decided to capitalize on the fact that his state was going through one of its periodic bouts of angst over immigration. The governor came out in support of a ballot initiative called Proposition 187, which sought to discourage immigrants from entering the country illegally by stripping them of state benefits, including access to public schools. Wilson also began to air a television commercial on the subject, complete with an ominous voice-over line: "They keep on coming—two million illegal immigrants."[20] The gambit seemed to work. Wilson was elected to a second term. Proposition 187 was also approved.

The campaign sparked an angry backlash that would haunt Republicans for years, however, giving the GOP an anti-Latino image as that group emerged as the nation's fastest-growing demographic and its most valued swing constituency. Non-Cuban Hispanics across the United States became even more loyal to Democratic candidates. Both Jeb and George W. Bush decried Proposition 187 as bad for their party and for their states. Jeb, whose Hispanic children had experienced prejudice when they lived in Tallahassee in the late 1980s, was especially sensitive to what Wilson had done. But it was George, in his new capacity as governor of Texas, who would carry the challenge into the national spotlight.

In late November, as governor-elect, George W. Bush announced that he would attend the inauguration of Mexico's new president, Ernesto Zedillo. The move underscored his opposition to the anti-immigrant initiative that California had just adopted.

"I believe it's good public policy for Texas to make sure immigrant children are educated so that they're available for the workforce later on," Bush said in announcing the trip to Zedillo's inauguration. "And I believe the Mexican government, Mexican officials, will appreciate this position."[21] Lest some think he had gone too far on the sensitive issue, Bush added, "Both of us agree we ought to enforce the borders. Both of us agree the federal government ought to pay for services mandated. I just happen to believe we ought to educate our children once they're here, once the ability of the federal government to enforce our borders is broken down."[22]

Bush's announcement coincided with a public challenge to Wilson's immigration views during a governors' conference in Williamsburg, Virginia. Wilson's victory in California made him the reigning expert within the party on the immigration issue. But the challenge by Bush in Williamsburg stood out, particularly to Wilson himself. "I was disappointed," Wilson said in an interview years later. "And I was obviously curious as to what the reasoning was."[23] Wilson said he thought Bush might have staked out an anti-187 stance during his campaign merely to set himself apart from Richards, whose administration had sued the federal government for financial assistance in dealing with the influx of illegal immigrants. He also attributed the difference to a cultural divide between Texas and his home state. "The so-called Latino voters there were for the most part third-generation Texans," Wilson said. "It was a very different situation than in California, where you did have this very, very large illegal population"[24]

Across the country, Republican leaders took notice that the new Texas governor was different. "George W. Bush made a very powerful impression and an early impression on other governors when he took on Pete Wilson on the immigration issue," recalled former Michigan governor John Engler, who observed the exchange.[25] "He really minced no words. He told Wilson, 'You're wrong,' and that it was . . . a catastrophic position. He was very clear. He felt that Wilson had made the issue one where it had become an anti-Hispanic issue rather than a solution to illegal immigration." Bush's challenge stunned the other governors. Wilson had taken heat on the immigrant issue from established conservative icons such as Bill Bennett and Jack Kemp. But Bush was still an unknown, a rookie governor who had been expected to defer to his more experienced California colleague. Wilson, after all, was a former United States senator, former mayor of a border city, governor of the most populous state, and often mentioned as the party's next candidate for president.

The new Texas governor had made a name for himself when it came to immigration. And his careful attention to the ethnic dynamic did not stop with his election. In 1995 and heading into the GOP presidential primary of 1996, the Texas governor openly challenged conservative Pat Buchanan, who at the time was campaigning for the White House on an anti-immigration, antitrade platform. "No Cheap Shots at Mexico, Please," was the headline of an August 1995 *New York Times* op-ed by Bush, who wrote that as the presidential campaign moves forward, "discussion on immigration and Mexico can turn ugly and destructive very quickly." Days earlier, Bush said in a press conference timed to coincide with Buchanan's United We Stand conference being held in Dallas: "I don't want anybody, any race, to be used as a political issue in the 1996 campaign."[26]

Bush's tenure in Texas was marked by unusual alliances with Democrats who controlled the state legislature. He won plaudits for bipartisanship and moving forward his education plan, albeit one largely formulated by the Democratic lieutenant governor, Bob Bullock.

In Florida, the election results forced Jeb to reflect. He decided to tackle the legacy of "probably nothing." That meant finding a way to alter the damaging image without compromising the conservative principles that formed the foundation of his political life. The answer, it turned out, was to follow the example of his brother in Texas. Days after the Florida voting, while his brother jetted off to meet the new president of Mexico, Jeb placed a call to T. Willard Fair, the son of North Carolina tobacco workers and president of the Urban League of Greater Miami. Bush asked if the group could use some of his left-over campaign funds. Fair said he could use the money. That same day, Fair recalled, Bush came alone to Fair's modest office in the Urban League's northwest Miami headquarters. "I thought we were just going to have a photo op, but we ended up talking for about an hour and a half," Fair said.[27]

The two talked about the campaign, about their families, and about the desperate state of affairs in Miami's black neighborhoods and schools. Fair was a grizzled veteran of the civil rights movement, but he had left the Democratic Party in the 1980s because he felt the Reverend Jesse Jackson's bid for the Democratic presidential nomination was never taken seriously by the party hierarchy. Fair was also a man who saw the whole issue of blacks and poverty in a different light. He was registered as an independent, but he had voted for Jeb Bush in the gubernatorial campaign. He had known about Bush's "probably nothing" remark but had reacted far differently from the Democratic establishment. "I said, 'Oh, that's my man. That's my man,'" Fair recalled later. "What it meant to me was that he was prepared to take the public position that you have got to do it for yourself. . . . And for him to say that knowing how it could be misinterpreted, knowing how it could be used by those other people, be they of one particular race or one particular party, said to me that this is an honest man. That was the right answer. Whether it was motivated out of racism, whether it was motivated out of the fact that he didn't want to alienate a white conservative constituency, I don't care."

The conversation on that day in November 1994 moved swiftly from politics to family gossip to brainstorming. Jeb Bush wanted to know if Fair knew much about the school choice movement. A few cities were experimenting with charter schools—schools that are privately run but governed by school district policies—but the idea had not yet gained a foothold in Florida. "He said have you ever heard of the charter school? I said no, what's that?" Fair recalled. "He shared with me what a charter school is. Then he said have you heard of the voucher movement? I said no. So he explained it. I said I really liked that. I saw it as leverage to be used in the revolution to bring about change in a system that had not ever been forced to change."[28]

Over the next eighteen months, Bush lobbied lawmakers in Tallahassee to pass a law allowing charter schools. He created a think tank, the Foundation for Florida's Future, which churned out research reports promoting school choice. The foundation conducted a survey of black voters in 1995; it found potential openings for a Republican candidate who embraced school choice. The survey's conclusion: "The onus is on white conservatives, those of us who have talked a good game for years, but who have only recently achieved the political power to make a real difference."[29]

As George W. and Karl Rove had understood in Texas, an education platform based on school choice was tailor-made for the new Republican political formula: an intellectually serious policy that was based on free-market principles and undermined a reliably Democratic constituency by appealing to blacks who were desperate over the condition of local schools. Advocating choice was an affront to teachers' unions, which generally opposed charter schools and other forms of choice on policy and political grounds. The unions were a significant source of money and manpower for Democrats; defeating the unions on this issue might undermine their standing and thereby strike another blow at the opposition party.

The charter school law was passed in Tallahassee, thanks largely to the Republican-led State Senate and Florida's newly elected GOP education commissioner. Chiles had little choice but to sign it. Bush and Fair then moved quickly to open their own charter school, right in the heart of Miami's impoverished Liberty City. As part of their effort, Fair recruited parents to a Saturday morning meeting at the Urban League headquarters. "It was his first big meeting with a bunch of black folks, and he didn't know how it was going to go," Fair recalled. The session was awkward at first. Jeb and a staffer were the only whites in the room. Several parents could be seen shaking their heads and looking askance at the Republican politician. "You could tell they were skeptical," recalled Cory Tilley, a longtime aide to Jeb Bush who was involved in the school's creation. Tilley said his boss worked hard to gain credibility, sticking around afterward to help stack folding chairs and talk one-on-one with parents.

Bush assigned aides such as Tilley to the project and drew on his massive fund-raising network to raise money for renovations and computers. "People had maxed out to the campaign, but they wanted to make sure they stayed in good graces with the future governor," chuckled Fair. Within two months, the new school had recruited a principal, rented a building, hired some teachers, and signed up sixty kids. Bush stayed involved, making sure the venture did not founder, and that no one forgot his role in it. During the first year of operation, he frequently stopped by for visits, sometimes surprising the staff. At Christmas he dressed up as Santa, donning a fluffy white beard and a pudgy tummy and bearing gifts for the children.

Jeb changed in other, ways, too. That he would run for governor again in 1998 was a given. But next time some things would have to be handled differently. The previous campaign had cast a pall over his family life. It had taken him away from home for long periods at a time. His marriage had grown tense. The experience prompted Jeb to convert to Catholicism, and to promise his family that in 1998 he would strictly limit overnight stays away from the family's Coral

Gables home. The family crisis and the religious conversion added another set of parallels in the lives of the Bush brothers. George's heavy drinking had threatened to break his family apart; in 1986, he had turned his back on alcohol, recommitted himself to his family, and become a born-again Christian. And once again, the common perception of the two brothers had been proved wrong. The apparently unfocused and unserious, late-blooming George had proved to be the more poised and canny politician. Now, when it came to putting his personal life on a sounder footing, the seemingly more mature Jeb had proved to be ten years behind his older brother.

For both, the changes in their personal lives brought with them significant political benefits. Family values were part of the conservative litany, of course. And George's religious conversion made him one with evangelical conservatives, while Jeb's Catholicism created a potential bond with Hispanic voters.

Jeb entered the 1998 campaign a new man and a smarter politician. In hindsight, he and his advisers decided the 1994 campaign had been too rigidly ideological; the candidate would follow his brother's example and adopt an outwardly more flexible approach. Meantime, the Liberty City charter school, where students wore red, white, and blue uniforms and were subject to corporal punishment, quickly became a symbol of the candidate's political transformation. It was a major theme of his 1998 campaign, which featured a renewed emphasis on attracting support from African Americans. In September 1997, it was a black woman, accompanied by a child from the Liberty City school, who filed the papers making Jeb's candidacy official. At a rally several weeks later, the candidate was introduced to an audience by one of Tallahassee's most prominent black ministers, the Reverend R. B. Holmes, who called Bush a "new spirit."[30] The first campaign swing that month included stops at a black school in West Palm Beach, the historically black Bethune-Cookman College in Daytona Beach, and a vocational school in Jacksonville. There, black cosmetology students gave the candidate a facial as the cameras rolled. "Democrats have taken African American voters for granted," Bush said. "Republicans haven't tried. I'm going to break the cycle."

The new rhetoric was a far cry from the words that drew so much scorn three years earlier in that Tampa debate. "To me, the question of race is one of the more compelling challenges our country faces," he told a reporter aboard his campaign jet. "One thing you can do is reach out and listen and not be fearful of getting beaten up."[31]

In Texas, George W. was cruising toward an easy reelection. In addition to his surprisingly smooth relationship with Democrats in the legislature, he had appointed several Latinos as top aides and senior state officials, including Alberto Gonzales, whom he named to the Texas Supreme Court and would later make the country's first Latino attorney general. Bush had seized on another opportunity to reap rewards on the education issue. Court rulings had struck down affirmative action in the admissions policies of Texas universities. Bush put forward an alternative approach dubbed "affirmative access," which promised that every student in the top 10 percent of every high school graduating class would be admitted to a state university or college. It was a quota system in all but name, because it meant good students in poor high schools might be offered college spaces ahead of better students from stronger high schools. But the political euphemism proved acceptable.

While the Bush brothers moved forward in their respective states, events at the national level were conspiring to improve their fortunes as well, though good luck for the brothers came in the form of what looked like disaster for their party. The proximate cause of both was Pete Wilson's use of the immigration issue. At first, it had seemed to succeed. Californians had approved the ballot initiative. And in 1996, the GOP-controlled Congress passed harsh immigration controls. The changes cut off welfare and health benefits even to some legal immigrants. But in 1996, it was the Republicans' turn to be stunned. President Clinton had recovered from his mismanaged first term to score a massive reelection victory against the hapless Republican challenger, Senator Robert Dole of Kansas. Many factors besides immigration policy went into the 1996 presidential returns, but it was hard to miss the fact that Republicans netted the lowest percentage of the Latino vote ever. And a backlash among Latinos and moderate voters over Pete Wilson was widely credited with playing a significant role in moving California, a state that Republicans once hoped to dominate, into the Democratic column. Among nationally known Republicans, George W. Bush and his brother Jeb were conspicuous in having stood up against Wilson's ideas from the beginning.

Realizing the depth of their problem, congressional Republicans rolled back some of the most onerous restrictions on immigrants. Speaker Gingrich traveled to Miami's Little Havana shortly after the election to celebrate a blanket amnesty that saved thousands of Cubans and Nicaraguans from deportation. As Jodi Wilgoren reported in the *Los Angeles Times*, Gingrich had pushed for the amnesty in the final days of the congressional session, and he was welcomed in Miami by cheering throngs as he stood behind a banner emblazoned with the words "Hispanics Love Newt." Before leaving Washington, Gingrich had told a group of Hispanic Republicans of the importance of improving the party's image on immigration and race. "If we extend *un gran abrazo* [a big hug] to everyone," he said, "they will extend it back to us and we will be a big American family."[32]

Gingrich was too late with too little. He and other Republicans had overinterpreted their 1994 victories and overplayed their hand in Washington. Pete Wilson's use of immigration had cost them Hispanic support. Gingrich's overreach on almost everything else had cost them more. As George W. seems to have sensed from the beginning and Jeb had learned in 1994, conservative principles could form the basis for political success, but they had to be handled carefully. George and Jeb had won because they combined conservative values with policy positions that appealed to more centrist voters as well as to their conservative base. They came across as "compassionate conservatives," to use the phrase George would soon make famous. Gingrich had run into trouble because Americans were put off by his take-no-prisoners approach to wielding government power. The 1998 elections cost Republicans five seats in the U.S. Congress. The disappointing results led to an announcement that Gingrich would not seek another term as Speaker.

Governor Bush, on the other hand, held onto his job as governor of Texas with a landslide victory that made him the front-runner for the Republican presidential nomination in 2000. Even the most hard-core

Democratic counties in the Texas border country, an area that had overwhelmingly backed Clinton in 1996, supported Bush. And for Jeb Bush, the makeover paid off. This time, he won. Both Bushes improved their share of the vote among blacks and Latinos. Suddenly, talk of another dynasty permeated American politics: the Texas governor would run for president; the Florida governor was well situated to help, presiding over twenty-five Electoral College votes that belonged to the fourth-largest state in the nation.

Watching all of this closely was a Harvard-educated lawyer named Ken Mehlman, then working as chief of staff to a Texas congresswoman, Kay Granger. Since college, Mehlman had been obsessed with the intricacies of electoral politics. A conservative with a computer nerd's appetite for numbers and precise organization, Mehlman had long dreamed of an era of GOP dominance and had concluded that achieving it depended on making gains with the country's rapidly growing minority populations. He was impressed that November with the Bush brothers' victories, but also noticed something ominous for the one-party movement: Democrats had refined their get-out-the-vote techniques, the one area of campaign mechanics where Republicans still lagged behind.

Thanks to strong support from the labor movement, Democrats had long had an advantage in delivering personal political messages and getting voters to the polls. In 1998, the Democrats exploited that advantage and it made the difference in close congressional races.

Republicans, meantime, had followed a more traditional route, pumping their resources into a barrage of cookie-cutter television ads that conveyed national themes that were less effective than the Democrats' narrowly tailored messages delivered door-to-door.

"They had a niche message and beat us [in House races]," Mehlman said later. "It was like they had all the planes and the bombers, and we had horses. They were communicating in a new way, and we were doing it the old way."[33]

Mehlman wanted to learn more—about the Bush brothers and about the strategies Democrats had deployed so successfully. Before long he was in Austin, as a member of Karl Rove's team. Rove had already begun plotting his boss's White House strategy, and he and

Mehlman experienced what Mehlman called a *Star Trek*–like "mind meld" over the importance of understanding demographic changes, wooing minorities, and taking a page from the Democrats' communication and get-out-the-vote playbook. Mehlman's technical skills and his faith that shrewd management could lead to Republican dominance made him just what Rove needed to develop the Bush-for-president strategy. As in the earlier races, that strategy would nurture the powerful conservative base, but it also would seek to make inroads in traditional Democratic constituencies. The key to attaining the two goals was unusual, but it proved effective.

Traditionally, politicians appealed to their base to get nominated, then moved toward the center to win general elections; the conventional wisdom was that the base might be irritated by such shifts, but it would fall into line by Election Day because it had nowhere else to go.

Rove and George W. Bush thought they had a better idea. The governor would not compromise his basic conservative positions in the slightest, but he would use his personal charm and aggressive outreach to recruit conservative voters even from within minority neighborhoods and union halls that were traditionally part of the Democratic base. The goal was not to win by a landslide but with just enough votes to attain a majority. And the result, according to the plan, was the ability to govern as a true conservative.

The strategy would work in the short term, but it was high risk and foreshadowed a question that would haunt the GOP's one-party plan: can a truly durable majority be built in a country evenly divided?

Rove's effort to lay the foundation for a run at the White House in 2000 began with a series of outreach meetings he organized at the governor's mansion. The guest lists showed how broadly he intended to cast his net: there were African American pastors, white evangelicals, economic conservatives, industry lobbyists, even activist Muslims and Indian American physicians.

Days after the 1998 election, Rove summoned Grover Norquist to meet with the newly reelected governor. Norquist had written an article for the *American Spectator* that summer titled, "Five Things a

Governor Can Do to Be Presidential." His list included longtime conservative favorites: tax cuts, school choice, protection for business from lawsuits, and changes in pensions and health benefits that would promote private market investment.[34] Nothing on the list was a problem for Bush, but there had been hard feelings between Rove and Norquist: the antitax activist and his Americans for Tax Reform had sponsored radio commercials lambasting a budget proposal by Governor Bush that could have led to higher taxes. Rove was furious at the time. But past differences were smoothed over when he and Bush sat down with Norquist in the breakfast room of the mansion and a sense of common purpose emerged from the meeting. "It was clear to me from that conversation and certainly from the meeting with Bush that I wanted to help Bush get to be president," Norquist recalled later.[35]

At the meeting, Bush, Rove, and Norquist talked about the importance of cultivating minorities. Democratic candidates had maintained strong support from African Americans, but Republicans—especially the Bushes—had increased their share of Hispanic voters. In the early 1980s, the average support for Republicans among Latino voters was only about 20 percent. In Texas, George W. Bush had received 47 percent of the Hispanic vote in 1998.[36] Jeb had also done well with Hispanics in his 1998 campaign. The trio discussed the need to build on those numbers if they were to win Democratic-leaning states such as Florida and Texas. The latter seemed secure, but a problem had arisen in Florida.

Jeb Bush was pursuing a plan to improve the state's schools, partly as a way to appeal to African Americans. But his effort was threatened by the arrival in the state of California businessman Ward Connerly, who had run a successful but contentious campaign for a ballot initiative called Proposition 209, which banned racial preferences in college admissions. Jeb, whose education foundation and involvement with the Liberty City charter school had persuaded some black voters that they could feel at home in the GOP, repeatedly denounced Connerly's 2000 effort as "divisive." Connerly pushed ahead anyway, seeking to put his amendment on the Florida ballot for 2000.

Conservatives like Connerly, it seemed, could never leave well enough alone. That put the newly elected governor on the spot. He could not appear to be endorsing quotas, even indirectly. He also could not afford to let Connerly take over the political agenda, especially at a time when George W. Bush was the likely GOP presidential nominee and would be counting on his brother to deliver a crucial state. GOP strategists feared the initiative would spark anger and drive up African American turnout, to the benefit of the presumed Democratic nominee, Vice President Al Gore. So in November 1999, the new governor proposed a preemptive initiative he called One Florida. To thread the political needle, Jeb would eliminate affirmative action in higher education and state contracting, while also establishing programs designed to bolster minority participation. One Florida required executive orders and legislation, but it stopped far short of the constitutional amendments proposed by Connerly. The governor said his plan would encourage a new kind of "race consciousness" that was more effective than outdated ideas that had not succeeded in giving minority firms and students the access enjoyed by whites. "This is not the end of affirmative action," Bush said. "This transcends affirmative action."[37]

A new office was opened to direct minority firms to state business. A so-called Talented 20 program guaranteed admission to state colleges or universities to the top 20 percent of every high school graduating class—an idea modeled after his older brother's "affirmative access" program in Texas. A prominent black state senator, Democrat Daryl Jones, had even agreed to endorse the plan once Bush announced it; Jones was to head a special task force that would examine funding disparities between low-performance and high-performance schools. "I want to help him succeed," Jones said at the time. "As long as his motives are pure, then I'm going to be with him."[38]

But if Bush hoped One Florida would fit with his goals of wooing blacks to the Republican fold—and protecting his brother from a backlash—he was quickly proved wrong. Connerly's drive for an amendment to the state constitution faded, but fierce opposition to Jeb Bush's plan broke out among Democrats and black leaders across the state. They charged that the governor's supposed compromise was really another plan to abolish affirmative action altogether. Things got so hot that Jones backed out. Karl Rove's worst fears seemed to be coming true. Florida was being engulfed by racial controversy and it looked like Republicans would be punished for it. Certainly the controversy over One Florida was spurring enthusiasm for an NAACP-led voter-registration drive.

Tensions did not subside as 1999 faded into 2000. Late on the afternoon of January 18, 2000, two African American state legislators, Kendrick Meek of Miami and Tony Hill of Jacksonville, entered the governor's office and refused to leave until he agreed to rescind his executive orders enacting portions of One Florida. "This is affirmative action. This is something people lost their lives for," said Meek, who later was elected to Congress. "I wouldn't be a state senator today if somebody didn't do what I'm doing right now."[39] The governor, who typically had his emotions under tight control, was visibly rattled. He stood by his position and warned the lawmakers they might want to get blankets, since they would be there a while. The situation was not helped by the fact that someone overheard Bush say, "Kick their asses out."[40] Some initially thought he was referring to the black lawmakers, but staffers later said the governor was angry at reporters, who insisted on remaining in his office to cover the sit-in.

Eventually, the sit-in was finessed. But two months later, as the state legislature convened its annual session, thousands converged on the capitol for a march protesting Bush's initiative. The events that spring, coming as George W. Bush was battling for the GOP presidential nomination, formed a precarious backdrop for the fall campaign.

At the outset of the presidential campaign, most analysts believed Florida would go Republican despite the local battle over quotas. Republicans had enjoyed steady gains there, and Jeb Bush remained a popular governor with ready access to a well-heeled and disciplined political machine. But as Election Day 2000 neared, Jeb Bush and his strategists grew more and more concerned. Gore had abandoned the traditional swing state of Ohio and had transferred staff and resources into Florida. African American households in central Florida were reporting personal visits from pro-Gore volunteers and recorded telephone messages from President Clinton. In heavily Jewish areas of south Florida, voters were revved up over the selection of Senator Joseph Lieberman of Connecticut, an observant Jew, as his running mate. That gave the Democratic ticket a potential edge in the vote-rich condos of Broward and Palm Beach counties. Meantime, turnout—particularly among blacks—was forecast to break records.

From their painful experience six years earlier with Lawton Chiles, Jeb Bush and his team had developed keen noses for Democratic surges, and in September and October they smelled one developing. It wasn't just instinct. The governor and his aides were receiving data from narrowly targeted polls that seemed to spell trouble, particularly in certain legislative districts that had gone solidly for Jeb Bush in 1998 but now seemed to be tipping against his brother. At the presidential campaign's headquarters in Austin, however, Rove and other strategists saw no cause for concern. Their own polls were not picking up a shift, and Austin strategists were assuring their Florida counterparts that Bush held a five-point lead.[41]

This mantra continued until about a month before the election, when Jeb Bush had heard enough. He and his aides had tried unsuccessfully to see national headquarters' polling data, and Rove and his team were making strategic decisions about ads, candidate visits, and the targeting of direct mail and phone calls in Florida without advice from Tallahassee. Florida strategists worried that Austin was counting on a one-size-fits-all national message, instead of developing specialized appeals to different parts of Florida's exceptionally diverse electorate. Jeb called at least three fellow Republican governors, including John Engler in Michigan, to get their sense for the campaign. He heard similar gripes. Next, he called Rove and demanded answers.

The result was an emotional, tension-filled meeting in the Florida room on the first floor of the colonial-style governor's mansion in Tallahassee. Jeb was joined by his advisers and several representatives from Austin, including Ken Mehlman and strategist Chris Henick, one of Rove's top deputies. The governor, clad in a V-neck sweater, was seated in a chair with pages of polling data in his lap and half-glasses on the tip of his nose. He was stern. "Something's got to give,"

Jeb told his brother's staff. "You guys are not listening." Henick recalled years later that Jeb, who understood Florida politics better than anyone on his brother's staff, had broad disagreements with the strategy Rove and pollster Matthew Dowd were advancing in Florida. Jeb wanted large rallies that led to impressive images on the local television news and on the front pages of regional newspapers. Rove preferred smaller settings, where the content, dialogue, and message could be more tightly controlled. Jeb wanted a say in where his brother went in Florida, and what voters were told. At the meeting, Austin strategists assured the governor that they would address his concerns with the folks back in Austin.

"We'll let them know," one Texas aide kept saying. "We'll let them know."[42]

"Who's them?" an exasperated Jeb Bush finally demanded. Henick, a longtime GOP operative and Mississippi native who had known the Florida governor for years, was stuck. "I'm them. I'm them," Henick said in his native Mississippi drawl, knowing full well that the "them" Jeb Bush had in mind was Rove and Dowd but hoping to diffuse the tension and give the Florida governor a sense of satisfaction.[43]

In some ways, Rove's resistance to taking advice from outside campaign headquarters was understandable. So much of it came pouring in that it could turn the campaign into an incoherent mess if he listened to everyone. Michigan governor Engler, for instance, was pestering Austin to put Lee Iacocca in a television ad, though the utility of that in attracting blue-collar voters was hard to see. Besides, in Florida it was too late to change. "Even if we did understand [what Jeb was saying], the strategy was set," Henick said in an interview years later.[44]

Henick knew better than to say that to Jeb, however, and the meeting went on for more than three hours. At one point the governor had to leave, so the strategists stepped outside onto a brick patio to calm their nerves and soak in the brilliant sunshine of a northern Florida fall afternoon. Everyone on the terrace understood what was at stake. The campaign could not afford to lose Florida. Jeb carried an added burden as the candidate's younger brother. Beyond the humiliation of letting his brother down, failing to deliver could leave the first-term governor badly damaged when he sought reelection in 2002 and would cloud his own national future. Jeb returned a few minutes later and demanded that his brother's staff get back to him quickly with proposed changes to the Florida plan. Days went by, and little seemed to change. Published polls showed wildly different results in Florida. An MSNBC-Reuters survey of Floridians had Gore leading by eleven points, while a Los Angeles Times poll showed Bush ahead by four.[45]

In the final week, Jeb took matters into his own hands, ordering the state Republican Party to commission its own poll using his campaign's Washington firm, Public Opinion Strategies. The new poll showed that Gore had pulled ahead by at least one percentage point. Even among white males, the Texas governor was struggling. Sally Bradshaw, Jeb's chief of staff, took the results to her boss. "What do we do with these numbers?" she asked. Jeb directed Bradshaw to call Austin immediately. But instead of moving swiftly to deal with the apparent erosion of support, Rove and his brain trust were furious that Jeb and his team had done a poll on their own. Campaign officials believed their numbers were better. The conversation grew so tense that at one point Bradshaw called Rove "a jerk."

The rest is history. Down the stretch, Gore and Lieberman had pounded George W. Bush's proposal to add private accounts to Social Security as a threat to the elderly. "The Bush plan would turn Social Security into a grab bag where everyone is out for himself," Gore told several hundred cheering supporters at the Kissimmee Civic Center. "You might call it Social Insecurity, and that's wrong for our values."[46]

On Election Day, Rove finally recognized there was a problem in Florida. Early exit polls there suggested Gore might be on the verge of achieving an upset that would be catastrophic for the Bush campaign. Around lunchtime, he called Bradshaw. "What do you need?" he asked. She told him to pour hundreds of thousands of dollars into phone calls—recorded and live—with special emphasis on the Panhandle, a conservative region where many of the precincts were in the central time zone and would be open an extra hour.

By 3 A.M. the next morning, Rove had a different kind of problem. The Florida vote count would decide the entire presidential election; Gore had won a majority of the popular vote nationwide, but if Florida's twenty-five electoral votes went to Bush, he would become president. Well before dawn, both campaigns were scrambling to get lawyers and recount experts into the state, though neither side had yet figured out exactly what to do. In the wee hours of Wednesday morning, Ken Mehlman and five other Bush campaign officials climbed aboard the private jet owned by the candidate's longtime friend Donald Evans to fly from Austin to Miami. They were exhausted. "I said, 'Okay, let's come up with a plan for how to deal with this,'" Mehlman remembered saying. "Ten minutes later we were all sound asleep."[47]

The days of seesaw vote counts and legal battling were hell for both campaigns and the legions of lawyers who invaded hotels and courtrooms from Tallahassee to Miami. For five weeks, the nation was riveted by allegations of black voter disenfranchisement and twenty-four-hour coverage of dimpled chads and butterfly ballots. One element of the Florida vote drew little if any notice: a dramatic shift in the Latino vote. While record black turnout nearly put Gore in the White House—and the butterfly ballot in Palm Beach County probably led thousands of befuddled Gore backers to vote for Pat Buchanan—Hispanic voters may well have saved the state for George W. Bush. Like every other aspect of that election, exit-polling data is subject to dispute. But exit polls showed that Bush received more than half of the Latino vote statewide and close to 80 percent of Miami-Dade County's massive and traditionally Republican Cuban American vote.

The world focused on the recount battle and the 5–4 vote of the U.S. Supreme Court that ended it. But while Rove, Mehlman, and others in Bush's tight-knit circle of advisers knew they had barely escaped—and vowed to do better in the future—they also took heart from their strong showing with Latino voters. The new president might enter the history books with an asterisk beside his name. In the space of just six years, however, first in gubernatorial elections in two of the most important states in the country and now in a presidential election, George W. Bush and his brother Jeb had profoundly changed the Republican Party's base of support. Despite the continuing clamor, that change might prove to have more enduring value than almost anything else that happened in the 2000 campaign.

CHAPTER 4

The Rove Doctrine

You know, every conspiracy needs a leader of vision who thinks long into
the future, who plays the game in his head many moves ahead.

— KARL ROVE, ADDRESS TO THE FEDERALIST SOCIETY DINNER,
WASHINGTON, D.C., NOVEMBER 10, 2005

Several days before George W. Bush was inaugurated as the forty-third president of the United States, a fleet of yellow Security Storage Company vans arrived at the White House to cart away the belongings of Bill and Hillary Clinton. Officially, the Bush family and the new White House staff could not move in until Bush and Vice President–elect Dick Cheney took the oath of office at noon on January 20. But the Bush transition team had elaborate plans for refurbishing the executive mansion and it was impatient to begin, starting with the Oval Office. Early that morning, the cherry-and-white-striped sofas that Bill Clinton had installed there were wrapped in protective film and loaded up, along with the gold curtains and royal blue rug. Within hours the bold colors were replaced by the

Bushes' more conservative palate: couches covered in cream brocade and a pastel yellow rug emblazoned with the presidential seal.

But the transformation that began to unfold in the weeks before Bush's inauguration went far deeper than changing Oval Office aesthetics. In addition to a new carpet and couches, the incoming president brought with him Karl Rove, who was more than the mastermind of George W. Bush's political rise. Rove was the architect of a breathtakingly ambitious plan to use the embryonic Bush presidency to build an enduring Republican majority. After decades of political seesawing and divided government, Republicans in 2001 controlled the White House and both houses of Congress. And even though the incoming president owed his office to one of the most disputed elections in American history, Rove intended to treat it as the political equivalent of Franklin D. Roosevelt's landslide victory of 1932. Indeed, Rove planned to use the next four years in the White House to do for conservatives exactly what FDR had done for liberals. And he meant to do it by bending every element of federal power to his political ends. All presidents, at least since John Adams, had worked to help their friends and hinder their enemies, but Rove meant to take that time-honored tradition to a new level. He would see to it, for example, that government actions and policies, down to the smallest detail, supported his goal. Tests of political purity would be applied not just to those serving inside the new administration but to lawyers, lobbyists, and scores of others outside the government whose livelihood depended on dealing with it.

By tradition, new chief executives used their first inaugural address to set the stage for their presidencies. Rove did much the same thing for the new administration's political vision, but he did not wait until Inauguration Day. Instead, while many Republicans and future White House staffers used the first few weeks of January 2001 to recuperate from the frenzied campaign season and the even more draining recount battle, Rove was busy making the rounds of the organizations that represented his party's base. Those appearances, little reported in the news media, gave clear indications that Rove was intent on achieving more than the customary transfer of executive power from one political party to the other. To each group, Rove made a pledge and extracted a commitment: in due course, he promised, all would be rewarded. But from the outset, he insisted, all must commit themselves to making absolute loyalty to the president and support for his agenda their paramount concern.

Rove's speeches, many of them in private receptions and luncheons, suggested that Bush, despite his narrow victory and the frequent pledges to be a "uniter, not a divider," would govern as an ideological conservative and not as the consensus-builder many expected. But that approach could have long-lasting effects, Rove told his audiences, if the administration and its partners outside the government focused on concrete goals. His words signaled a concentration on four: to foster a sweeping realignment in government and politics; to seek out and cultivate new Republican voters, especially minority voters and most especially Hispanic voters; to roll back the legacy of big-government programs that had helped cement the Democratic base since the New Deal; and—as conservative strategists had with redistricting—to construct so many obstacles to Democratic success that a liberal resurgence would be all but impossible. If they could achieve those goals, Rove believed, Republicans could rule the country according to their conservative lights for at least a generation.

At a lunchtime gathering hosted by longtime social conservative leader Paul Weyrich a few days before the inauguration, Rove said Bush would govern as "a philosophically driven president who is a conservative." Only one journalist was permitted to attend the gathering, political columnist Donald Lambro from the reliably Republican *Washington Times*. Although he was granted entry only on the condition that he quote Rove sparingly, Lambro characterized the presidential adviser's address as unequivocal. "The most important message Mr. Rove came to deliver," Lambro wrote, "was that Mr. Bush needs the full and faithful support of his conservative soul mates if he is to enact his conservative agenda: cutting income-tax rates, reforming the Social Security system, lifting educational standards, and helping poor and low-income people through faith-based institutions and programs." Rove noted that Bush, despite the election's photo finish, had won 11.3 million more votes than GOP nominee Bob Dole did four years earlier. But, Lambro wrote, paraphrasing

Rove's remarks, "The challenge now is to hold on to these voters and to build upon their support. That means bringing the high-tech, New Economy workers—the fastest-growing part of the American electorate—into the Republican coalition." In an early preview of the "Ownership Society" proposals that later became a rhetorical centerpiece of Bush's domestic agenda, Rove added that growing the GOP coalition meant "being on the side of those who are struggling to climb into the middle class."[1]

Conservative leaders in the audience were delighted. "It's quite evident from what you've said here today that we are going to agree 80 percent of the time," Weyrich, who had frequently disagreed with past Republican presidents when they strayed from the strict conservative line, told Rove after his remarks.[2]

In other such appearances, Rove laid out other pieces of his strategy for building the new majority. For example, he pointed out to members of the Republican National Committee that Bush won 35 percent of the Hispanic vote—the highest GOP share of that bloc since Reagan's reelection in 1984. Sensitive to the importance of demographic change from his days as a direct-mail fund-raiser, Rove said the committee must do better. "Our mission and our goal," he declared, is to attract more Latinos, a goal that would "require all of us in every way and every day working to get that done."[3] He went on to tell the Republican National Committee that Bush had scored in the paltry single digits among African American voters—worse than Dole. "As a country and as a party," he said, "that has to be unacceptable to us."[4]

But he told his fellow Republicans to take heart. Bush had drawn more moderate voters than Republicans had in the past—proving, Rove posited, that there was a "gigantic coalition" available to the party if Republicans simply framed their arguments correctly.[5]

Even many close political watchers missed the importance of Rove's inaugural addresses. But for party officials and those who would join Bush in the White House on January 20, Rove's remarks defined a mission—unique in its intensity—that would guide the administration and the party's national leadership from the moment the forty-third president took his oath.

Days after addressing the Republican National Committee, Rove moved into the West Wing. His new digs, a single cramped room on the second floor, lacked the outward trappings of power and mystique that most of Washington would associate with his role. But Rove knew better. The office previously belonged to the former first lady, Hillary Rodham Clinton, and it was just a flight of stairs away from the Oval Office. The change of occupants was in many ways a symbol, as *Time* magazine noted, of one political marriage replacing another.[6] Bush and Rove, after all, enjoyed a rapport that dated back years in Texas politics. It had endured despite blunders that might have cost other political gurus their jobs—Rove's failure to recognize John McCain's strength in the New Hampshire primary in 2000, for instance, and the decision to invest millions of dollars and even more valuable time in Democratic-leaning California while neglecting Florida, which was up for grabs. Bush and Rove were more than just candidate and consultant. They had a closeness derived from sharing an extended journey. They had traveled from the traditional old-guard Republicanism of George H. W. Bush to the new, values-driven conservative Republicanism, a philosophy they considered a perfect match for an America that was changing its political geography, its ethnicity, and even its sense of itself. Those who observed the interplay between Bush and the man he variously dubbed "the architect," "boy genius," and "turd blossom,"[7] reminded some longtime friends of an old married couple. To Deborah Burstion-Donbraye, the press adviser who traveled with the two during the early months of the 1994 gubernatorial campaign, Bush and Rove were "like twin brothers. They spoke in their own language, a kind of shorthand," she said. Often, she recalled, they could finish each other's sentences. Though Burston-Donbraye spent hours with the two, she said their language was such that frequently, "I wouldn't have the foggiest idea of what they were talking about."[8]

In some ways, Bush and Rove could not have been more different. In other, deeper ways that may have mattered more, they had much in common. In family background, they were alpha and omega. Bush came from a tight nuclear family. He could trace his ancestry back many generations, and it was Establishment all the way—studded with famous names on Wall Street and in the Social Register. His middle name, Walker, came from Great-Grandfather George Herbert Walker, the prominent and prosperous St. Louis financier who, among other accomplishments, established the Walker Cup, one of the most venerable prizes in golf. The Texas governor's resume began with Andover, Yale, and Harvard, but he was notoriously lacking in intellectual curiosity. Rove, by contrast, dropped out of college and never graduated, yet became a self-taught intellectual who delighted in parading his knowledge of history and political theory. Unlike Bush's family, Rove's parents divorced when he was an adolescent; his mother later committed suicide. And, in an emotionally wrenching episode when he was a young man, Rove learned from other relatives that the man he had always thought to be his father was in fact biologically unrelated.[9] Some have suggested that in associating himself with the Bush family—he was helped up the political ladder by George H. W. Bush—Rove gained some of the strength and support of the stable family he never had. At the same time, Bush seems to have felt more at home in Rove's world of nitty-gritty retail politics than in the more refined realm of Bush's father. Moreover, both Rove and the younger Bush had felt the sting of scorn from "elitists" who failed to appreciate their talents. Both rejected some of the expectations of their birth and remade themselves. Both took satisfaction in doing things their own way, proving themselves smarter, tougher, more disciplined, and more competitive than their opponents.

They had come together as young adults, in an era when the Republican Party's future was hardly bright. The Nixon White House was embroiled in Watergate, and George H. W. Bush was the chairman of the Republican National Committee, loyally parroting the Nixon line and trying to avoid sullying his own image. Meantime, Rove, barely into his twenties, had quit the University of Utah to campaign for chairman of the College Republicans, a rough-and-tumble organization that spawned legions of future politicians and consultants who now occupy key roles in the conservative movement. As the elder Bush struggled with Watergate, Rove was fighting his way to the top of the College Republicans in a campaign for the organization's chairmanship that would become legendary among GOP political operatives. To win, Rove and his ally, Lee Atwater, traveled the college campus circuit full-time, building up a network of like-minded comrades. They also devised a system for challenging delegate selection rules at state College Republican meetings around the country. Their opponents complained of dirty tricks and—during the course of the disputed election—even leaked to the *Washington Post* a tape recording of Rove describing election espionage tactics. The result was that both Rove and his opponent claimed victory.[10]

The dispute became so heated that it fell to the elder Bush, as the national party chairman, to investigate and resolve the impasse. He ultimately chose Rove, absolving him of charges of dirty pool. In fact, he was so impressed with Rove that he was soon part of his entourage.[11] Rove moved to Washington, and on the day before Thanksgiving in 1973, he was dispatched on a fateful errand—to pick up the chairman's eldest son at Washington's Union Station and to give the visiting Harvard Business School student the keys to the family car.

As Rove later described it—in words that might have brought a blush to the cheeks of George W. Bush's adoring but ill-fated Supreme Court nominee Harriet Miers—he was awed at first sight. "I can literally remember what he was wearing: an Air National Guard flight jacket, cowboy boots, blue jeans, complete with the—in Texas you see it a lot—one of the back pockets will have a circle worn in the pocket from where you carry your tin of snuff, your tin of tobacco," Rove said in an interview with journalist Nicholas Lemann writing in the *New Yorker*. "He was exuding more charisma than any one individual should be allowed to have."[12]

Collaboration did not begin immediately. It was to Atwater that the younger Bush seems to have been drawn first. But partnership with Rove was a natural outgrowth of Atwater's death and George W.'s decision to go into politics in Texas. By that time, they had discovered they saw the world and its prospects in similar ways. Each thrived on the assets of the other and, in a sense, compensated for the other's deficiencies. The bookish Rove, who had little future as a political contender, saw in the charismatic young Bush the picture of the winning candidate, a man who could win and take over once-Democratic

Texas. Bush, for his part, benefited from Rove's discipline, partisan acuity, and political vision. The Democrats' oft-repeated notion that Rove is Bush's brain undervalues the president and the nature of this extraordinary partnership.

Close, almost symbiotic relationships between presidents and individual advisers dot the pages of American history. Early in the nineteenth century, Andrew Jackson had Amos Kendall. A political strategist and polemicist, Kendall is now largely forgotten, but he helped make Jackson the putative father of patronage and the spoils system, came to dominate Old Hickory's "Kitchen Cabinet," and played a central role in the defining domestic issue of Jackson's presidency, his fight against the country's first central bank. Late in the nineteenth century, William McKinley had Marcus Hanna, who served as his conservative political strategist in the campaign of 1896 and during McKinley's subsequent years in the White House. Early in the twentieth century, Woodrow Wilson had his Colonel House, who became almost a surrogate president after Wilson was incapacitated by a stroke. And in the modern era, Franklin Roosevelt had Harry Hopkins. All, to varying degrees, combined a wide-ranging impact on politics, policy, and the overarching philosophy of the presidents they served.

But the relationship between Roosevelt and Hopkins may come closest to matching that of George W. Bush and Karl Rove.[13] Like Rove, Hopkins was close to the president personally; at times, Hopkins even lived at the White House. Hopkins also carried a broad portfolio. He helped craft the New Deal, always keeping in mind the potential political benefits for Democrats, much the way Rove helped Bush develop the idea of the Ownership Society as an approach to policy making and to growing the party base. Like Hopkins, who was a close adviser to Roosevelt during World War II, Rove helped map Bush's political strategy around the war on terrorism, the invasion of Iraq, and even hurricane recovery in the second term. But there were differences: far more than Bush, Roosevelt was intensely involved in the running of his administration and he cultivated a far larger circle of advisers to serve his varying needs. Moreover, Hopkins did not run campaigns; Rove did.

Bush often said that he approached the presidency the way a strong CEO would approach the leadership of a major corporation, embracing the techniques of delegating authority and accountability that he had learned at the Harvard Business School. To Rove, he delegated a job of historic proportions: mixing—to an extent seldom if ever seen before—responsibility for the functioning of the government and the advancing of long- and short-term political goals. And in Bush's first term, Rove and his lieutenants embarked upon the brashest, most dramatic effort to politicize the day-to-day functioning of the executive branch that Washington had ever seen. It was a vastly different approach than that of the president's father, who rarely fretted political tactics and only considered them late in his term as the 1992 elections approached. The younger Bush and his team saw that as a fateful miscalculation. They were convinced that, in the elder Bush's White House, senior aides underestimated the crucial relationship between policy and politics, allowing the president to stumble into the tax increase deal with Democrats that led—predictably and avoidably—to a humiliating defeat. Rove and his aides admired Bill Clinton for his simultaneous proficiency in politics and policy. But Clinton's political consultants were a changing cast—James Carville, Paul Begala, Doug Soznik, Harold Ickes, Dick Morris. Rove and Bush, on the other hand, were disciplined, stayed together, and mixed policy with political strategy so that the two became indistinguishable. In the White House, Rove reshaped the way the political office functioned. Every president since John Kennedy has relied on a polling or poll-tracking operation in the White House. Rove and his aides tracked national polls and the outlook for congressional races in every state. But he also created structures to bring senior members of the White House staff and other top government officials together on a regular basis to discuss both practical politics and decision making on the policy issues that Rove saw as integral to the GOP's political strategy. He established a weekly meeting in the old Executive Office Building next door to the White House, for example, at which a dozen members of the senior staff would gather to discuss pressing matters, such as the effort to shepherd the new president's massive tax cuts through Congress or how best to position the GOP for the 2002 midterm elections. As *Washington Post* reporter Dana Milbank revealed, Rove christened those who attended these meetings the "Strategery Group," after the *Saturday Night Live* lampoon of Bush's famous tendency toward malapropism. Rove and former chief of staff Andrew Card also launched a group, nicknamed with comparable irony the "Conspiracy of the Deputies," to mull campaign themes for Bush's 2004 reelection. Then, to coordinate these efforts to institutionalize politically savvy policy making, Rove established the Office of Strategic Initiatives, which operates as a kind of war room to push White House policies with campaign-style techniques and intensity.[14] The official White House Web site notes that "the office conducts research and assists in message development" for presidential priorities.

A key figure in all this was Ken Mehlman. A former Hill staffer and campaign field director, Mehlman had risen quickly in Rove's estimation in 2000 after he engineered a Bush victory in the Iowa caucuses by employing the kind of finely tuned grassroots strategies that had largely been absent from prior Republican campaign efforts. Impressed with Mehlman's work, Rove gave him the responsibility for the entire Midwest in the general election. Bush carried Ohio and Missouri, both of which had gone for Clinton in 1996, while holding the Great Plains states of North and South Dakota, Nebraska, and Kansas. Following the campaign, Rove tapped Mehlman to be the White House political director. Reporting directly to Rove, he orchestrated an after-action review of the 2000 strategy and canvassed state GOP leaders for policies and ideas that could boost election hopes in 2002 and beyond.

Rove also placed loyal staffers at the Republican National Committee and in key positions at cabinet agencies. He often called together small groups of aides to work—war-room style—on a specific issue or problem. Often, the focus of Rove meetings was on press coverage and how to influence it. Although Rove granted few on-the-record interviews after entering the White House, he understood the norms and habits of the Washington press corps and maintained daily communication with top political journalists and commentators. He had a point of contact with every major news organization and used off-the-record communications with them to convey his messages and build goodwill. He sometimes used those contacts to deal with political enemies as well. One of the White House teams that Rove helped lead, the White House Iraq Group, came under scrutiny by the special prosecutor who investigated the leaking of the name of covert CIA operative Valerie Plame. The leak apparently had been arranged to undermine the reputation of her husband, Joseph Wilson, who had challenged White House claims about Saddam Hussein's efforts to obtain nuclear material from Africa.

Those who worked with Rove in the White House knew his power and his ambition, and not everybody liked what they saw. One of those was University of Pennsylvania academic John J. DiIulio Jr., who was taken on board to launch the White House program to increase government reliance on faith-based organizations to deliver social services to the poor. The initiative was part of the president's "compassion agenda." DiIulio quit during the first year, largely out of frustration with Rove and his injection of partisan considerations into the process. "Karl is enormously powerful, maybe the single most powerful person in the modern, post-Hoover era ever to occupy a political-adviser post near the Oval Office," DiIulio wrote in a now-famous e-mail exchange with author Ron Suskind. As a result, DiIulio said, policy was entirely subordinated to the demands of winning the next election.[15] Though DiIulio may have been the first White House official to remark on Rove's methods publicly, he saw only one piece of a larger puzzle. Rove thought about winning the next election all right, but he also thought about winning the election after that, and the one after that. He was a rare species of political consultant, a short-term and a long-term thinker. "Bifocal politics," as his ally, Grover Norquist, calls it. Bush political strategist Mark McKinnon, a former Democratic consultant who worked on Bush's second gubernatorial campaign and both presidential campaigns, once described Rove as having "more bandwidth" than any operative he had ever worked with, citing his uncanny knack of assessing poll numbers, policy initiatives, and other factors all at the same time.[16]

From the day Rove moved into Hillary Clinton's old office, he also brought meticulous planning to the White House, using his underlings in the West Wing and his disciples throughout the executive branch. Everywhere, the goal was not just to win President Bush a second term but to make him a transformational figure as well. Rove described the vision in a 2003 interview with the *New Yorker*, laying out his view of the Bush presidency as a catalyst for political realignment. He said that by the outset of the twenty-first century, the two major political parties had "sort of exhausted their governing agendas." Those agendas, he said, "were originally formed, for the Democrats, in the New Deal, and, for the Republicans, in opposition to the New Deal—modified by the Cold War and further modified by the changes in the sixties, the Great Society and societal and cultural changes. It's sort of like the exhaustion of two boxers fighting it out in the middle of the ring."[17] The party that refreshed and reinvigorated itself with new ideas and a new agenda, Rove was suggesting, was the party that would win the fight and dominate the government for the foreseeable future. He drew another parallel—with America after Reconstruction, a time when the principles on which the existing parties had been organized before and during the Civil War no longer fit the nation's altered circumstances. "This happened in 1896, where the Civil War party system was in decline and the parties were in rough parity and somebody came along and figured it out and helped create a governing coalition that really lasted for the next some-odd years," he said. "Similarly, somebody will come along and figure out a new governing scheme through which people could view things and could, conceivably, enjoy a similar period of dominance."[18]

What Rove meant to do in the White House was make sure that "somebody" was George W. Bush. To that end, he injected his larger political calculations into even the most obscure federal issues and the most local of election campaigns. The Rove doctrine demanded that special attention be paid to closely fought regions and states that could prove important not only to Bush's reelection as president in 2004 but to GOP campaigns at every level far into the future. Rove and Mehlman devised plans for the early days of Bush's presidency that revolved around two goals: project the image of a consensus-minded president most concerned about topics such as education reform, while tending assiduously to the needs of the party base and looking for ways to expand it. Feverish behind-the-scenes work had already begun on Mehlman's after-action review of the 2000 results. To this was added the development of new, systematic tactics to increase grassroots activity in upcoming races.

There were setbacks, like the stunning decision by Vermont's Republican senator Jim Jeffords to shed his party affiliation during that first year, putting Democrats in charge of the Senate. But the White House remained focused, especially on bolstering the president's standing in key states.

Bush and Rove settled on education reform as their first initiative. It made sense in all respects. Staking their claim on a traditionally Democratic issue would help soften Bush's image and expand his base of support while neutralizing Democratic critics on Capitol Hill. It was also an issue Bush felt comfortable with after his experience in Texas. Chiding opponents for embracing the "soft bigotry of low expectations" helped paint an ideologically conservative plan as sensitive to minorities. And by dubbing the school accountability program No Child Left Behind, the White House sought to drive a wedge between two core Democratic constituencies: the teachers unions opposed to linking standardized testing to school ratings on the one hand, and the African American and Latino parents who were desperate over the condition of their children's schools on the other. "Our hope was to move the party, and to move the party on important issues, to not simply accept the Congress as it was and the image of the Republican Party as it existed, but to change it," Rove told an audience at the American Enterprise Institute.[19]

That was the high-profile part of Bush's agenda in the opening months of his presidency. There was also a low-profile agenda, and in terms of building the new Republican majority, it was at least as important. This low-profile agenda was designed in part to ensure the Republican Party's financial base. In the popular phrase, that meant "taking care of business." And what mattered most to this constituency were not the big, ideological issues—abortion, gay marriage, the role of religion in public life, and such. What the major corporations, the leading industries, and the senior executives who ran them wanted were changes in government policies that affected the bottom line: environmental requirements, public land policies, court liability restrictions, and the myriad federal regulations that defined the competitive landscape for American business.

Within hours of Bush's inauguration, his chief of staff issued a memo imposing an immediate two-month freeze on all regulations, across all agencies, that had been enacted in the final days of the Clinton administration but had not yet taken effect. That Inauguration Day memo served as an early signal to Bush's business supporters—the "country club Republicans," as they are sometimes called—that this president was a friend and an ally, and that their millions of dollars in campaign contributions would be rewarded. The move against new regulation was also the first concrete indication of a strategy that grew to characterize the Bush White House in its first term: the high-flying rhetoric of fixing schools suggested a reasonable president committed to helping all Americans, but much of the real work went into actions that would strengthen the president's political operations and expand the conservative base. The import of that strategy was not lost on those it was meant to serve. "We have come out of the cave, blinking in the sunlight, saying to one another 'My God, we can actually get something done,'" gushed an ebullient Washington lobbyist named Richard Hohlt, who represented banking, energy, and other interests that had funneled financial support into the Bush campaign.[20]

Illustrating his commitment to helping business, Bush tasked two trusted aides, deputy chief of staff Joshua Bolten and economics adviser Lawrence Lindsey, to scrutinize the regulations adopted by the previous administration. And their approach to the assignment left no doubt about what the results would be. The pair met almost daily with industry lobbyists, conferring at conservative think tanks and on Capitol Hill as they invited corporate leaders to offer suggestions and recommendations. Bush also signed an executive order reinstating a requirement first imposed by his father and rescinded by Clinton that labor unions instruct members that they were entitled to refunds if they objected to the unions' automatically withholding dues from their paychecks.[21] The move reflected a goal shared by Rove and one-party architects like Norquist: hastening the disintegration of organized labor's already diminished political strength. The disclosure requirement, it was hoped, would choke off at least some of the money that the AFL-CIO and its affiliates used to support Democrats. In the same way, the decision to lavish presidential attention on the seemingly obscure issue of shielding business from tort liability lawsuits sprang in part from a belief that reducing consumers' ability to take corporations to court would dry up campaign contributions from wealthy trial lawyers who had been supporting the Democrats.

In the White House political office, Mehlman and his staff reviewed potential appointees to key administration posts. Washington tradition held that big donors and other important political supporters should be rewarded with suitably prestigious jobs, and that would hold true in many parts of the Bush administration. But Rove and Mehlman were more selective than many of their predecessors, carefully screening applicants to ensure that they believed in the administration's long-term goals. "If you want to be transformational, policy is transformational," Mehlman said later. "Patronage isn't."[22]

One of the most important appointees was John Graham to head the White House office responsible for overseeing the regulation of industry. Graham was an industry favorite for his work as the head of Harvard University's Center for Risk Analysis, a respected analytical center that gets most of its funding from private sources including corporations and trade associations. While there, Graham had made his name as a critic of the cost of regulation. His appointment sent a message to career bureaucrats throughout the federal government: the decisions of even midlevel managers would face closer scrutiny from political appointees. The subtext was "Be careful about imposing burdens on the business community." Rove knew that seemingly routine decisions by government agencies could win or lose support and thereby potentially swing local and state as well as national elections. The day after Graham was confirmed by the Senate, he issued the first of a slew of memos halting plans to impose new regulations and demanding further review. These so-called return letters—numbering fourteen by the end of Bush's first year in office, compared with just thirteen that had been sent during Clinton's eight years—sought almost uniformly to restrain agencies from increasing financial burdens on businesses.[23]

One such rejection related to a Transportation Department proposal to reduce the risk of trucking fires by requiring companies to retrofit cargo tanks that carry hazardous materials. In his rejection letter, Graham dressed down the agency for overstating the risk of fires and questioned whether the benefits were worth the costs of compliance. He suggested requiring retrofits only for tanks that were at least fifteen years old as one way to lessen the burden on trucking companies. Another letter chastised the Environmental Protection Agency for offering a "limited analytical basis" to justify new clean-water standards proposed for Indian tribal lands and called for a full examination of the "costs and benefits" of the new standards. Yet another questioned the Federal Aviation Administration's plan to require digital flight recorders in Boeing 737s to provide more data for crash investigations; Graham cited concerns about the "relative cost-effectiveness" of such a change.[24]

Many of the Bush administration's pro-industry moves attracted little public attention because they occurred after the September 11, 2001, terrorist attacks. The attacks transformed the public face of Bush's presidency, shifting his rhetorical focus to security and a broad war on terrorism that ultimately dominated the next two campaign cycles. As Bush emerged from 9/11 a self-styled "war president," ousting regimes in Afghanistan and Iraq and hunting suspected terrorists in caves and hideouts around the globe, the more stealthy war on industry regulations ratcheted up as well in the conference rooms and office suites of the federal bureaucracy. A memo from Graham dated just nine days after September 11 alerted agency regulators and industries that the White House had developed new guidelines for drafting rules. The new guidelines would take into account costs to businesses instead of just considering health, safety, and other possible public benefits. The latter had been the chief concern of regulatory decision makers in the previous administration; this one, to borrow Vice President Cheney's phrase, "had other priorities."

"If not properly developed, regulations can lead to an enormous burden on the economy," Graham wrote.[25] His actions—invoking the powers of the White House Office of Information and Regulatory Affairs to force agencies to reconsider their treatment of businesses— marked a sea change in how the federal government would approach regulatory issues in the coming years. Environmentalists, consumer advocates, and left-leaning activist groups were outraged, of course. And many would reap huge rewards from the Bush administration's unabashed tilt toward business in terms of fund-raising and member- ship. But they were no longer active participants when decisions were made. Frequently, they would not even be invited to the table at all.

The administration's decision to move aggressively in this area from the very beginning reflected what Rove and Bush considered a fact of life: political capital was perishable. "You build up capital through right action, and you spend it," Rove said during a 2001 speech to the American Enterprise Institute. "If you don't spend it," he said, "it's not like treasure stuck away at a storehouse someplace. It is perishable. It dwindles away." It was a measure of the new team's shrewdness that it spent its capital first on the business community, not the religious or social conservatives who were the foot soldiers of their army. Making the changes yearned for by the latter would take time; it would also take more muscle and political capital than the new administration had. So the first order of business was business— feeding the cash cow that would provide the wherewithal for gaining strength in 2002 and 2004.

It was clear that scoring gains in the 2002 midterm elections would not only increase the Republicans' freedom of movement in Congress but would lend legitimacy to a president elected under a cloud of controversy. To that end, Rove and Mehlman ventured to nearly every cabinet agency to share key polling data and to deliver a reminder of White House priorities, including the need for the presi- dent's allies to win in the next election.

Cabinet agencies under previous presidents had seen the occa- sional visit from a White House official, but such intense regular communication from the political office had never occurred before.

"One of the things that can happen in Washington when you work in an agency is that you forget who sent you there," Mehlman explained in an interview years later. "And it's important to remind people you're George Bush people. You work for the secretary, but you are George Bush people. And it's very important because Washington becomes a town where it's very easy for everyone to build their own little empires. If there's one empire I want built, it's the George Bush empire."[26]

Building the George Bush empire in 2002 meant regaining control of the Senate. In early January 2002, Rove stood in a darkened Interior Department conference room before a screen displaying maps and brightly colored bar charts. In Oregon, Republican senator Gordon Smith, who had to face voters in the fall, was taking heat over an issue that pitted environmentalists against farmers. The latter wanted to divert precious water from the Klamath River basin to quench their parched fields. Environmentalists argued that permitting more water to be siphoned off for irrigation would endanger the state's prized salmon runs. But the farmers were major GOP players, and Bush could not afford to let his party lose a seat in an evenly divided Senate. The Interior Department meeting followed a January 5, 2002, visit to Portland by Rove and Bush in which they met with Smith. The president signaled his desire to accommodate agricultural interests, saying, "We'll do everything we can to make sure water is available for those who farm." The next day, Rove made sure that commitment didn't fall through the cracks. He visited the fifty Interior Department managers attending a department retreat at a Fish and Wildlife Service conference center in Shepherdstown, West Virginia. In a PowerPoint presentation similar to one Rove used to solicit political contributions from wealthy donors, he brought up the Klamath controversy and made clear that the administration was siding with the agricultural interests that made up the Republican base.

His remarks were not entirely welcome, especially among officials who had to deal substantively with an issue that affected farmers, sportsmen, environmentalists, and Indian tribe members who depended on plentiful supplies of salmon for their livelihood. Neal McCaleb, then an assistant Interior secretary, recalled the "chilling effect" of Rove's remarks on his ongoing effort to negotiate a settlement. Wayne Smith, then deputy assistant secretary with the department's

Bureau of Indian Affairs, said Rove reminded the managers in attendance repeatedly of the need to "support our base." He also recalled Rove making a reference to the importance of other electoral battlegrounds, including an upcoming Florida governor's race—and the impact that department policy could have on it.

In addition to that meeting, Wayne Smith said that the White House regularly sent over polling data linked to administration priorities. On occasion, he said, Mehlman would come by the managers' meetings to hammer home the point. "We were constantly being reminded about how our decisions could affect electoral results," Smith recalled.[27]

A few months after Rove's presentation, Interior Secretary Gale Norton stood with Senator Smith in Klamath Falls to open giant floodgates sending millions of gallons of river water into irrigation canals. Tens of thousands of salmon subsequently died in one of the largest fish kills in the history of the West; but Smith survived. And the Bush-led GOP restored its control of the Senate.[28]

Few industries benefited more from the Bush administration's approach to policy making than coal. Its executives had played a major role in helping Bush defeat Al Gore in Democrat-dominated West Virginia by accentuating Gore's support for regulations that company officials believed hurt their business. West Virginia hadn't backed a nonincumbent Republican for president since Herbert Hoover in 1928. After a campaign fueled in part by coal industry money and activism, however, the Mountaineer State had given Bush its five electoral votes. He would not have become president without them. Now the Bush White House rolled back key labor and environmental rules—and industry officials were not shy about declaring the new president's allegiance to their cause as payback. "You did everything you could to elect a Republican president," a joyous William Raney, director of the West Virginia Coal Association, told 150 industry executives during a conference in Daniels, West Virginia, held in early 2001. Now, he said, "you are already seeing in his actions the payback, if you will, his gratitude for what we did."[29]

Rove knew that coal remained a key political ally and that West Virginia remained a closely fought state where Democrats continued to dominate elections. And other Ohio River Valley states were battlegrounds as well, centers of America's dwindling but still important manufacturing sector and one of the last bastions of organized labor. Mehlman took responsibility for that region, personally working with Raney and other industry leaders, including union workers the White House saw as potential supporters because of their social conservatism and their opposition to environmentalists. By its fifth month in office, the new administration pleased industry by reneging on a pledge to cut coal-related carbon-dioxide emissions, backed coal advocates for key political jobs in the Interior and Energy departments, and unveiled an energy policy that made no effort to wean the nation off the environmentally troublesome fuel. The administration also began to ease regulation on the industry's most controversial practice: blowing the tops off of mountain peaks to expose lucrative coal seams below.

The technique, which involved removing the top eight hundred to a thousand feet of a mountain in one fell swoop, saved companies the time and expense — and the risks — of digging shaft mines or using conventional strip-mining methods. Environmentalists and some local community activists objected that decapitating mountains with explosives sent tons of debris into the valleys below, often covering streams, lakes, forests, and sometimes whole towns. The Clinton administration had angered environmentalists by permitting this activity as well. But mountaintop removal mining increased in intensity during the Bush years, thanks to a series of regulatory decisions that were encouraged by Bush appointees at the Interior and other departments. By 2003, the coal industry had flattened nearly one fifth of the mountaintops in some West Virginia counties.[30]

The drug industry was equally intertwined with the Bush White House. Pharmaceutical companies, after all, were the biggest spenders of any industry in the 2000 and 2002 elections. In those cycles, the industry directed money to nonprofit groups with names like Citizens for Better Medicare, which spent $50 million on broadcast ads in key states. Ostensibly reflecting the companies' right to free speech by focusing on "issues," the ads usually supported positions taken by Republican candidates and attacked Democrats. The investment paid off in December 2002, when the United States stood alone in the 144-member World Trade Organization to block the distribution of certain drugs to fight acute health problems in underdeveloped nations. The major drug firms had lobbied hard for the United States position, a turnabout from earlier years, claiming that widespread dissemination of patented drugs would cut prices on the world market and eliminate incentives for research and development. The companies backed a far narrower plan focused on fighting AIDS, tuberculosis, malaria, and a few other diseases in only the very poorest nations. Industry officials argued that the World Trade Organization proposal would have allowed too much leeway for nations to decide when to override patent protections to treat a health crisis — giving countries like Brazil, China, and India the freedom to copy Viagra or cures for skin rashes or baldness and sell them at cut rates.[31]

International relief workers and foreign diplomats argued that the drugs were needed for devastating illnesses such as cancer and asthma. And they charged that it was the drug companies' pressure on the White House that led American Trade Representative Robert Zoellick to backtrack on an earlier United States commitment to make the drugs available to needy countries everywhere. "The U.S. had agreed to find a solution to the problem the poorest countries have accessing affordable medicines," said Jennifer Brant, trade-policy adviser for the international antipoverty organization Oxfam. "Now, at the behest of powerful lobbyists, the U.S. has become the obstructionist."[32]

The growing string of industry victories suddenly transformed Washington as industry groups sensed almost unprecedented opportunities. According to an analysis by Washington Post reporter Jeffrey H. Birnbaum, the number of registered lobbyists in the capital doubled between 2000 and 2005, to nearly thirty-five thousand.[33] The chamber of commerce's vice president, Stanton Anderson, said major corporations expanded their lobbying operations during Bush's first term "because they were impressed with the ability to get things done in Washington and realized the window may not be open forever."[34]

Antitax maven Grover Norquist had launched the K Street Project years before that was designed to encourage business associations and corporations to hire as lobbyists philosophical fellow travelers instead of left-leaning Democrats. His operation was backed subsequently by House majority leader Tom DeLay and, later, Senator Rick Santorum and other conservatives, and their loosely affiliated efforts began to change the nature of Washington, its economy, and its hiring patterns. These efforts, coupled with the dramatic rise in the number of lobbyists, were critical in shaping the new Republican political machine and promoting one-party dominance. In effect, the Washington lobbying corps was morphing from a small fraternity of policy wonks and politically connected former pols of mixed-party loyalties to a doctrinally purified army of Republican operatives that was prepared to provide money, expertise, and links to local power centers during future election campaigns.

For business, times had arguably never been better. Whole industries—forest products, chemicals and pesticides, utilities and energy to name a few—enjoyed a new relationship with once-pesky regulators. Oil and gas executives had complained for decades about environmental restrictions blocking them from valuable deposits in the West and off American coastlines. The Interior Department, they groused, required permits that could delay exploration for months or years. The Environmental Protection Agency's water experts often slowed projects, even on private lands. But the Bush administration, headed by two former oilmen, quickly wiped away many of those impediments. An energy task force headed by Vice President Cheney called for opening once-restricted lands in Alaska and the West to exploration and a reduction in regulation across the board.

The White House quietly moved in on the regulatory turf of the Interior Department, opening a little-known White House Office of Energy Permit Expediting that acted as a complaint desk for industry executives, passing along energy company concerns directly to federal land management employees in the field. The *Los Angeles Times* broke the story of the obscure new office in 2004. A Bureau of Land Management field archeologist told the newspaper about an unusual call he'd received from the White House. He said the caller had told him he was with a White House task force and wanted to know about a pending application for a single gas well in a remote part of a western state.

The archeologist was so stunned to get a call from the White House about such an obscure topic that he thought the call was a joke. "You guys must have things with Iraq taken care of if you have time to call somebody in a field office about a gas well," the archeologist told the *Times*'s Alan C. Miller.

But when he realized the call wasn't a joke, the staffer paid attention. "I know it's political," the archeologist said. "I know it's hot. It becomes a top priority because you don't want the bosses to jump down your throat. I've worked for the federal government since the Reagan administration and that's never happened before."

Thanks to this kind of effort, the Bureau of Land Management issued drilling permits at a record pace during Bush's first term, an increase of 70 percent over the Clinton administration. The pressure was so intense in the oil- and gas-rich Rockies that some federal workers took to calling the region "the OPEC states."[35] In fact, the Bush White House sided with the oil industry in nearly every case — except one. That conspicuous exception came in a familiar state: Florida.

If ever there was a question about what mattered more to the White House — ideological devotion to regulatory relief or winning elections — the handling of oil exploration in Governor Jeb Bush's state cleared it up. The president's younger brother was preparing his own reelection campaign for 2002, an election that both national parties viewed as a midterm referendum on the president and an early indication of whether the state that decided the 2000 election would be deadlocked again. Rove knew that in a state dominated by retirees and tourism, the only issue more explosive than Social Security was the environment. Resort owners, hoteliers, airline executives, elected officials from Pensacola to Key West — nobody wanted the sight of oil rigs off Florida's coasts. Jeb had vehemently opposed offshore oil drilling in his 1998 campaign and, facing a potentially tight reelection, was promising to use his Washington connections to preserve the state's coastline. In his early 2002 meeting at the Interior Department, Rove referred to the importance of the Florida race and cited specific Interior Department issues that could affect it, according to one participant, Wayne Smith. In July 2001, the Interior Department announced it would limit the number of new oil and gas leases to be sold in the Gulf of Mexico, thus shielding Florida's shores. Environmentalists in the state praised the announcement.

Yet in California, where Democratic governor Gray Davis wanted similar limits, there was no such White House response — proof, Democrats charged, that the administration was playing politics. Then, in May 2002, Jeb Bush stopped by the White House for an Oval Office meeting with his brother and another big announcement: the federal government would pay Chevron and two other oil companies $115 million to block their plans to drill for natural gas in the Gulf of Mexico's Destin Dome area within thirty miles of the Panhandle coast renowned for its white, sandy beaches. The leases had been granted during the Reagan administration but long opposed by Florida officials. The president also announced a proposal to pay $120 million to the politically connected Collier family for mineral rights under four hundred thousand acres of land near the Everglades. Oil and gas drilling was already taking place there, but the Bushes said the deal would ensure future protection of the ecologically sensitive water system. The proposed deal, which was never consummated, won nods of approval from environmentalists, who for years had been pushing for more safeguards around the Everglades.

But the announcement was blatantly inconsistent with the policy priorities of the Bush administration. Its energy priorities so far had consistently supported oil and gas drilling from Alaska to the Rockies. Critics denounced the decisions as political, and they argued that both the Collier deal and the money paid to the oil companies reflected a vastly overblown estimate of the value for the leases and the property. The Collier land was considered highly speculative, but critics noted that the family had donated thousands of dollars to the state Republican Party.

Nonetheless, the Florida governor did not shy away from basking in the potential benefits of the deal, which softened his image with moderate voters. On a sunny spring day at the White House, standing with Interior Secretary Gale Norton, Jeb Bush was asked by reporters if the agreement would boost his reelection prospects. "I hope so," he said, quickly adding, "But more importantly, it is good public policy. And when there's a convergence of good politics and good public policy, I don't think we should be ashamed about it."[36] One of Florida's Republican congressmen, Representative Mark Foley of West Palm Beach, brazenly couched the deal in campaign-style sloganeering: "The River of Grass is now Bush country."[37] On the other hand, Phil Clapp, president of the National Environmental Trust, called the agreements a "$235 million campaign contribution to the Reelect Jeb Bush Committee, courtesy of U.S. taxpayers."[38] Later an Interior Department inspectors general report concluded that the proposed payout to the Colliers was many times the value of the oil and gas holdings. The report concluded that the Colliers were "exploiting a combination of public policy, politics, and environmentalism," and that their company "took complete advantage of a negotiating environment weighted heavily in its favor." The report said the behavior of Interior Department officials in approving such a large payment—which had been announced in the May 2002 White House ceremony designed to burnish the Bush brothers' green credentials—remained a mystery. It never mentioned Rove's prior appearance at the Interior Department managers meeting when he referred to the importance of Florida in the upcoming election.

Several years later, after both Bush brothers had secured reelection, they would relent somewhat on their hard-line antidrilling policies off of Florida's coast. Their willingness to compromise—which came at a time of rising energy prices and increasing pressure to find more energy sources—underscored the long-term interest in keeping a critical pro-GOP industry happy. But back in 2002, as the White House eyed the importance of Florida in the Bush family's immediate future and the Republican Party's long-term goals, the Rove model of tapping executive branch power and resources for political gain dominated decision making.

A scene in April of that year prompted one Florida newspaper to propose a new joke: "How many Bush cabinet secretaries does it take to introduce a new species of bug into the Everglades?" The question poked fun at an incident that month when Agriculture Secretary Ann Veneman and Interior Secretary Norton appeared at Everglades Holiday Park with loads of Australian insects known as *melaleuca psyllid*. The bugs were to be set free to attack the Australian melaleuca tree, which was growing out of control in the Glades, choking native plant life and causing problems for animals. Under normal conditions, the *St. Petersburg Times* reported, "the task of releasing these bugs might have fallen to a humble government scientist or a lowly bureaucrat. But the presence of two Bush cabinet members underscored the message that the administration was knocking itself out to preserve the environment in Florida."[39]

Throughout the first term, critics noted that Florida—the state that put Bush in the White House—seemed to receive more than the usual share of federal grants and visits by top-ranking officials. One prominent example came in July 2002, when the Senate rejected a proposed drug benefit for some seniors, a vote that Republicans feared would hurt their party's candidates in states like Florida. But on the very same day, the White House announced a special federal waiver permitting Florida to offer drug coverage to poor seniors through its Medicaid program.[40]

The attention to Florida illustrated how carefully the Rove-led White House political team was willing to calibrate administration policy to match political needs. At the same time, strategists knew they needed to counter a growing negative reaction to broader national policies on energy, worker issues, and consumer rights. Environmental groups, for example, were viewed as highly effective national advocates whose opposition could hurt the president's attempts to appear green-friendly. So, in response, the White House moved to solidify ties with hunting and fishing organizations, effectively exploiting divisions with environmental allies. At Rove's direction, leaders of the National Rifle Association, Ducks Unlimited, and other hunting groups gathered with the president in the Theodore Roosevelt Room to discuss wilderness policy. The president later invited leaders of some of these groups to his home near Crawford, Texas. Members of the Bush cabinet would sit down repeatedly with these leaders, including once meeting in September 2004, to answer preelection concerns about oil drilling in the west and its impact on big game.

The immediate target was the 2002 midterms, though, and as they drew near, Rove continued to study polls and examine the electoral map. His standard for backing potential congressional candidates was simple: he recruited based on who was likely to win, not who was the most ideologically pure. And he micromanaged individual midterm campaigns from his White House office, working closely with political director Mehlman to devise a new "seventy-two-hour initiative" to turn out Republican voters in the final three days of a campaign. The idea, inspired by the near-loss in 2000, would finally put Republicans in the same league as Democrats when it came to the old-fashioned get-out-the-vote techniques of machine politics. Rove's iron hand was felt that year by one Minnesota Republican, Tim Pawlenty, a favorite of conservatives, who was preparing to announce a challenge to liberal Democratic senator Paul Wellstone. The day before Pawlenty was to address a town hall meeting in southern Minnesota to make his big announcement, his cell phone rang. It was Rove, calling to explain that the White House had decided to bless Norm Coleman, the better-known moderate mayor of St. Paul, for the bid to take out Wellstone. As first described by *New York Times Magazine* writer Matt Bai, Rove asked Pawlenty to drop out.[41] When Pawlenty balked at the suggestion, Rove arranged for Vice President Cheney to contact Pawlenty and make the argument. The next day Pawlenty announced that he had decided not to run for the Senate.[42]

Rove's intervention wasn't limited to Minnesota. In Georgia, he backed a moderate congressman, Saxby Chambliss, to challenge incumbent Democrat Max Cleland. He pulled a Missouri congressman, Jim Talent, into the Senate race and then helped Talent with advice and fund-raising to effectively challenge the incumbent senator, Jean Carnahan. In South Dakota, he persuaded Representative John Thune to challenge Democrat Tim Johnson, the state's junior senator. In North Carolina, he pushed behind the scenes to help Elizabeth Dole secure the nomination.[43]

Conventional wisdom had long held that an incumbent president's party performed poorly in a midterm election. But on Election

Day 2002, it appeared that Rove and his team had one-upped that conventional wisdom. Just two years after Al Gore nearly won the White House with the help of the Democrats' masterful grassroots, door-to-door politics, Rove and his lieutenants had harnessed government, handpicked the best candidates, and put together a massive get-out-the-vote effort without precedent in Republican politics. That election marked a turning point: a moment at which the GOP actually beat the Democrats at the game the Democrats had won for so many decades. On election night, Rove, Bush, and a handful of advisers gathered in the family quarters of the White House to watch returns. The president kept an eye on the Fox News projections as Rove thumbed his BlackBerry. As *Time* magazine would later describe the scene, when Talent's campaign manager phoned from Missouri with news of victory, the president lit up a cigar.[44] The call signaled that Republicans would retake control of the U.S. Senate. North Carolina and Minnesota brought more good news. South Dakota would provide an ultimately disappointing cliffhanger, but Thune was in position to try again two years later. It was the best performance by the presidential party in a midterm election in nearly a century.

More important for the future, the leap forward in voter registration and get-out-the-vote performance meant the Republicans would no longer enter a campaign ceding that factor to Democrats; indeed, before long they would gain a clear advantage in that area. Such things do not win elections if time and tide favor the opposition. But year in and year out—when no epochal issue was wracking the country—they would make a difference. And they were a piece of Rove's overall strategy: to gain an edge here, put up an obstacle there, until the sum of all the parts equaled a political organization that would be very hard to beat in the best of times, impossible under ordinary circumstances.

Poring over exit polls, Rove also saw improvement in support from evangelical voters and minorities.

He wanted more.

CHAPTER 5

The Organized Shall Inherit the Earth

The elite media thinks the only black political stories are Barack Obama, Jesse Jackson, and Al Sharpton. Meanwhile, 23 million black church-attending folks are making independent decisions about what they think is important.

—REVEREND EUGENE RIVERS III, PASTOR OF AZUSA CHRISTIAN COMMUNITY CHURCH, *BOSTON GLOBE*, JANUARY 10, 2005

S ix weeks after marking the Republicans' midterm election victories with a celebratory cigar, George W. Bush stood on a stage in Philadelphia before a blue backdrop bearing the message "Compassion in Action." As he spoke, he sounded like a Baptist preacher, his voice filled with a rare combination of confidence and poetic cadence as he told a White House–sponsored conference about the promise and power of private, religious charities in fighting poverty, drugs, and crime. "Our economy is growing, yet there are some needs that prosperity can never fill," he said. "We arrest and convict dangerous criminals; yet building more prisons is no substitute for responsibility and order in our souls. No government policy can put hope in people's hearts or a sense of purpose in people's lives. That is done when someone, some good soul puts an arm around a neighbor and says, 'God loves you, and I love you, and you can count on us both.'"

Members of the audience shouted, "Amen," and then burst into the sort of cheers and sustained applause that feed a politician's soul. And it must have been all the more satisfying for Bush, because this was no Republican crowd, nor was it a typical gathering of religious conservatives who would naturally applaud a born-again message. This audience was mostly African American, a mix of lay black church leaders and ministers from across the nation, individuals who have traditionally constituted a pillar of the Democratic Party. And collectively, African Americans had emphatically rejected Bush in the past. In 2000, he received just 9 percent of the black vote and the Florida recount battle that gave him the presidency drew massive civil rights protests and allegations of minority voter disenfranchisement. The stated theme of this day in Philadelphia was faith and social problems. It was an effort to renew interest in his faith-based initiative, a foundation block in his much-advertised compassionate conservatism. The president had spent the morning meeting with the children of prison inmates who were being nurtured by a church-based mentoring program. But the larger subject of race in politics—and the Republican Party's tortured history on the subject—hovered over the meeting.

The Bush presidency had quietly dedicated itself to repairing relations with African Americans, a population that left the party of Lincoln for the Democrats during the New Deal and never came back. African Americans' links to the Democratic Party grew stronger during the era of the civil rights movement and the Great Society. And it had intensified in the decades after that, as Republicans pursued their Southern strategy. Bush had renounced that Southern strategy, but he and Rove knew that was not enough. Moving away from an indirect form of race baiting only meant the GOP would stop rubbing salt in old wounds. To begin healing the wounds would require something more. And what Bush was offering was his so-called faith-based initiative, a proposal to provide federal funds to religious and other charities. Beyond its untested value as a tool for attacking acute social problems, offering federal money had three political advantages when it came to African Americans. First, it showed Republicans making a direct effort to help blacks with problems they cared about—a better answer than "probably nothing" to the classic voters' question, "What have you done for me lately?" Second, it was an acceptably conservative variation on the Democrats' old game of giving federal dollars to an important voting bloc. And third, it used as its point of contact perhaps the most influential leadership network in the black community: its clergy. As Bush political adviser Matthew Dowd put it, "The minister is the number one influencer in the African American community."[1]

Bush and his advisers had no illusions about winning overwhelming numbers of black votes. Rove played a more subtle game than that. In large part, his formula for dealing with the Democrats was the political equivalent of the death by a thousand cuts. The outreach to black ministers was meant to be one of those little nicks. In a close election, reducing black support for Democratic candidates by even a few percentage points could make a difference. Overall, Republicans got 11 percent of the black vote nationwide in 2004. That was up two percentage points from the previous presidential election cycle. And GOP strategists credited the faith initiative with helping to erode the Democrats' hold on the African American base in Ohio and other key states.

When Bush talked about his faith initiative with black audiences, the larger topics of civil rights, race relations, and traditional social values almost always came up. The speech in Philadelphia was no exception. Days before, Senate Republican leader Trent Lott had sparked headlines for suggesting the country might have been better off had Strom Thurmond been elected president when he ran as a segregationist Dixiecrat back in 1948. Lott, an old-guard Mississippi lawmaker with enormous influence in Washington, was the face of Republican power on Capitol Hill. But his words—coupled with his own history, along with that of Thurmond—symbolized the racially motivated shift of whites away from the Democratic Party in the South as the GOP exploited the ferment over such issues as desegregation, affirmative action, and school busing.[2] Lott had tried to deflate the controversy, appearing on Black Entertainment Television to apologize. But Democrats were calling for his ouster. For Bush, this was a golden opportunity, a chance to show African American voters that this son of Midland, Texas, was not his father's Southern Republican. "This great and prosperous land must become a single nation of justice and opportunity," Bush told the faith-based meeting that day in Philadelphia. "We must continue our advance toward full equality for every citizen, which demands the guarantee of civil rights for all. Any suggestion that the segregated past was acceptable or positive is offensive, and it is wrong."

He then dug deeper: "Recent comments by Senator Lott do not reflect the spirit of our country. He has apologized, and rightly so. Every day our nation was segregated was a day that America was unfaithful to our founding ideals. And the founding ideals of our nation and, in fact, the founding ideals of the political party I represent was, and remains today, the equal dignity and equal rights of every American."

Trent Lott and his wife were watching the speech on television from a relative's home in Key West, where they were seeking a respite from the controversy. Bush's speech turned Lott's mood first to rage, then to worry and depression. "When Bush said 'He has apologized and rightly so,' his voice hammered away those last three words in a tone that was booming and nasty," Lott wrote later. "Watching from Florida, Tricia and I were totally flattened emotionally. If we hadn't realized the desperate nature of our fix, Bush's obvious anger drove it home."[3] Six days later, with Lott still fighting to save his career despite Bush's rebuke, the senator took another hit. This time, chiming in from Tallahassee, was the president's brother Jeb, who had won his second term as governor with surprisingly high minority support. "Something's going to have to change," the governor told the *Miami Herald* in response to a question on the impact of Lott's remarks on the GOP's outreach efforts. Lott wrote later that he was told Jeb's remarks followed a morning telephone conversation with Karl Rove.[4] Within days Lott stepped down as the Senate's Republican leader, removing a blemish on the party's outreach strategy and indirectly burnishing the

Bush brothers' image as beacons of a new Republican approach to race. Not incidentally, it would also allow the White House to install in the Senate a more reliable majority leader who would cooperate more closely with the White House than Lott had done.

In his Philadelphia speech, Bush placed himself on the side of the traditional civil rights community. Then he made an elegant pivot, comparing racial discrimination of the past with what he said was persistent religious discrimination in the present. And he took dramatic action. From the stage, Bush signed an executive order directing all government agencies to treat religious charities like any secular social service organization in issuing grants. "I'm here today to stop unfair treatment of religious charities by the federal government," he told the fourteen hundred religious leaders in the downtown Marriott Hotel ballroom. "The days of discrimination against religious groups — just because they're religious — are coming to an end."

The audience applauded as Bush signed the order from a desk onstage. It was the second faith-based order he had signed that day. The other had been signed in Washington that morning, expanding faith-based programs throughout the federal bureaucracy. All told, the two executive orders accomplished by signature much of what Bush had sought and failed to get from Congress the previous year. His orders created faith-based centers in the Department of Agriculture and the Agency for International Development, expanding to seven the number of government agencies with offices devoted to making taxpayer-financed grants more available to religious organizations. And in each case, the president had established a rhetorical link between the civil rights battles of old and what he described as a new fight against religious bigotry. "If a charity is helping the needy, it should not matter if there is a rabbi on the board, or a cross or a crescent on the wall, or a religious commitment in the charter," Bush said.

His action produced immediate criticism from Democrats. "Today, the president endorsed the practice of hanging signs on doors that say 'No Jews or Catholics Need Apply,'" complained Representative Jerrold Nadler, a Democrat from New York.[5] Another leading critic was Representative Chet Edwards, a Democrat whose Texas district included Bush's home in nearby Crawford. Edwards, who is deeply religious, said he feared that government support of religious institutions would weaken those groups by threatening their independence. "Religious freedom will survive and thrive the most if you put it up on a pedestal above the reach of politicians in the federal government," he said.[6] Edwards also cited specific examples of cases in which he said the Bush initiative threatened the Constitution's prohibition on any law "respecting the establishment of religion." Edwards pointed to the Department of Housing and Urban Development, which acted the day Bush signed the orders to change its rules so as to permit federal dollars to pay for the construction of church buildings; the only caveat was that the buildings were required to be used partly for community activities. Edwards's complaints brought results—of a sort. Republicans targeted him in his 2004 reelection campaign with ads saying he opposed prayer, even for U.S. troops in battle. The antiprayer campaign backfired, and Edwards, a locally popular politician known for the depth of his faith, won reelection.[7]

Edwards's philosophical concerns were echoed to a certain extent by a handful of conservatives, including for a time the Reverend Pat Robertson. They worried that local charitable enterprises would be compromised once they began receiving government funds.[8] Robertson dropped his objections after 2003 when his organization, Operation Blessing, received a $500,000 grant from the Department of Health and Human Services.[9]

When Bush spoke that day in Philadelphia, Congress bore the brunt of his complaints for failing to act. But, in fact, a part of Bush's originally promised faith agenda—a tax break for charitable giving—had been dropped by the White House.[10] As detailed by *Washington Monthly* writer Amy Sullivan the tax breaks lost out in internal White House budget discussions because other tax cuts were deemed greater priorities. Nonetheless, in the rhetorical campaign preparing the way for the president's reelection in 2004, it was Congress and "secular extremists" who got the blame for a lack of progress.

The Philadelphia speech coincided with the release of an *Esquire* magazine article that quoted the departed director of the White House office that handled the faith-based initiative, charging that he was forced to follow orders from "Mayberry Machievellis" in the administration who were more concerned with politics than with helping people in need.[11] The former director, John DiIulio, had returned to his home in Philadelphia and was well known to many in the president's audience on that December 12, 2002, visit to the city. DiIulio was, in many ways, an architect of the faith-based initiative, a University of Pennsylvania professor who provided advice to both Bush and Democrat Al Gore and whose ideas were very much a part of President Clinton's "charitable choice" initiatives.

Bush expanded on Clinton's approach. Encouraging religious organizations to battle poverty and other social ills became the heart of his self-styled compassionate conservatism. Bush embraced the concept during his first months as Texas governor. In advance of his White House run, Bush's strategists viewed compassionate conservatism as a winning label that could comfort moderates and religious conservatives simultaneously. The phrase first arose in Bush's conversations with outspoken Texas evangelical Christians. He credited the idea to Marvin Olasky, a Yale-educated Jew, antiwar activist, and communist who later converted to Christianity and became a leading advocate of the faith-based approach to social problems. Under Olasky's influence, then Governor Bush began pushing a range of state legislation promoting faith-based social services, from day care to drug treatment.

On a 1999 campaign trip to Indianapolis, Bush called for more faith-based programs, including billions in tax credits to encourage private organizations, firms, and people to donate to charities.[12] That high-priced incentive program was a key component of the faith initiative as it was originally planned, but Bush would drop it in favor of tax cuts after he arrived in Washington.

That decision foreshadowed the tensions that would continue to grow between two pillars of the GOP's one-party temple: religious conservatives and business lobbyists. When DiIulio left in 2001, his "Mayberry Machiavellis" charge was aimed in part at administration officials he believed had failed to make tough decisions that would have truly helped the poor by expanding social service programs and encouraging charitable giving through changes in the tax code.[13] Instead of being increased, social service programs had been cut. The modest increase in faith funding fostered by the Bush initiative did not nearly offset those cuts. And the faith programs that were funded were rarely if ever subjected to the scrutiny and evaluations that Bush had advocated. The plan to help charities raise billions by giving millions more Americans a tax incentive to donate had been dropped entirely. Where the faith initiative once seemed a potentially beneficial policy and a brilliant political symbol, the exit of DiIulio followed by his blunt assessment had instead embarrassed the White House and left the young initiative in shambles.

With Bush that day in Philadelphia was the man he's asked to succeed DiIulio, James Towey, another Catholic veteran of social causes. A registered Democrat and former state social services official under Florida Democratic governor Lawton Chiles, Towey brought sterling credentials. A gentle, soft-spoken father of five, Towey had been a top aide to former senator Mark Hatfield, the deeply religious Oregon Republican who advocated for refugees and an end to armed conflict. Towey had worked as counsel to Mother Theresa, was a pioneer advocate for the rights of the frail elderly, had authored a popular living will format that helped thousands prepare to die with dignity, and had long pushed the government to support the needs of persecuted and destitute people around the globe.

He was also a close friend of the president's brother Jeb. As an opponent of abortion, Towey felt disaffected from the Democratic Party. He had never been a political operative, but perhaps because of his own experience with the abortion issue, he understood the potential alliance between the Bush White House and groups of people who had traditionally been alienated from the Republican Party. "African Americans are really starting to question some of these fundamental precepts that the Democratic Party is there for them," Towey said in a 2005 interview from his office next door to the White House. "They're starting to say, 'What do we have to show for that? What has that done for our community? I see President Bush is trying to leave no child behind. He's trying to rattle these miserable schools that our grandparents went to, that my mother went to, that I went to, that my kids are going to.'"

"They're frustrated," Towey added. "They want change." Towey said the frustration stemmed from a sense among many black churches that they were excluded from federal grants in the past, due largely to complicated rules and a preference for large, well-established charities. That, he said, explained why black clergy in particular might respond so enthusiastically to the faith-based initiative, and why they dominated attendance at White House–sponsored conferences across the nation such as the Philadelphia meeting where Bush rebuked Trent Lott. "The first thing, you look at [at a typical conference] is you say, 'Whoa, that's a Republican gathering? Half the room is minority. Wow,'" Towey said.[14]

When Towey was named to replace DiIulio in early 2002, Bush said that his new faith-based chief understood that "there are things more important than political parties. And one of those things more important than political parties is to help heal the nation's soul."[15] But Towey proved an effective political weapon as well. As the 2002 midterm campaign entered its final months and eased into the early stages of Bush's own reelection, Towey's faith-based office was at the center of the GOP strategy to find new voters and expand its base. As staffers planned conferences and meetings across the country, they appeared to pay close attention to a blue- and red-shaded map that Rove and Mehlman had distributed to nearly every executive branch agency to illustrate competitive states and races for 2002 and 2004. The map served as a less than subtle suggestion of where government officials might want to focus their energies.

The mixture of politics and policy in the faith-based office led to more controversy. The deputy director, David Kuo, would ultimately quit following the 2004 elections, outraged by the discrepancy between the White House's ability to milk political gain from the program and its commitment to some of the initiative's big-dollar requirements. Kuo was most upset over the tax break for charitable giving that Bush had promised but never delivered. Some had estimated that the tax break would cost more than $30 billion over ten years. Writing for the online religion newsletter Beliefnet, Kuo described the faith-based office as the "cross around the White House's neck," an adornment that made the politically beneficial statement that the president was a man of faith. "The White House discovered urban faith leaders had been so neglected for so long that simple attention drew them in," Kuo wrote.[16]

In the case of the faith-based office, this meant planning high-profile meetings in key districts and towns, and, often, following up with grant recipients who could help the president. In 2002, the GOP appeared to be offering federal grants as a way of luring support for Republican candidates, often targeting black voters in states and districts with tight races.[17] Towey, his director of outreach at the time Jeremy White, and other White House staffers also appeared at Republican-sponsored events with candidates in half a dozen states. During the summer of 2002, for instance, the *Washington Post* reported that Towey appeared with numerous other Republicans in close races, including Representatives John Shimkus of Illinois, Tim Hutchison of Arkansas, and Shelley Moore Capito of West Virginia. After a South Carolina event for black ministers, participants received a follow-up memo on Republican Party letterhead explaining to ministers how they could apply for grant money.[18]

Of twenty publicly financed trips taken by Towey between the 2002 and 2004 elections and publicized through press accounts or releases, sixteen were to battleground states. Towey declined to release copies of his full calendar. But he defended his frequent travel, arguing that key electoral states such as Florida, with the nation's first faith-based prison and the active support of the governor's office, were hotbeds for the initiative. "If you look at where the battleground states are, it's where the action is in the faith-based initiative," he said.[19] After 2002, Kuo said that more than fifteen thousand religious and social service leaders attended free White House conferences in battleground states, and many of the attendees were black and Hispanic. "They were hardly pep rallies for the president," Kuo said. "But the conferences sent a resounding political message to all faith-oriented constituencies: President Bush cares about you. . . . By traveling across the country, giving useful information, and extending faith-based groups an open hand, powerful inroads were made to 'non-traditional' supporters.'" Kuo described one "senior Republican" who was ecstatic over the racial diversity at an early conference. "This is what Republicans have been dreaming about for 30 years," Kuo said the Republican told him.[20]

Some of the work performed by Towey's office won plaudits from across the ideological and political spectrum, even as it benefited the president's reelection. In June 2004, Towey, a longtime advocate for refugees, personally intervened to convince Bush that the United States needed to loosen post–September 11 restrictions that had prevented tens of thousands of persecuted refugees from entering the United States. Towey arranged for two young African refugees to meet privately with the president in a back room at a Washington hotel shortly before Bush was scheduled to address a faith-based conference. The meeting was scheduled to last only a few minutes but stretched closer to an hour as Bush listened intently to the refugees' sorrowful stories. Still, critics believed politics outweighed purity in the White House faith office. Robert Wineburg, a professor of social work at the University of North Carolina at Greensboro, said he thought an electoral calculus overrode most decisions. "Look at where they planned their large-scale meetings," said Wineburg, author of several books on faith-based social programs. "A grant-writing workshop in St. Louis in September before Missouri was a lock, in Miami in October before Florida was sealed. I wouldn't call it honest technical assistance based on communities that needed that assistance most at that specific time. I'd call it honest American, or maybe old-style Chicago, politics." Wineburg said that the meetings were designed almost exclusively to appeal to Christian pastors. Early sessions, he said sometimes opened with a prayer to Jesus. Wineburg said he did not object to prayer but wanted one that would be inclusive.[21]

A Bush administration political appointee to a federal agency later leveled the same accusation in stark legal terms. Eugene Lin, a Republican who worked on Bush's presidential campaigns and a political appointee at the United States Agency for International Development, was convinced that the agency's faith office had become a hub of Christian evangelism and effectively discriminated against other religions. The federal agency distributed hundreds of millions of dollars in grants around the world. But Lin, who is Jewish, said he came to believe the agency's recently established faith-based office served as an "instrument of the religious right," building political support from that critical GOP constituency in an election year. Also, he said that the office actively discriminated against him because of his religious beliefs. Lin was dismayed by what he saw and what he experienced in the faith office. In 2004, he filed a discrimination complaint with the agency, its inspector general, and the Equal Employment Opportunity Commission.[22]

Lin, a tall red-haired man in his early thirties with Nordic features, is the son of a Holocaust survivor, a fact that he says makes him "especially sensitive to any level of discrimination not only toward Jews but against all religious or ethnic minorities." He said he began to feel uncomfortable and isolated in the agency headquarters as his supervisors crusaded for Christian causes. But Lin said he was amazed to see that the office's deputy director, Linda Shavlain, a conservative Catholic, had mounted a two-foot-tall crucifix on the wall of her office, next to a conference table frequently used for meetings between staff and visitors. He said he walked out of one meeting that began with a Christian prayer but was later reprimanded by Shavlain, who called him into the conference room for what she called a "come to Jesus" meeting.

An investigation file from the department shows that Lin's superiors viewed him as a troublesome employee. Lin said in an interview that investigators talked only with other managers and not with witnesses he had recommended. Even so, the file verifies much of his account. It includes a photograph of the crucifix and an acknowledgment that meetings sometimes began with a Christian prayer.

Lin's superiors at the agency suggested in affidavits to investigators that his discrimination complaint may have resulted from his poor performance reviews and inability to secure a pay raise. Lin has acknowledged dissatisfaction with his supervisors but said his formal complaint was entirely related to his feelings of discrimination and a sense that the office was using taxpayer dollars to curry favor with an influential GOP voting bloc, the Christian right. He said that he first grew disconcerted as he arranged and tracked outreach meetings with faith-based groups. Of 165 outside groups invited to meet at the Agency for International Development, 161 were conservative Christian organizations, Lin said. Following his expressions of concern, two Jewish groups along with one Muslim and one Hindu organization were invited into the agency. When he asked why more Jewish groups were not invited, Lin said he was told that Jews were more active on domestic issues, not foreign—an explanation he said was incorrect.

Lin said that his office was obsessed with promoting abstinence overseas and discouraging abortion rather than pressing concerns such as combating hunger and improving relations with the Muslim world. "As a social moderate I found I had to keep my mouth shut or be ostracized in the office," he said.[23]

An agency spokesman declined to respond specifically to Lin's charges in late 2005. But he said the agency "responded proactively when Mr. Lin first voiced his concerns in 2004." An internal inquiry found that there was "no merit to any of Mr. Lin's allegations," the spokesman said. Lin would pursue his discrimination claim, charging that the faith office advocated for the interests and political priorities of Christian conservatives, a key component of the GOP base.[24]

As the 2004 campaign progressed, James Towey plunged deeper into politics. He publicly disparaged the faith-based proposals of Democratic nominee John Kerry, even though the Massachusetts senator issued a campaign position paper proposing a similar program to Bush's. "My own sense was that he would stick it in the Smithsonian," Towey said of Kerry. "He had gotten enormous pressure from . . . all the secular extremists to stop this thing from moving forward."[25] (Towey's sharply worded comments—and political acumen—proved helpful in the 2002 and 2004 campaigns. But Towey would not be available for the challenging 2006 midterms. He left the White House in the middle of that year to assume the presidency of St. Vincent College, a small Catholic school in Pennsylvania.)

In the critical months before the 2004 election, grants awarded by the faith office revealed a political pattern. In October 2004, for example, the administration issued press releases announcing $7.8

million in faith-based grants, mostly to African American organizations. The announcements were made in Pennsylvania, Ohio, and
Florida, the states given the highest political priority by the Bush
campaign, the very states that were expected to be pivotal in elections beyond 2004. The outreach was especially aggressive with black
ministers. Some recipients of faith-based money were Democrats and
often declined to support George W. Bush. Others waved off invitations. One black minister, Reverend Amos Cleophilus Brown Sr., pastor of San Francisco's Third Baptist Church, said he received regular
offers from the White House and from the Bush campaign to attend
faith-based meetings and conferences. Brown called the entreaties a
"sinister attempt at realignment" and ignored them.

Another word of caution came from the Reverend Timothy
McDonald, an Atlanta-based minister and president of the African
American Ministers Council, who warned fellow preachers to be wary
of the federal funds and the invitations to apply for them at meetings
like the one Bush addressed in Philadelphia. "I think a lot of black
churches will suffer because they will lose their prophetic voice when
they accept government dollars," he said. "Imagine Dr. King with a
$100,000 after-school program funded by the state of Alabama and
Rosa Parks comes to him about the bus."[26] Nevertheless, the recipient
list would eventually include a number of prominent black pastors,
some of whom had been outspoken supporters of the president.

"I asked Congress to not fear faith," Bush told a meeting of black
religious leaders in New Orleans nine months before his own
reelection.[27] "We ought to say, 'We want results, we welcome
results, and we're willing to fund programs that are capable of delivering results. We want to fund programs that save Americans, one
soul at a time.' So, I called on Congress to join me in passing laws
that would open up the federal treasury to faith-based programs, and
they balked."

Republicans conveyed that message to conservative, religiously
observant voters of all kinds, often communicating below the radar in
private, untracked communications. One video distributed to evangelicals laid out in stark terms the president's legacy on faith and the
"secular humanistic" motives of his opponents. Daniel Lapin, an

Orthodox rabbi and talk-show host with ties to lobbyist Jack Abramoff and the Bush White House, couched the battle as a struggle between those with Judeo-Christian values and those who viewed such values as "obstructions" to progress. During 2004, he encouraged fellow religious activists to back the president's faith agenda. "The future of our nation depends upon the outcome of this struggle," Lapin said in the video.

The film, *George W. Bush: Faith in the White House,* carried a less than subtle subtitle: *His Faith Will Inspire You.* And it included testimonials from some of the president's closest and best-known friends in the evangelical world, including Ted Haggard of the National Association of Evangelicals and Texas-based religious broadcaster James Robison, who recalled praying with the president on a quiet hilltop on his Texas ranch. Another witness to Bush's faith, Tom Freiling, author of *George W. Bush on God and Country,* offered this: "I've heard several accounts of the president being found in the Oval Office on his knees in prayer."

The overriding point: Bush was a divinely inspired president who was told by God to seek the highest office, presumably because September 11 was looming. Viewers learned about his 1986 conversation with the Reverend Billy Graham when, during a stroll at Kennebunkport, Bush realized he wanted to be "right" with God. They learned how he promoted government funding for faith-based programs as governor of Texas despite a hostile bureaucracy, and how he decided to run for president. As Bush told Robison, according to the evangelist's testimony, running for the White House was "something God wants me to do. . . . I can't explain it, but I believe my country's going to need me at this time." The film showed Bush speaking in a church about his faith. The camera focused on a massive portrait of Jesus Christ, draped in a yellow robe. As the camera slowly panned down, Bush appeared at the podium, his face perfectly positioned beneath the body of Jesus. "My faith has made a big difference in my personal life, and my public life as well," Bush said. "And I pray. I pray for guidance. I pray for patience. I firmly believe in the power of intercessory prayer. And I know I could not do my job without it."

Despite the producers' claims that the video was a politically independent enterprise, the film was shown several times for delegates to the Republican National Convention in New York. Producers told the conservative Web site WorldNetDaily.com that they planned to distribute the seventy-minute film to every church with a mailing address, totaling about three hundred thousand, and that it was to air on several Christian broadcasting networks, reaching millions of viewers.

Much of the president's communication to evangelicals was similarly shielded from larger public view. Supporters used church directories to reach potential voters. The president himself often spoke using veiled references, a kind of code that could energize religious conservatives without offending moderates. He frequently referred to a "culture of life" rather than outright opposition to abortion. He studiously avoided saying whether he felt the landmark abortion ruling *Roe v. Wade* should be overturned, insisting he opposed any litmus test for appointing judges. But he found ways to score political points, sometimes with more than one constituency at a time. In one debate encounter with Democrat John Kerry, Bush cited the 1857 *Dred Scott* decision by the Supreme Court affirming slavery, calling it one of the worst rulings in American history. For many viewers and for the mainstream news media, the remark at first seemed random and bizarre. But to abortion foes, who long viewed the 1973 *Roe* ruling as the *Dred Scott* of its time, the meaning was clear. And to socially conservative African Americans, there was double meaning: the president was acknowledging the country's horrific history on race and couching abortion as a civil rights matter. "It was a poignant moment, a very special gourmet filet mignon dinner," said the Reverend Louis P. Sheldon, the chairman of the Traditional Values Coalition, a prominent conservative advocacy group. "Everyone knows the *Dred Scott* decision and you don't have to stretch your mind at all. When he said that, it made it very clear that the 1973 decision was faulty because what it said was that unborn persons in a legal sense have no civil rights."[28]

The Bush administration sent signals through quiet policy changes that likewise escaped wide public notice. At the Department of Justice, led in the first term by John Ashcroft, a favorite of the evangelical movement, lawyers adopted a unique approach to protecting the rights of religious organizations. In 2002, the department established within its civil rights division a separate "religious rights" unit that added a significant new constituency to a division that had long focused on racial injustice. When the Salvation Army—which had been receiving millions of dollars in federal funds—was accused in a private lawsuit of violating federal antidiscrimination laws by requiring employees to embrace Jesus Christ to keep their jobs, the civil rights division for the first time took the side of the alleged discriminator. In siding with the Salvation Army, the department launched a legal revolution to protect religious organizations that the president believed had been targets of past discrimination. That change occurred as the White House was pressing—unsuccessfully—for a new law permitting faith-based groups to discriminate in hiring by choosing employees based on whether their faith matched that of the organization.[29]

No story better illustrates the political power of the faith-based initiative than that of Bishop Sedgwick Daniels, the venerable leader of Milwaukee's Holy Redeemer Institutional Church of God in Christ and a longtime Democrat.

Gospel hymns echoed through Holy Redeemer's modern sanctuary on a cool Sunday in October 2004. Hundreds of black parishioners stood clapping their hands and singing "A Closer Walk with Thee." A visiting preacher, Rita Twiggs, an understudy of the Dallas preacher T. D. Jakes, warned of the danger of gay marriage, or as she put it, the "devil comin' in from San Francisco." Twiggs pointed to moves by San Francisco's mayor and judges in Massachusetts to allow gay marriage as a prime example of the decline of the family and of moral values.

When the singing subsided, parishioners leaned back into their cushioned pews. Holy Redeemer's charismatic preacher stepped to the pulpit. Bishop Daniels, a stocky, round-faced man, wore a black ministerial robe decorated with a brilliant purple sash. He reminded his followers that an important judgment day was close at hand. It was late October. Wisconsin was getting regular visits from President

Bush and John Kerry, both of whom viewed the state's electoral votes as crucial to their carefully mapped strategies for cobbling together an Electoral College victory. Daniels exhorted the worshippers to vote. He said he would not tell them who to vote for. "That's not my place," he bellowed. But everyone in the sanctuary that day knew exactly where this lifelong Democrat stood when it came to George W. Bush. One of Milwaukee's most beloved black pastors, the scion of a locally famous family and patriarch of a growing church empire, Daniels had supported Democrats in past presidential elections. He backed Bill Clinton and Al Gore. But in the week before Daniels took the pulpit that October day, black voters across the city had received glossy Republican Party fliers dominated by the preacher's photograph and his endorsement of the Republican president. The flier quoted Daniels saying that Bush "shares our values."[30]

What changed in 2004 for Bishop Daniels? After Bush's contested victory four years earlier, Daniels felt the pull of the most powerful of earthly forces: a call from the White House. In the months after that 2001 call, Daniels conferred with Rove and other top administration officials and, the following year, hosted the president himself in Holy Redeemer's sanctuary. The bishop gave Bush a CD featuring his sermons and showed the president plans for a new complex being constructed on the church property that would house a combination parochial and public school. Bush showered Daniels with praise, declaring the bishop a "social entrepreneur."

"It's a word that's applicable to the bishop and the congregation and the church; the willingness of people to use the great power of faith to revitalize neighborhoods is inspiring," Bush said that day in the sanctuary. A few months later, Daniels's church received $1.5 million from the government through Bush's faith-based initiative to support church-affiliated social service organizations.

Daniels said it was not the federal money that led him to endorse a Republican after so many years of backing Democrats for president, but rather the values of Bush and other GOP party leaders. "This is not some new conversion. To say that is not accurate," Daniels said. The bishop said he made his decision to back Bush based purely on issues, including the faith-based initiative, same-sex marriage, and school choice—the same issues highlighted in the GOP flier bearing his picture that was sent to tens of thousands of Milwaukee-area voters. Despite his endorsement, Daniels said, Democrats such as John Edwards and Howard Dean campaigned during the 2004 presidential primary at his church. And the Reverend Jesse Jackson appeared there on a Sunday before the general election on Kerry's behalf. "I cannot say to you that I would not support anything Democratic in the future," he said. Then, holding a Bible in his left hand and tapping it with his right, he added: "Where I am, the number one thing is this. This is what I believe. This is what I embrace."

The White House built ties to such ministers in nearly every major city, from Boston to Los Angeles, from Detroit to Dallas. These next-generation black leaders enjoyed regular White House meetings with Bush and other top officials. And in return, like Daniels, their churches gave Republicans unprecedented entrée into a world long dominated by the opposition.

For White House political strategists, Daniels's migration to the GOP marked a stellar chapter in their ambitious effort to transform the government and realign the country politically. Daniels's conversion was not a lightning bolt on the road to Damascus. Rather, it was the result of a painstaking, costly effort to move minorities and other traditional Democrats away from their post–New Deal home. In Daniels's case, the White House won a particularly influential friend, a charismatic preacher and a powerful community leader who presided over a fast-growing church with a flock of thousands. The vast majority of Daniels's followers remained Democrats in the 2004 election, but with Daniels on board, GOP strategists reasoned that a portion of his parishioners could later form at least part of a long-lasting Republican majority.

Daniels's church, located amid abandoned warehouses and modest homes, symbolized the kind of potentially GOP-friendly turf sought out by Bush's campaign strategists. The $25-million complex, including a school, a health clinic, a credit union, and senior housing units with plans for a retail center and a water park, represented the kind of entrepreneurial mega-churches (black, white, and Latino) that Republicans targeted across the nation. Holy Redeemer's membership in 2004 was eight thousand and growing.

On that Sunday in late October 2004, Daniels remained playfully neutral in his remarks from the pulpit. But he quickly turned the microphone over to one of President Bush's most prominent African American advocates, Maryland lieutenant governor Michael S. Steele. "We know what faith-based can do every single day," said the guest, drawing head nodding and shouts of "yes" and "Amen" as he referred to the president's initiative.

The enthusiasm that greeted Steele that day at Holy Redeemer was echoed in battleground states across the country, particularly in Pentecostal congregations that drew the most conservative black Americans. On-the-ground activists later said the faith initiative was a driving force behind Bush's ability to increase his share of the black vote, along with the White House position on school vouchers and gay marriage. Those issues gave many longtime black Democrats a reason to consider voting for Bush.

"For the first time," recalled Deborah Burstion-Donbraye, a one-time Bush staffer who in 2004 headed black outreach efforts for Ohio Republicans, "even those who may have been most against what the administration stood for realized they had a friend in the White House."

The faith-based initiative provided an especially appealing and long-lasting draw to black voters, Steele said. When the president cited the initiative's emphasis on funding small and independent church organizations that had never received government funds before, the message had special resonance with congregations like Holy Redeemer. "That's part of the strategy to create some realignment, to demonstrate to the African American community that your issues are the same as our issues," Steele said in an interview.[31] The White House courtship of black evangelical ministers would continue long after the 2004 elections. Daniels joined other GOP-friendly pastors and community leaders for White House meetings to discuss the faith-based initiative and other ideas. The bishop and about two dozen other pastors, such as the Reverend Eugene Rivers of Boston's

Azusa Christian Community Church and Bishop Charles Blake of the twenty-four-thousand-member West Angeles Church of God in Los Angeles, would huddle six months after the election with Bush's new secretary of state, Condoleezza Rice, to mull over giving black churches faith-based grants to operate in Africa. T. D. Jakes, the Dallas-based televangelist who leads the massive and influential Potter's House ministry, took an even bigger step in Bush's second term. He stood by the president in the wake of Hurricane Katrina, the devastating storm that exposed to the world the black poverty of the South, even when a disastrously slow federal response left thousands of poor African Americans suffering in squalid conditions.

Some Democrats seemed to understand that the faith-based initiative and the White House's careful courtship of black ministers were scoring points. One participant in the Rice meeting was former Atlanta mayor Andrew Young, a former aide to Martin Luther King Jr., and a longtime liberal activist, who actually stood and offered an emotional tribute to the first black woman to hold the country's top diplomatic job. Even Senator Hillary Rodham Clinton gave a nod to the faith-based idea. In a postelection appearance at Rivers's Boston church, the potential future presidential candidate offered an endorsement of the initiative that sounded as though she were reading from a Bush White House script. "We cannot come in, through the government, and dictate to faith-based organizations how they should best minister in their streets, and in their churches, and in their synagogues and mosques," she said. "We need to not have a false division or debate about the role of faith-based institutions; we need to just do it and provide the support that is needed on an ongoing basis."

While the support from Bishop Daniels and some others came after years of cultivation on myriad issues, other black ministers fell quickly into the Republican camp over the singular issue of same-sex marriage. The issue erupted as a motivator for Christian conservatives and some black voters during the 2004 election after the decisions in Massachusetts and San Francisco to permit gay marriages. Evangelical leaders, with the backing of the White House, fought to place antigay marriage initiatives on ballots in battleground states.

"African Americans are more opposed to gay marriage than whites are," said David Bositis, senior political analyst for the Joint Center for Political and Economic Studies, a Washington, D.C., think tank. Forty-six percent of African Americans surveyed in 2004 opposed any legal recognition of homosexual relationships, compared with 37 percent of whites who opposed it, he said. These strong views provided a powerful point of entry for conservative evangelicals who wanted to encourage African American congregations to join their cause—and they won support from some of the country's most high-profile black evangelists. In Atlanta, the daughter of the late Martin Luther King Jr. marched with one of that city's mega-church pastors, Bishop Eddie Long, to protest gay marriage. The march drew fifteen thousand people.

The Reverend Louis P. Sheldon, the Traditional Values Coalition chairman, wooed black pastors in 2004 and later by showing a video, *Gay Rights, Special Rights*, that emphasized tensions between blacks and gays and assailed Democrats such as President Clinton for supporting the "homosexual agenda." Also featured were scantily clad gay and lesbian activists dancing at rallies and invoking Martin Luther King Jr. during their protests. A narrator accused gays and lesbians of hijacking the traditional civil rights movement to pursue special protections for a group that chose to be different as opposed to one that was brought to the United States in slavery. Graphics illustrated the economic disparities between gays and blacks, noting that gays enjoyed higher incomes, often held management positions, and frequently traveled overseas.

Other conservative groups such as the Heritage Foundation sponsored events in this period for black pastors promoting the "family values" agenda. As Election Day 2004 loomed, both Democrats and Republicans realized that a handful of swing states would determine the outcome. None was more important than Ohio. Kerry supporters, bolstered by massive voter registration drives and other ground-level organizing by independent groups such as America Coming Together, were confident they could turn out the votes to win. What they didn't realize was that the Republicans—organizing quietly through black and Hispanic Pentecostal churches—had made enormous inroads into those traditionally Democratic constituencies. In the final weeks before the election, the GOP and its allies among conservative church leaders concentrated on perfecting get-out-the-vote campaigns. In essence, they were hoping to beat the Democrats at their own game.

CHAPTER 6

Death by a Thousand Cuts

Building the network from the ground up was what we did.

—KEN MEHLMAN, PORTLAND, OREGON, SEPTEMBER 14, 2005

A
s the 2004 presidential campaign entered its final weeks, strategists for Bush and Democratic nominee John Kerry narrowed the list of competitive states—those that might go either way—from the original eighteen to only a handful. The election would come down to New Mexico, Nevada, Florida, New Hampshire, Wisconsin, Pennsylvania, Michigan, and, most important of all, Ohio. With the race so tight and the nation so polarized, conventional wisdom held that the next president would be chosen by a small number of undecided voters in those states. Rove, Mehlman, and the rest of the Bush team had a different view. As they saw it, the race would be won by the campaign that was most successful in getting its core supporters to the polls.

That might seem like a truism, but campaign managers who truly believe it are relatively rare, because it dictates very different tactics than those usually employed in American presidential elections. Instead of wooing the wavering middle, such a campaign will preach to the choir—and, more important, it will work hard to arrange car pools and whatever else it takes to make sure everyone in the choir gets to the church. And, to the puzzlement of many political pundits, that is exactly what the Bush campaign did in the battleground states of 2004. Instead of edging toward the middle, Bush ran hard to the right. Instead of trying to reassure uncertain moderates, he worked hard to stoke the passions of those who needed no convincing. Meantime, his field commanders worked tirelessly to strengthen the mechanisms responsible for getting every last Bush voter to the polls, mechanisms they had spent more than four years putting together. As Election Day drew near, they redoubled those efforts.

That is why presidential speechwriter Noam Neusner got a strange, eleventh-hour assignment. On the Sunday before the election on Tuesday, November 2, Neusner was asked to visit a nightclub in the Cleveland suburb of Mayfield Heights. A Russian Jewish immigrant owned the Sherwin-Gilmour Party Center, and while it was a popular venue for weddings, anniversaries, and other celebrations, the area's Russian population also used the club as a kind of cultural gathering spot. Republican organizers had long before identified Russian immigrants as potential GOP voters. They hated Communism; many had settled in the United States after fleeing the Soviet Union. They had warm memories of Ronald Reagan. They were open-minded about party affiliation, and—except for a large group living in the New York City borough of Brooklyn—Russian immigrants had seldom been courted aggressively by Democrats or Republicans. If anything, when it came to Russian Jewish voters like those in Mayfield Heights, it was widely assumed that the prosperity of the 1990s had turned them into supporters of Bill Clinton and Al Gore. And, in a tight race with limited time and resources, Republicans would have ignored the Democratic stronghold of Cleveland and concentrated on the Republican suburbs and regions beyond.

In 2004, both sides scoured the landscape of the battleground states for every possible vote. But Rove's team had a critical advantage: a substantially better computerized system for pinpointing small but significant pockets of potential supporters and even individual voters. The GOP also developed a more nuanced understanding of ethnic voting blocs, as well as more disciplined tactics for going after them. That meant they could find and reach out to the Russian immigrants who frequented the Sherwin-Gilmour Party Center even though it lay in the middle of one of America's most staunchly Democratic urban centers. And not just in Ohio. The capability of finding conservative voters in unlikely places had been developed on a broad scale as part of the overarching quest for a one-party country. Like the other pieces of the strategy, it did not seek to gain long-term dominance by bringing about a sea change in public attitudes or values. Rather it approached the task as a matter of maximizing the size and impact of the GOP's natural base, nibbling away at the edges of the Democratic base and, wherever possible, putting obstacles in the path of the opposition. It was a strategy that required immense amounts of time, energy, stamina, and money. It also required an obsessive-compulsive's capacity to focus on the details. But as it happened, Karl Rove and his Republican cohorts had all those things in abundance.

For example, the Bush campaign had built up a massive and growing database called Voter Vault. Its operation was the key to surgically precise microtargeting of voters. Voter Vault was what led the campaign to send emissaries to the Russian Jews in Cleveland, to thirty-something whites in Midwestern exurbs, to Puerto Rican barrios in Orlando, to new immigrants in New Mexico, and to middle-class, churchgoing black suburbanites in Pennsylvania. There were similar outreach programs for business-oriented Asians in the Pacific Northwest, for second-generation Indian Americans in the South, and for hopeful young entrepreneurs everywhere. The tactic succeeded because the GOP matched voter files with marketing data obtained from magazine sales, grocery stores, and other retailers. Then the campaign devised narrowly focused materials—mailers, phone calls, even door-to-door canvassing by neighbors—to touch millions of potential voters in a personal way, voters who would have been overlooked by traditional campaigns. Previous Republican candidates had ignored many of these targeted constituencies. Some of the groups had voted heavily Democratic in the past—blacks, for instance, 90 percent Democratic, and Jews, 75 percent Democratic. Latinos had historically leaned Democratic as well, but at a lower rate—in the 60 percent range in 2000.

The more scientific strategy has transformed the way political campaigns are fought, and it has put the Republicans in the lead. While the old-model campaign sought to educate voters about a candidate and his or her views, the new strategy almost completely reversed that approach. Instead of trying to educate voters about Bush, Rove worked at educating himself and his staff about voters— and about how to target them with narrowly cast appeals. One could ask why it mattered if a handful of Jews in Cleveland or Latinos in Orlando or labor union members in West Virginia voted for Bush. The answer was that the Republicans' ability to send custom-tailored messages to relatively small numbers of voters inside Democratic precincts in swing states enabled them to slice away pieces of the enemy's base. Each slice might seem inconsequential standing alone, but taken together the slices might add up to something very consequential. Moreover, because these once-Democratic swingers were trimmed away in so many carefully selected but disparate places— creating Bush blocs only where they were needed—the shift did not always register in national opinion polls, or on the radar of Democratic strategists. It was the political equivalent of stealth technology in air power: Democrats would feel the bombs explode, but they could not see the bombers.

Bush campaign officials were so committed to this new playbook, they spent $120 million on grassroots politicking in 2004, six times the budget for such tactics in 2000.[1] Party officials on both sides later said it was this sophistication that helped the Republicans outmaneuver the Democrats at the grassroots level. And the rising sophistication of the GOP operation was reinforced by the declining effectiveness of organized labor, which had been the heart of the Democrats' grassroots success for decades. As the unions withered and the GOP system became ever more powerful and sophisticated, the Republicans gained an institutional advantage that could be maintained and enlarged in future election cycles.

That advantage was clear among Orthodox Jewish communities in the Cleveland area, where as many as twelve thousand Russian Jews had settled and become citizens. The latter lived in a handful of neighborhoods with extended families crowded into multistory apartment buildings. That created an easy-to-reach social network that had never been tapped politically, until the Bush reelection campaign.

On that Sunday before the election, elderly immigrants and their families gathered at the Sherwin-Gilmour Party Center for what is believed to have been the first Republican presidential campaign rally ever conducted entirely in Russian. The Ohio GOP provided free transportation from the apartments. At the party center ballroom, a vast windowless space with chandeliers and linen-draped tables, the Russians clustered around buffet spreads munching familiar appetizers—deviled eggs, dark breads, bagels, and lox.

Neusner, the guest speaker, was a conservative Jew who held two jobs at the White House: speechwriter and the head of Jewish outreach. He had driven to Ohio with three college-age volunteers, taking unpaid vacation time to help the campaign in its final days. With polls showing Ohio a dead heat, the Bush campaign threw the Russian rally together in less than forty-eight hours. At 2:15 P.M. on that Sunday, a broad-shouldered, graying Russian American GOP leader from the Sheepshead Bay neighborhood of Brooklyn, New York, made his way to the center's white-painted podium and quieted the noisy audience. Oleg Gutnik, a gynecologist who had emigrated from the former Soviet Union in 1980, spoke rapidly in Russian. The crowd grew rapt as he gesticulated and sometimes banged the podium for emphasis. His remarks were for the most part unintelligible to Neusner and other non-Russian speakers except for certain English words that kept recurring: *Bush. Israel. Reagan. Republicans.*[2]

The crowd applauded Gutnik as he introduced the next speaker, Lawrence Valery Weinberg, the editor of a New York–based Russian newspaper called *Novoye Russkoye Slovo*, America's only Russian-language daily. Weinberg's Russian speech was punctuated with the same words and was interrupted several times by applause. He distributed reprints of his newspaper's endorsement of Bush—perhaps the first Russian-language campaign literature ever distributed for a

Republican presidential candidate. To Neusner, the speeches seemed to drag on and on, making him nervous that the event was turning into a bust. But he was reassured when a fellow Republican told him that Russians like long speeches. Neusner then heard his own name spoken as Weinberg motioned him to the podium. He was unsure what to make of this crowd, which included one elderly man who wore Russian military medals from his service in Afghanistan. Another elderly man waved his cane menacingly at the presenters when asking questions. Neusner had been told that these new citizens were friendly, but would they commit to Bush?

They had concerns about Medicare and Social Security. But Neusner also knew that the Russians had a healthy skepticism of appeasement—and a long memory of Reagan. So he began his speech, halting at first, by recalling Bush's record of fighting terrorism since September 11 and the president's heartfelt solidarity with Israel. Soon, the thirty-three-year-old Neusner was delivering an impromptu stem-winder, pausing after every phrase for his translator to catch up.

"Who said no to Arafat?" he boomed.

"Boosh!" the crowd replied in a thick accent.

"Who said no to Saddam?"

"Boosh!"

"Who said no to the Taliban?"

"Boosh!"

As he got to the end, Neusner's audience was on its feet, napkins and glasses in hand. He had one final question: "Who are you going to vote for on Tuesday?"

"Boosh! Boosh! Boosh!" the audience shouted in response.[3]

A former journalist, Neusner had seen plenty of political speeches and rallies. Even so, this scene near Cleveland of Russian Jews chanting the name of the incumbent Republican president stunned him. Weinberg, too, was stunned. On the plane that morning, he had wondered what he would find. What they had found was one small part of the most sophisticated presidential campaign in the history of American democracy.

Jews, after all, were overwhelmingly loyal Democratic voters; their views on social issues and domestic policies were usually liberal.

But the White House had identified three core issues on which its strategists believed certain Jews could be swayed: Israel, terrorism, and anti-Semitism. On every topic, Bush boasted an appealing record. The war in Iraq was supported by Israel and considered vital to its security, while the post–September 11 war on terrorism struck a chord with Zionists who had long feared Islamic fundamentalism. Bush also had denounced anti-Semitism in Europe, visited Auschwitz, and, unlike his predecessors, barred Palestinian leader Yasser Arafat from the White House. The leaders of the nation's best-known Jewish organizations, all of them non-Orthodox, had long said they felt closer to the Clinton administration than to the White House of George W. Bush.[4] And many Jews had felt far closer to past Republican presidents Eisenhower, Nixon, and Reagan than to the first Bush, who was not considered a close ally of Israel and left many Jewish voters with chilly feelings toward the family.[5] But aides to the second President Bush believed their record could help the Republican incumbent chip into the religious Jewish communities in Cleveland, Detroit, and south Florida—the three biggest concentrations of Jewish voters in those battleground states. What the Bush strategists saw more clearly than their Democratic counterparts was that the Jewish vote was not monolithic. They viewed communities of Orthodox and other observant Jews as untapped Republican strongholds, filled with voters who appreciated not just the president's support for Israel but his personal faith, opposition to abortion and gay marriage, and other traditional values. The Orthodox were also considered easy to reach—frequent attendees of synagogues and kosher butcher shops—and respectful of authority. "They didn't vote, but if the rebbe told them to vote, they'd do it. And they were Bush supporters," said one strategist.

The goal was never to win a majority of Jewish voters. And the raw numbers of Jewish voters were just a tiny percentage of the overall population. But surveys showed that the GOP had an opening with observant and pro-Israel Jews, and strategists knew their numbers were large in three of the most important places in 2004: Ohio, Michigan, and Florida. Motivated by the vice presidential candidacy of Senator Joseph Lieberman, an Orthodox Jew, Jewish voters had been viewed as a crucial factor in Al Gore's ability to make Florida so competitive in 2000; eroding his support among these voters could make Florida safe for Bush in 2004. Moreover, increasing the GOP share of the Jewish vote in New York and New Jersey—while not likely to carry those Democratic bastions for Bush—would fatten his total in the popular vote, an important goal for a campaign eager to claim a mandate four years after a bitterly contested election. Bush aides hoped to add a few points to Bush's 19 percent share of Jewish votes in 2000 and create a buzz that would help build GOP-Jewish ties in future elections. Also, they hoped to force Democrats to spend money wooing a group that was long considered a given.

The party's aggressive courtship of Orthodox Jews received public attention from community leaders during the Republican National Convention in New York, when Bush campaign officials hosted a meeting at the Waldorf Astoria for three hundred Jewish leaders. In the meeting room, a glossy, twenty-three-page booklet called "President George W. Bush: A Friend of the American Jewish Community" was placed on each chair. Produced by the White House Office of Public Liaison, the division responsible for outreach to evangelicals, the booklet declared Bush a "steadfast" supporter of Israel and a defender of moral values. It laid out a time line of the president's attention to Jewish concerns, starting with a March 2001 meeting in the Roosevelt Room with Jewish leaders and an April visit by the First Couple to the Holocaust Memorial Museum in Washington. The president and Laura Bush were pictured holding hands as Laura laid a ceremonial stone on a memorial during their May 2003 visit to Auschwitz. The booklet highlighted Bush's decision in September 2001 to boycott a United Nations conference in Durban, South Africa, when some countries tried to equate Zionism with racism, and a 2003 kosher dinner at the White House hosted in honor of the Holocaust Memorial Museum's tenth anniversary. Other photos showed Bush at a menorah-lighting ceremony in the White House, addressing the American Jewish Committee, speaking with Israeli prime minister Ariel Sharon, and standing around his desk in the Oval Office with at least ten bearded Hasidic rabbis wearing black hats.

As the rabbis and spiritual leaders poured into the Waldorf-Astoria meeting room, they were greeted by Tevi Troy, an Orthodox Jew and White House aide who was helping to lead Jewish outreach efforts. Troy regaled the audience with stories of the president's closeness to religious Jews. He said Bush had met with a group of rabbis a year earlier in the period between the holiest Jewish holidays of Rosh Hashanah and Yom Kippur. Bush told the rabbis of al Qaeda threats against Jewish targets, and how the United States would protect them.

Troy called the meeting a "double hit," because the holidays marked the biggest synagogue attendance days of the year and the rabbis no doubt recounted all the details of the session with Bush for their packed sanctuaries.

Back on the ground in Cleveland and its heavily Jewish suburbs, Bush volunteers obtained the local Orthodox community's most important database: the "Mikva list." It contained the names of every Orthodox household in the area and typically was used to help families connect for babysitting, schooling, and other activities. Just as Republican officials in Ohio and elsewhere were tapping Christian church membership directories to reach evangelicals, the campaign had found a portal into the world of religious Judaism in an important urban hub. Volunteers called every home (about 10 percent of greater Cleveland's 81,500 Jews are Orthodox) to make sure they were registered to vote and that they would support Bush. Recipients overwhelmingly responded that they would back the Republican president. The response seemed to reflect an election-year survey of Jews nationwide by the American Jewish Committee, which showed that at least six in ten Orthodox intended to back Bush—compared with nearly eight in ten Reform Jews who intended to support Kerry.

The Republican campaign's greatest achievement came when Bush volunteers convinced the region's most prominent Orthodox leader, Rabbi Chaim Stein of Rosh Yeshivas Telshe, to sign a "Kol Koreh," a special religious instruction, calling on every Orthodox Jew to vote. Jewish GOP organizers said this had never happened before. But after Stein issued his order, several other rabbis signed the decree too, which was then posted on community bulletin boards and at kosher butcher shops, where Orthodox Jews flocked on the Thursday before the election just as they did every week to prepare for the Sabbath. On the Saturday morning before Election Day, Orthodox rabbis across Cleveland underscored the importance of voting, mirroring a message that would come the next morning from the Christian pulpits whose occupants also backed the president. The clergy did not necessarily tell their flocks to vote for the president—many of them understood that their federal tax exemptions required them to refrain from endorsements—but the congregations knew who their leaders backed. Bush campaign workers asked the rabbis to make one point clear to their congregants, who adhered to strictly traditional gender roles: men and women alike were expected to vote.

In the final days of the campaign, the White House also dispatched one of its highest-ranking Jews, budget director Joshua Bolten, to boost the president's bona fides in Cleveland. Appearing in the city in late October, Bolten addressed local Jewish financial leaders and granted a rare newspaper interview. He spoke not to the New York Times or the Los Angeles Times, or even the Plain Dealer, but to the Cleveland Jewish News, which referred to him as Bush's "only Jewish Cabinet member" and quoted the presidential aide describing Bush's stances against terrorism, anti-Semitism, and some anti-Israel United Nations initiatives as evidence that Bush was a friend to the Jews. Former New York mayor Ed Koch appeared in Cleveland, Detroit, and southern Florida, emphasizing his intention to vote for Bush solely because of his support for Israel in the war on terrorism. Highly targeted mailers distributed by the Republican Party and independent groups such as the Republican Jewish Coalition featured an attractive, young Jewish couple backing Bush's views on Social Security and tied Kerry to Arafat.

On Election Day in Cleveland, yeshivas gave their students the day off so teenagers could babysit while mothers went to the polls. Local Jewish leaders said this was a first. "Even if that meant getting just a few thousand votes, at that point after the Florida election of 2000, every vote counted," said David Heller, a Jewish real estate developer in Cleveland who coordinated Orthodox outreach events with the Bush campaign.[6]

Though the raw numbers of Orthodox Jews were small in the battleground states, Republicans concluded that the heavy courtship proved important to Bush's victory. The analysis showed that in the heavily Orthodox Cleveland suburb of Beechwood, Bush improved from finishing fifty-five hundred votes behind Al Gore in 2000 to winning twenty-two hundred votes more than Kerry four years later. Similarly, the president improved his showing by more than 30 percent in several targeted Jewish precincts in Florida's Broward, Palm Beach, and Miami-Dade counties.[7] Even in the densely Jewish precincts of Brooklyn, New York, and New Jersey—hardly swing districts—the Orthodox turned out in big numbers for the president. His vote total increased by at least thirty thousand in Brooklyn's Flatbush and Boro Park neighborhoods, and in one precinct his performance more than doubled. Support for the president among the Orthodox totaled more than 80 percent in some places.[8] Bush also performed well among young Jewish men, a point Republicans believe bodes well for the one-party vision. "That is certainly a good sign for Republicans going forward—perhaps as good a sign as the fact that quite a few Jews gave generously to the president's campaign," wrote Jay Lefkowitz, a Washington lawyer and former White House staffer who offered advice on Jewish outreach and later described the success of that effort in a 2005 article in the magazine *Commentary*. "A number of 'Rangers' and 'Pioneers'—those raising more than $200,000 and $100,000, respectively—were Jews, and several of these had been large Gore-Lieberman givers in the previous election."[9]

The GOP in 2004 did not succeed in converting masses of Jews from the Democratic to the Republican column. But it did shift the allegiance of a small percentage of formerly reliable Democratic voters, and it discovered new voters as well. The Republicans repeated this microtargeting model with every other part of the Democratic base.

The emergence of this precision targeting was a natural consequence of the twenty-first-century political reality of the United States, in which the electorate was polarized in a sort of freeze-frame capturing the moment in November 2000 when George W. Bush and Al Gore finished in a virtual tie. That freeze-frame, which is illustrated in the now ubiquitous Electoral College maps shaded red in the heartland for GOP country and blue along the coastlines for Democratic strongholds, marked a milestone in GOP strategy: old-style national campaigns did not suffice. No longer could strategists rely on a unified message aimed at masses of voters from coast to coast, transmitted through national media. While pundits became obsessed with two Americas, one blue and one red, the GOP became obsessed with many Americas, of all colors. While the Republicans exploited data and targeted voters with masterful efficiency in 2004, they cannot take credit for inventing this approach. Strategists for organized labor, which pioneered modern get-out-the-vote techniques, concluded in the mid-1990s that campaigns needed to change. "We realized that we were spending millions on television advertising and losing our real strength, which was using personal contact to get our members to the polls," said Steve Rosenthal, the former political director of the AFL-CIO and an architect of labor's get-out-the-vote strategies. Labor first stressed personal voter contacts to boost President Clinton's reelection in 1996, dramatically increasing turnout among union voters. The strategy was executed with greater precision in 2000, particularly in Florida, nearly putting Al Gore in the White House. Many believed the strategy did, in fact, win the election for Gore, who fell 537 votes short of taking Florida and the White House. Bush's political team knew better than anyone that the Democrats had outperformed them in getting supporters to the polls and that the GOP victory was the result of ballot confusion, aggressive legal maneuvering, and luck. In 2001, the Republicans vowed to learn from the Democrats, whom they had just barely defeated.

In their systematic review of the 2000 debacle, GOP strategists, led by Mehlman, determined that they had lost an average of five percentage points in several key states between publication of the final public opinion polls and Election Day. That meant Republicans needed to improve their get-out-the-vote efforts or they would lose. "We were even or slightly ahead in just about every one of those states, and of course we know what happened," Christian Coalition founder and Bush campaign operative Ralph Reed told PBS's Charlie

Rose. "We ended up winning by 537 votes in a single state. Because in the last roughly three to five days, they did a better job of getting their vote to the polls than we did."[10] Mehlman and Rove designed a series of military-like operations to change that, the most important of which was the seventy-two-hour plan to reach likely supporters and get them to the polls.

In the twenty-first century, both parties are relying increasingly on their ability to tailor messages to relatively narrow slices of potential supporters and get them to the voting booth. So long as voters remain polarized and no great issue arises to transcend the current divisions, campaigns organized in this more targeted way are likely to succeed. Such campaigns put a premium on the kinds of below-the-radar tactics and strategies that outside analysts, including the news media, often miss entirely. It also means that traditional methods of predicting outcomes—namely public opinion polling—may become less reliable. With half of the electorate not voting, pollsters have long faced a challenge in accurately estimating preelection support for candidates. Their solution has been to use statistical weights to estimate the likelihood that a respondent will actually cast a ballot. But microtargeting is designed in part to mobilize voters who do not usually turn out. Lawrence Jacobs, a polling expert at the University of Minnesota's Hubert H. Humphrey Institute of Public Affairs, called it a "subterranean strategy that offsets general turnout patterns and can be very surprising for pollsters, particularly in close elections."

The result is that George W. Bush, or any Republican after him, can win a general election even if his approval ratings fall below 50 percent—so long as the GOP maintains its database supremacy and continues to find messages that motivate selected groups of voters to turn out for their candidate. "In this era it is not about anticipating the general electorate, it's about activating your voters," Jacobs said.[11]

All such calculations may go out the window if voters become concerned about topics that transcend the GOP's narrow appeals—issues such as war or peace, government corruption, or economic calamity. But dominating themes like that don't come along very often in American campaigns. The Civil War and slavery spurred political transformations that lingered for more than 150 years. The

Great Depression and World War II, likewise, changed the way millions of people looked at government and politics. Those were historic moments, however, precisely because they were exceptions to the general rule. The Vietnam War churned the nation and split the Democratic Party, but it did not produce a major political realignment. Even after the riotous divisions of the 1968 Democratic National Convention, Vice President Hubert Humphrey almost turned back Richard M. Nixon. In the same way, Watergate elected a passel of Democratic congressmen, but Nixon's heir and pardoner, Gerald R. Ford, came within a whisker of beating Jimmy Carter in 1976.

So it was not far-fetched for Rove, Mehlman, and their team to suppose that getting the small details right—righter than their opponents—offered them their best shot at continuing to win elections for a very long time.

Following through on their vow to never be outdone in the final days of an election, Rove and Mehlman studied what went wrong in battleground states down to the level of individual precincts. They decided to adopt nineteenth-century-style precinct communications but to do so with a twenty-first-century twist, relying increasingly on database technologies to identify potential voters.

Both parties engaged in this microtargeting, amassing data files on registered voters and segmenting the data by using sophisticated computer programs. But strategists on both sides agreed that the depth of the Republican files grew far greater, included more information, and were put to smarter use in the field, thus increasing the data's predictive power. The Republicans also raised more money to buy top-of-the-line consumer data from retailers. They knew, for instance, that bourbon drinkers were more likely to be Republicans, while gin was a Democrat's drink. Military history buffs were likely to be social conservatives. Democrats preferred Volvos; Ford and Chevy owners were most likely Republicans. People with call-waiting service on their telephones were predominantly Republican. Cross-referencing such seemingly disparate data produced powerful correlations and drew a road map for targeting messages to specific voters. Where voters lived, what cars they drove and what magazines they read were all used to predict their positions on specific issues—and to determine what the odds were that they could be persuaded to support GOP candidates if the appeals were made in particular ways.

From his 2004 campaign headquarters in a nondescript Arlington, Virginia, office building, Mehlman went about his job as though he were the sales director of a shoe company rather than the manager of a presidential campaign. "If you live in a world of niche marketing, what's the most powerful form of niche marketing?" he asked. "It's word of mouth. Why does Hush Puppy hire models to sell their shoes as opposed to ad people? Well, it's in part because they understand that word of mouth is an important campaign."[12]

Voter Vault, the master list, helped Republicans execute Mehlman's seventy-two-hour word-of-mouth plan to near perfection. Every county chairman in Ohio had been given lists of names to contact and was responsible for putting together teams, team captains, and legions of callers who would contact each voter. The party purchased cell phones so that impromptu GOP calling centers could open and close rapidly around the state. Volunteers were assigned wireless PDAs so they could update the master list on the spot after a voter had been contacted or driven to the polls. If someone said they needed a ride or a babysitter on Election Day, the information was added immediately to the file and noted by the appropriate department.

The fact that the plan worked on Election Day was not happenstance. Mehlman had insisted that his organization in each battleground state test its seventy-two-hour plan before the election. "It drove us crazy to have to do these test runs of our get-out-the-vote strategy," recalled the Ohio state Republican Party executive director, Chris McNulty. "We were busy. But each time we would catch some glitches and when Election Day finally rolled around we were confident and ready."

In all of these efforts, the Republican machine enjoyed a major logistical advantage: its highly centralized control over data, targeting, and strategy. In contrast to this concentrated management, the Democrats permitted state parties to establish their own systems while relying on labor unions and other independent activist groups to get out the vote. Those groups had struggled to establish voter data files in the wake of newly passed bans on corporate and union contributions to federal campaigns that had made it harder for the Democratic National Committee to raise the cash it needed to keep a top-of-the-line database. Because the Democrats had relied far more on "soft money," the new law hurt the Democratic National Committee more than it did the Republican National Committee. Worse from the Democrats' point of view, the new laws prohibited the independent groups from sharing such data with political parties. "These groups did a lot, but much of it was redundant and unconnected," said Michael Erlandson, the former Democratic Party chairman in Minnesota. "The day after the election, many of these groups leave the state, and their voter files and experience leave with them."[13]

In Missouri, which Democratic strategists initially believed would be closely contested but Kerry ultimately abandoned, this decentralized approach was evident to Steve Rosenthal, who in 2004 led the largest of the pro-Democratic groups, America Coming Together. He sought a voter list that had been developed by a vendor with close ties to that state's venerable Democratic power player, former House minority leader Richard Gephardt. The list was considered the most complete directory of active Democratic voters in the state. But when Rosenthal approached the vendor who maintained the list, she agreed to turn it over—for a fee of $1.3 million. Rosenthal said he could not afford it, leaving the pro-Kerry forces further depleted in Missouri.

With the Republican National Committee maintaining and updating Voter Vault, GOP volunteers faced no such barriers. They easily accessed names, addresses, and phone numbers of potential Republican voters through a Web-based program that allowed ground-level operatives to segment targets by street, demographic, or political leanings. At the national level, Democratic officials took heart in battleground states because they saw Bush's declining approval ratings, an unpopular Iraq war, and a sagging economy. But Democrats on the ground acknowledged that a serious lag in the mechanics of twenty-first-century party building was preventing them from making gains even when public opinion and other factors seemed to swing in their favor. "The Republicans have been working on this for a decade, and that's why they kick our asses," said Dennis L. White, who was the Democrats' chairman in Ohio during the election, referring to the GOP's technological advantage. "We are still three years behind."[14]

While the Democrats struggled to keep a database of their own core backers, Republicans in 2004 began using Voter Vault to nibble away at the Democratic base and find new supporters, both of which would advance the longer-term goal of a one-party country. The database led Republican strategists to voters like Felicia Hill, a suburban Ohio mother of two who, at first glance, seemed to fit the profile of a loyal Democratic voter. An African American married to a General Motors union worker, Hill had voted for Democratic presidential candidates Michael Dukakis, Bill Clinton, and Al Gore. Nonetheless, in the weeks before Election Day 2004, the thirty-nine-year-old was deluged with telephone calls, invitations, and specially targeted mailings urging her to support President Bush. The intense courtship of this longtime Democrat was no coincidence. A deeper look at Hill's lifestyle and politics revealed a voter who could be persuaded to switch sides. Among the clues: she was a church member uneasy about abortion and she lived in a golfing community in a growing suburb and sent her children to a private school. Hill had once worked for a black Republican mayoral candidate, as well. But Republicans had not courted her in a national election before, and she had rarely considered voting against the Democrats.[15]

This time, she wasn't sure what to do. The outreach had such an effect on her that she was unable to decide who to vote for until she was in the booth. She ultimately chose Kerry over Bush, with great reservations. Still, Hill could be counted as a success in the one-party plan. She said she was open to Republican arguments in a way she never had been before, reflecting what GOP strategists viewed as a broader foothold among socially conservative minorities who were growing increasingly comfortable with the idea of voting Republican. And when Ohioans choose a new governor and decide whether to reelect Republican Mike DeWine in 2006—and then when the state plays a central role in the 2008 presidential election—Hill will be considered a potential GOP pickup. And the GOP knows where she lives. "I saw people I could relate to," she said, describing conversations she had with Republican professional women during telephone outreach calls and at party events. During one campaign function in Dayton, the president was introduced by Hill's friend Donald K. McLaurin, the black mayor of suburban Trotwood. "I saw families there who seemed like our family, and I found that their ideology lined up with mine," she said.

The GOP's targeting of previously overlooked voters extended beyond the Jewish precincts of Cleveland and Felicia Hill's subdivision. As Rove and Mehlman strived to ensure that 2004 would not be a repeat of 2000, they sought new ways to build the GOP voter file, sending remarkably specific orders to precinct captains and county GOP chairmen across battleground states.

One recipient of the instructions from Washington was Tom Grossman, chairman of the Republican Party in Warren County, about thirty-five miles outside of Cincinnati. The registration goals Rove and Mehlman set for him were so ambitious that they weighed heavily on Grossman's mind in the summer of 2004, so much so that he personally devoted night after night to registering new voters, sometimes in the oddest places. One evening in June, Grossman parked his blue convertible at a temporary home expo center set up under white tents at a newly constructed subdivision. He walked through the maze of booths that were hawking the necessities of upscale living—home security systems, Jacuzzi tubs, fancy kitchen fixtures, and wooden blinds—before settling into a booth of his own.

Grossman, of course, had not come to Chestnut Hill, one of southwestern Ohio's newest McNeighborhoods, to peddle home furnishings. He was there to hunt new Republican voters. "Hey there, have you registered to vote?" he asked passersby. "I can do it for you. Won't take but a minute." Grossman sat behind a table stacked with bumper stickers promoting Bush's reelection, an incongruous sight in a sparkling new neighborhood with cul-de-sacs and curvy streets dotted with mansion-style homes, replete with built-in movie theaters, fancy kitchens, and spacious patios. He was there because, back in Washington, Karl Rove and Ken Mehlman had concluded that success in November's election depended on searching for a new and perhaps more valuable prize: the "exurbanite." Just as the party was finding new voters among blacks and Jews, the hunt had extended to the new ring of towns and developments that were rising up around most American cities.

Fleeing older areas for the newest ring of developments beyond the suburbs, exurbanites in 2004 became a sensation among national political consultants. Pockets of these voters were sprouting up in nearly every state: a fast-growing population searching for commutable neighborhoods with more house for the money, better schools, less traffic, and an all-around easier, less-expensive opportunity to enjoy the good life. Exurban areas are booming and, according to demographers and GOP strategists, rapidly drawing a concentration of potentially conservative but unregistered, unaffiliated voters. Rove saw exurbanites as critical new additions to the voter registration rolls and to the GOP's massive database. He liked to point out that 88 percent of eligible adults who lived in the country's old-growth suburbs were registered to vote before the 2004 campaign, whereas in the predominantly conservative exurbs, that number was just 83 percent. Closing that small gap, Rove predicted, would make the difference for his party in tight races in 2004 and beyond. As Matthew Dowd, Bush's 2004 campaign pollster, said, "The growth potential is much bigger on the Republican side in exurban counties than it is on the Democratic side in urban counties."[16]

Rove was so taken with the potential in the exurbs that, during one interview, he rattled off the names of obscure counties in swing states across the nation, along with the percentages of people who had not registered to vote in each one. "It takes them awhile to get established, to find the best grocery store, the best dry cleaner, to pick out a church, to sort of fit into the community," Rove said of the residents of these new settlements. "And then it takes them awhile to figure out the local politics, and then presidential politics."[17]

The Ownership Society first outlined in George W. Bush's 2004 reelection campaign, with its emphasis on home ownership, low taxes, private Social Security retirement accounts, and health savings accounts, was in many ways designed with the thirty- and forty-something exurbanites in mind. Exurbanites, after all, owned homes, raised children, tended to be religious, and worked hard. They were sensitive to tax increases in part because—Rove did not emphasize this—their incomes had been largely stagnant and their household economies were often stretched.

Bush visited many of these new boomtowns on bus tours in his reelection campaign with events designed to spur more for the campaign than a one-day burst of publicity. Playing off the excitement of presidential appearances, strategists used the Bush visits to recruit volunteers for phone banks, canvassing, and voter registration efforts—building an enduring GOP machine in the hearts of present and future battleground states. Bush visited Warren County in May 2004, speaking to thousands in downtown Lebanon during a brief stop along a bus tour of southern Ohio. Voter registration instantly spiked, along with the list of party volunteers. Excitement over Bush's visit lingered for months, with locals buzzing about the day the president rolled into town in a red, white, and blue tour bus and spoke right in front of the town's historic inn, the Golden Lamb. On that day, more than twenty-five hundred people, many waiting at least three hours, welcomed the first sitting president to stop in Lebanon. The city's cable television station carried the event live—including the waiting—with color commentary from a local historian discussing the significance of Bush's presence. "We're talking about the leader of the free world here, the most powerful man on Earth right now, actually," gushed John Zimkus, a Lebanon history teacher, during the live broadcast. "It is an honor to have the president visit your town. How many communities can say that?"[18]

The presidential visit offered a critical boost to the campaign's on-the-ground efforts to find voters. "You have a bigger impact in a smaller area because it's more unique to them," said Dowd, Bush's pollster. "People in big urban areas are used to whoever it is, some rock star coming to town. The president has celebrity, but in these big urban areas they see a lot of celebrities."[19]

True to that theory, Bush's May trip to Lebanon helped turn Elizabeth Uptegrove onto politics. The twenty-eight-year-old mother of two moved from Charleston, South Carolina, to a subdivision north of Lebanon about five years earlier for her husband's job. She lived in the same neighborhood as the local Bush campaign volunteer coordinator, San Diego transplant Ricki Wilkins, who persuaded Uptegrove to help out with crowd control at the rally. She was one of about forty new volunteers Wilkins signed up for the event, and she remained on the volunteer list long after Bush left town. "It's amazing how much I've learned about grassroots politics," said Uptegrove, who later worked a phone bank for the Bush campaign. "I remember seeing all the television ads as a young kid, but now living where I do I can really feel the effect of the grassroots."[20]

Memories of the Bush visit drove conversations weeks later at Tom Grossman's voter registration booth at the home expo. Grossman estimated that he registered about ten GOP voters an hour. "You don't have to guess about it. They're clearly Republicans," he said, interrupted routinely with screams of "Go Bush!" and "All the way!" from passersby.[21]

In many ways, Warren County was a case study in Rove's exurban theory. Between 2000, when Bush narrowly won both Ohio and the White House, and 2004, the county grew more than 10 percent to about 180,000. The once-rural county of rolling green hills was transformed into a suburban mecca within easy commuting distance of both Cincinnati and Dayton. Strip malls, subdivisions, gourmet grocery stores, and churches popped up everywhere, even a massive new YMCA packed every day with mothers and their children. New schools were opening, and the existing ones were overcrowded. The roads, many of them still just two lanes, were often gridlocked with new SUVs and minivans.

The beauty of the new-age Republican battle plan was its ability to segment populations that, like the Jews, had long been courted as one single bloc. This segmentation proved critical to GOP gains among Latino voters as well, a constituency that is growing fast and already proving decisive in several battleground states. In 2004,

Republicans deciphered key demographic changes in the Hispanic population and capitalized on them, aggressively wooing first- and second-generation immigrants who had not had time to develop deep ties to the Democratic Party, along with third-generation Hispanics who were gaining wealth and, in some cases, becoming more GOP-friendly. That population was growing fast in Arizona, New Mexico, Florida, and across the South, and just like the Russian Jews, Hispanics became easy targets for a message that emphasized the dream of becoming rich and joining the fabric of American society. Many of these new transplants still spoke Spanish at home, a comfort zone for the younger-generation Bushes, who spoke the language and maintained close contacts to the immigrant communities.

In Ohio, home to a modest but potentially decisive Latino population, Republicans used a computer database to identify every Spanish surname in the state. Bilingual volunteers called every household, gathering information for the Voter Vault. John Perez, a Columbus businessman and lawyer who oversaw the GOP Hispanic outreach operation, said the campaign reached "every Hispanic household in the state several times."[22]

New immigrants were among the targets in January 2004, when Bush unveiled a controversial program to let millions of undocumented Spanish-speaking immigrants gain legal work papers. Immigration, though not necessarily a top-tier issue for longtime American citizens of Hispanic heritage, was a sensitive topic for newer citizens who still spoke the language and maintained close family contacts back in Mexico and other homelands. In his speech in the East Room of the White House, Bush stood with a bevy of immigrant advocates as he extolled the contributions of millions of citizens who were "Americans by choice."

"As a Texan, I have known many immigrant families, mainly from Mexico, and I have seen what they add to our country," Bush continued, drawing special attention to his understanding of new arrivals.

Across town at Republican headquarters, party strategists used their growing list of Latino contacts to segment the population and—as they had done with Jews—find new voters whose opinions and concerns made them friendlier to the GOP. In New Mexico,

Republican Party researchers noticed that just 19 percent of the state's Hispanic population identified itself as Republican. But below that dismal number, there was hope: 47 percent supported Bush generally and 80 percent liked his education initiative, the No Child Left Behind Act, which stressed improving the performance of struggling schools. So those 80 percent were targeted by a Republican telephone and mail campaign that emphasized the idea that Bush's education agenda had special benefits for Latino and other minority students.

In addition to carefully researched messages like that, voters with Hispanic surnames across the nation received a five-minute DVD barely noticed outside the Latino community that was narrated by Bush himself. In the video, the president sought again to strike a personal connection with Latino viewers, clearly differentiating himself from the increasingly loud anti-immigration wing of his party that was violently opposed to his guest-worker program and incensed by his soft rhetoric on immigration. He did so with language that would never be used in a more broadly circulated message, essentially describing millions of Americans who populated his native Texas and nearby states as the true foreigners in someone else's native land. "About fifteen years before the Civil War, much of the American west was northern Mexico," explained the president, pictured in jeans with his dog Barney, fishing in a lake on his property near Crawford, Texas. "The people who lived there weren't called Latinos or Hispanics. They were Mexican citizens, until all that land became part of the United States." Black-and-white images of Mexicans and other obviously Latino people flashed on the screen as Bush spoke. They were working in fields and factories, socializing with extended families. "After that, many of them were treated as foreigners in their own land," Bush said.

This emotional appeal was not based on social issues such as abortion or school prayer that many political experts had long believed influenced the nation's Catholic Hispanics. Instead, the message was rooted in the personal connection that Bush had built since that day in 1994 when he stood up to California governor Pete Wilson and his anti-immigration initiative.

The Bush brothers understood intrinsically the power of communicating directly with new immigrants whose households were still dominated by Spanish rather than English. Those households tended to be working class and took pride in their native countries as well as in their accomplishments in the United States. Hearing directly from a president in their own language—a president who was a Republican but understood their dual pride in their homeland and in their new country—easily trumped the message from some Democrats promoting social welfare policies that were arguably more beneficial to low-income immigrants. Pro-Kerry groups had tried to lure Latinos with messages promoting health-care reforms and programs to help more people go to college, but those messages did not permeate the way the Republican appeals did.

Sergio Bendixen, a Democratic pollster and an expert on Hispanic public opinion, credited the Bush brothers with transforming the GOP pitch to Latinos into a powerful issue-free appeal that tugged at the heartstrings rather than the purse strings. He cited a 2002 Jeb Bush ad in Florida featuring images of the flags from various Latin American countries, with a clip of the governor, speaking in Spanish, welcoming viewers to Florida.

Following the 2002 election, Bendixen worked for the New Democrat Network, an independent group that promoted Latino outreach in the 2004 presidential campaign, and presented the Jeb Bush ad to focus groups to gauge reaction. The spot was particularly effective in central Florida, home to hundreds of thousands of new immigrants from the very countries whose flags appeared on screen. He called it a "masterful commercial."

"People told me things like, 'My God, I haven't seen that commercial for a year and a half, and I miss it. I got emotional when I saw it. It made me so proud,'" Bendixen said.[23] Bendixen concluded that the Bush brothers' Latino outreach strategy was a success, pulling this important group away from their Democratic party moorings and putting them in play politically in a way they never had been previously. Bendixen called it the "I love you" strategy. It was most effective, he said, with those newer immigrants who maintained closer ties to home—a group that by 2004 made up nearly half of the Latino vote across the country. A report by the New Democrat Network hailed the Bush approach as "primarily based on a message that emphasizes cultural empathy, emotional connection, and personal charisma. Issues and party ideology are unimportant to the Republican Latino strategy."

Joe Garcia, former executive director of the Cuban American National Foundation who quit in 2004 to work with Bendixen at the New Democrat Network, said the Bushes' issue-free message succeeded in wooing a new generation of GOP voters among recent immigrants. "These are people who want to belong here," said Garcia. "The biggest compliment is to tell these folks, 'You're one of us.'"

All of this happened amid rocket-speed growth in the Hispanic electorate, from just 2.5 million voters when Ronald Reagan ousted Jimmy Carter to 7.6 million in 2004. That number is estimated to hit 20 million voters by the year 2020, according to the New Democrat Network's report. The GOP share of that vote rose rapidly after the Bush brothers became the iconic leaders of the party, from the 21 percent share won by Bob Dole in 1996 to 35 percent won by George W. Bush in 2000. Exit polls reported that Bush pushed that to 40 percent in 2004, with Democrat John Kerry's share of 59 percent a dramatic decline from Bill Clinton's 73 percent performance in 1996. Illustrating the differences within the Latino bloc, Bendixen's survey of several exit polls concluded that the Republican share of U.S.-born Hispanics had remained steady in the low 30s. The dramatic rise, Bendixen concluded, came in the immigrant vote—with the GOP share shooting upward from 18 percent in 1996 to 47 percent in 2004. That made it nearly even with the Democrats' 52 percent share that year.

In his video, Bush spoke about the growing Latino influence on the United States and, in a nod to the one-party aspirations of his top lieutenants, pledged to recruit them to the GOP. "As Latinos continue to influence every part of American life, our country will have more Latino senators and more representatives to the Congress," he said. "I'd like to help elect them. I hope they'll be Republican."

As Bush spoke, the background music—a Latin beat—grew

louder. The president was pictured waving a Mexican flag, hugging a Latino woman, and then holding a Latino baby. Words flashed in Spanish saying, "President Bush. We know him."

The video was shown at the Republican National Convention in New York, but its real power came in its wide distribution across the Southwest. Bush himself understood the effectiveness of the "I love you" approach. When the strategy's architect, noted Texas-based Latino adman Lionel Sosa, had laid out the themes during a 2000 meeting with Rove and the then governor of Texas, Bush turned to Sosa and asked "How much do you need for this?" Sosa replied that it would take $3 million. Bush then turned to Rove: "Give him five."[24] In 2004, when Sosa presented Bush the script for the DVD, he said the president was equally gung ho, changing nothing even though the White House faced growing attacks from the anti-immigration wing of the GOP.

As the Bush campaign increased its aggressive outreach to Latinos in 2004, the Democrats began losing ground, despite positive early signs. In July, for example, the pro-Democratic group Democracy Corps, led by pollster Stanley Greenberg and strategist James Carville, issued an upbeat survey of Latinos in key states suggesting that Kerry was already on track to win. The poll, headlined "Bush Faltering Among Hispanic Voters," showed Kerry securing 65 percent of that group in a two-way race, compared with just 30 percent for Bush. The poll seemed to reveal dramatic improvements for Democrats over 2000 with the potential for even more growth.

But as the campaign wore on, Greenberg said he could see that Kerry's performance with Latinos was not living up to expectations. Latino outreach was outsourced to a montage of independent, third party groups barred by law from coordinating directly with the Kerry campaign. Greenberg eventually joined the campaign in the fall, and posted internal polling data at strategy sessions, hoping to kick the Hispanic outreach effort into gear, but to no avail. He called the Kerry campaign's Latino vote effort "aimless." "I was putting up charts showing we were constantly underperforming with Hispanics," Greenberg said.[25] "The response, consistently, was, 'That's being handled from the outside.' But it should have been a central task of the strategy team."

Officials at the New Democrat Network, who had decided independently to focus on Hispanic outreach, were prohibited by campaign finance laws from coordinating with the Kerry campaign. So the group published results from Bendixen's polls publicly, hoping that Kerry strategists would at least notice and decide to refocus on getting out the Latino vote. But New Democrat Network strategists later learned that their numbers were being closely watched not by the Kerry campaign but by the operatives inside the White House political office. Months after the election, a White House official in charge of Latino outreach called Bendixen and invited him to stop by for a visit. Bendixen did so and said the administration made a case for him to work for the GOP. "They made me feel like a million bucks," Bendixen said, recalling an avalanche of compliments from White House officials about the accuracy of his Hispanic polling. Bendixen said he remained a Democrat, but he lamented that his own party failed to take note of the demographic changes that he and the Republicans have seen—a sophistication that served the GOP well on Election Day among Latinos and other targeted groups. Nationally, Republicans said the targeting produced a noticeable increase for their side among Hispanics, proving particularly beneficial in turning New Mexico from blue to red. In that state, Bush's Latino performance rose by twelve points between 2000 and 2004, according to the New Democrat Network study.

In Ohio, the number of Hispanic voters was so small it was difficult to know whether gains were made in that category. But there was no doubt, Republicans said, that microtargeting was powerful among African Americans, boosting support for Bush by seven percentage points in 2004, enough to enable the president to win Ohio— and the nation—outright on election night without a legal challenge.

But Rove and Mehlman did not rely on microtargeting alone to chip into traditional Democratic strongholds. In 2004, as Democratic strategists sought to appeal to workers by emphasizing concerns about the economy, Republicans had found a way to take their message directly to workers on the factory floor as never before.

CHAPTER 7

The Business of America Is Business — and Lobbying

The business community is very, very cautious about what they do. But in recent years they have been more effective in motivating people to participate, which is good for us.

— Ken Mehlman, Portland, Oregon, September 14, 2005

The frenzied weeks before Election Day marked a time of heartland bus tours by the candidates, mega-rallies in pivotal states, televised debates, and obsessive twenty-four-hour cable news coverage. At the same time, a little-known Midwestern manufacturing company was gearing up to play its own quiet but significant role in President Bush's reelection.

Politicking was new for Vermeer Corporation, a family-owned maker of hay bailers and trench diggers based in the prairie town of Pella, Iowa. But in 2004, Vermeer's executives were engaged, repeatedly urging their seventeen hundred employees to read specially prepared candidate guides and then to vote. The company did not make an overt endorsement. That can violate federal election laws under some circumstances. But the voter guides, prepared by the National Association of Manufacturers, rated the candidates on how well they understood the needs of business—and, implicitly, its employees. Bush won praise. John Kerry scored zero.

Vermeer was positioned to make a difference in 2004. Polls showed Bush and Kerry in a dead heat in Iowa. Mobilizing voters was considered critical in areas like Pella, a historic agricultural and industrial town of about ten thousand located an hour south of Des Moines. Iowa was once fertile territory for Democratic presidential candidates. While best known for growing corn, it also had a substantial manufacturing sector, led by agriculture-based companies such as Vermeer. Along with that manufacturing, Iowa had a vibrant labor movement that knew how to get out the blue-collar vote. Running against George W. Bush's father in 1988, Michael Dukakis achieved his second-highest voting percentage in Iowa. Bill Clinton carried the state twice. Al Gore also won Iowa in 2000, but just barely. Like other parts of the Upper Midwest, once dependably Democratic Iowa was changing. Republicans had already won four of the state's five congressional districts by the end of Clinton's tenure and had taken control of the State House in 1994 and the State Senate in 1996.

Iowa voters could still be lured by the economic populism that had once held an almost religious grip on many farmers and blue-collar workers there; during the Depression and other times of economic hardship after all, angry crowds of farmers had sometimes prevented local sheriffs from foreclosing on one of their number. But the modest family farms that formed the backbone of the Populist movement had been fading away for decades, replaced by larger farms whose owners operated and thought more like corporate executives than prairie radicals. As for manufacturing, by 2004 it was struggling against global competition in Iowa just as it was almost everywhere else in the United States. Workers understood that manufacturing jobs were evaporating. They no longer dared dismiss out of hand arguments that what was good for their employers was also good for them. Not that far east of Pella, for example, just across the Mississippi River in Peoria, Illinois, workers at Caterpillar had fought long, bitter, and largely unsuccessful strikes trying to preserve the wages and benefits that had come with union contracts in the years after World War II. So when Iowa businesses used their internal communications networks to challenge Kerry and the unions supporting him, as they did in 2004, those GOP-friendly messages had resonance. At Vermeer, a nonunion plant with warehouses and assembly buildings stretching along a two-lane highway just outside Pella, the company's e-mail and in-house newsletters repeatedly directed employees to an elaborate Web site designed by the Washington-based Business Industry Political Action Committee (BIPAC), a nonprofit organization founded in the early 1960s to get companies to engage in politics. The Web site, www.vermeervote.com, provided detailed information on voter registration, absentee ballots, polling stations, and the candidates for state and federal offices. It also contained descriptions of the issues that business considered important—issues that Vermeer's workers might want to think carefully about as well.

The notion that employers might distribute voter guides may not seem very dramatic, but it represented a notable change from the practices that prevailed in most U.S. corporations in the years after World War II. The U.S. Chamber of Commerce, the National Association of Manufacturers, the National Federation of Independent Business, and other such groups had always been major players in Washington, and their political leanings were generally Republican. But their views were not aggressively communicated to workers on the factory floor. Worker communication was generally the province of labor unions.

In earlier eras, the late nineteenth and early twentieth centuries, American business had considered one of its most important duties to be telling its employees how to vote—and seeing that they did so. But for many years after the Second World War, business had lowered its partisan political profile. It did not stop giving money to the Republican Party and its candidates on a scale that Democrats could only dream about. Nor did it pull back from the battle over specific government programs and policy. What it did do, however, was cut back on direct efforts to influence the political opinions of its employees. And it drew back from the public bear pit of debate over political ideas. Soon liberal academics and intellectuals had that arena largely to themselves. There was an unintended subtext to Barry Goldwater's slogan in the 1964 presidential campaign, "In your heart, you know he's right." Conservatives had to appeal to the heart; they had developed precious few arguments to appeal to the head.

That began to change after the debacle of the Goldwater campaign. Conservative strategists began to see a need to do more than wring their hands over what they saw as liberal bias in academia, the news and entertainment media, and the courts. Liberals opposed to the war in Vietnam were building huge grassroots organizations. So were groups fighting for civil rights and more generous programs for the poor. Ralph Nader and other consumer advocates were rattling corporate boardrooms. Environmental groups were springing up to challenge long-established business practices on grounds that they fouled the air, water, and soil. Organized labor, protected by union shop rules and employer-operated dues checkoffs, was helping to finance what seemed to be a rapid buildup of liberal strength. And an army of academics, lawyers, and other specialists were supplying the liberal cause with ideas, analysis, scholarly studies, and other resources that conservatives were hard-pressed to match.

Against this background of conservative disarray, a Richmond, Virginia, corporate lawyer named Lewis F. Powell Jr. penned a letter to the U.S. Chamber of Commerce urging business engagement across the board—in electoral politics, judicial selection, and influencing the media and academia. Often referred to simply as the "Powell memo," the document became legendary among activists, both left and right, for its clarity and prescience. Powell, who sat on the boards of a dozen major corporations and went on to serve fifteen years on the U.S. Supreme Court, was nominated to the bench by President Nixon shortly after drafting the manifesto.

"The time has come—indeed, it is long overdue—for the wisdom, ingenuity and resources of American business to be marshaled against those who would destroy it," Powell wrote to his friend Eugene Sydnor Jr., then chairman of the U.S. Chamber of Commerce Education Committee. "The American economic system is under broad attack," he said, from left-leaning intellectuals, from activists like Nader, and from complicit members of news, academic, and political institutions. "It is time for American business, which has demonstrated the greatest capacity in all history to produce and influence consumer decisions, to apply their great talents vigorously to the preservation of the system itself."[1] In the pages that followed, Powell's memo laid out a plan for business to transform the views and actions of scholars, the mainstream media, the courts, and elected officials.

The late Joseph Coors, heir to the Colorado brewery fortune, was "stirred up" by Powell's call to arms, convinced that his business and others needed to plunge into politics and public affairs. That led Coors to provide early support for the establishment of the Heritage Foundation.[2] At about this same time, the brothers who owned Koch Industries, an oil, natural gas, and land-management firm and the second-largest privately owned company in the United States, made their own investment in conservative think tanks, underwriting the formation of the Cato Institute and Citizens for a Sound Economy. They contributed more than $11 million to these two organizations between 1986 and 1990.[3] Another recruit to Powell's banner was the John M. Olin Foundation, established in the early 1950s with funds from the Olin family's manufacturing interests. It set about endowing chairs—to be occupied by conservative professors—at leading academic institutions and sponsoring seminars to train judges. The Olin foundation closed in 2005 after donating more than $300 million to conservative causes, including the Heritage Foundation, the American Enterprise Institute, and the Cato Institute.[4]

Nixon adviser and speechwriter Patrick Buchanan recognized the potential power of these foundations. In 1972, he authored a memo for Nixon on how to "make permanent the new majority" that centered on the need to train conservatives for top positions in Washington. His memo focused on three things: a "talent bank" for Republican officeholders, a "tax-exempt refuge" when they were out of office, and a nationwide communications center for conservatives wanting to exchange ideas.[5] The year after Buchanan wrote that memo, Heritage opened its doors in Washington, intent on helping to fulfill those goals. At first, the foundation focused on members of Congress, producing reports and fact sheets on topics that ranged from tax policy to national security.[6] The American Enterprise Institute, founded earlier, served much the same purpose, producing mountains of data to counterbalance the work of left-leaning scholars. Cato did likewise. The conservative think tanks differed in degree and emphasized varied topics and approaches, but all served to fill the intellectual void on the right and to provide ammunition for conservative politicians and activists.

A Milwaukee-based organization, the Bradley Foundation, had enormous influence in the development of the conservative intellectual base. Harry Bradley and his brother Lynde made their fortunes from the Allen-Bradley Company, which produced electronic devices and components. Harry Bradley was a contributor to the *National Review*, one of the nation's earliest and most important conservative voices.[7] The Bradley Foundation's longtime president, Michael Joyce, became a key figure in the world of conservative organizations, emerging as a leading proponent of school choice and voucher initiatives across the country. He retired in 2002 and, at the request of President Bush and Karl Rove, established Americans for Community and Faith-Centered Enterprise, a group designed to lend political grassroots support for the president's faith-based initiative.[8]

Changing the balance, and thus the political climate, was not a quick process and it took time for the conservatives to develop the complete arsenal of modern advocacy. But they kept at it. The conservative think tanks trained and supported journalists, sponsored internship programs for college students, and built up networks for aspiring politicians. Conservative scholars emerged as talking heads and pundits on cable television news shows alongside liberals. Quotes from conservative experts took their place in mainstream publications, and op-ed pieces by conservative thinkers began to appear regularly on editorial pages. Publications such as the *National Review* and the *Weekly Standard* became required reading in Washington. Eventually such efforts moved conservative ideas into the mainstream as Lewis Powell hoped they would.

Historians may conclude that the culmination of all this was the presidency of Ronald Reagan, who gave conservative ideology a warm and likable human face it had never had before. Yet Reagan, while dedicated to shrinking the role of government and to a more muscular approach to national security, held some of the social conservatives at arm's length. More important, he had little interest in building a national political organization that would seek to maintain conservative power after he left the White House. That role was left to George W. Bush and Karl Rove. For his part, Bush was generous in acknowledging what the efforts of conservative intellectuals and the organizations created at their suggestion had contributed to conservatives' strength in the twenty-first century. At one White House gathering, Bush said that the *National Review* and its founder, William F. Buckley Jr. had "helped move conservatism from the margins of American society into the Oval Office." It was hard to recall the days when "the only conservative game in Washington, D.C., was Bill Buckley and the *National Review*," the president said, but "today we've got, of course, an abundance of conservative columnists and radio hosts and television shows and think tanks and all kinds of organizations. I guess in an intellectual sense, you could say these are all Bill's children."

Yet for all it did to support this expansion of conservatism in the world of ideas and mass communications, the business community continued to limit its participation in retail politics largely to the writing of checks—predominantly for Republicans but also in significant measure for Democrats too. Typically, corporate campaign contributions through the 1980s were divided between Republicans who controlled the executive branch and Democrats who ruled the legislative branch. In the early 1990s, Democrats received generous contributions from business, often the result of aggressive fundraising tactics employed by party leaders such as Representative Tony Coehlo of California, the third-ranking House Democrat until he resigned in 1989 amid ethical questions about his financial dealings. The ability of Democrats to sustain support from corporate interests was limited by the party's obligations to its core constituencies—labor unions, trial lawyers, and environmentalists, whose agendas often ran counter to the goals of industry. And, as Republicans gained power during the 1990s, GOP strategists moved to exploit that vulnerability—a vulnerability that was increased by the fact that GOP gains in Congress reduced the necessity of business groups to cultivate Democrats. Rove, DeLay, Norquist, and their acolytes understood the changing dynamic and exploited it at every turn. Responding to the K Street Project and other initiatives, donations from businesses and their lobbyists began tilting more heavily Republican. And some business leaders began urging their colleagues to do even more. Among them was Michael Baroody, the National Association of Manufacturers' vice president whose father helped establish the American Enterprise Institute. Another was C. Boyden Gray, an heir to the R. J. Reynolds tobacco fortune and former White House counsel to the first President Bush; Gray had a central role persuading business to enter the fray on behalf of George W. Bush's policy agenda and judicial nominations.

Baroody, a gray-haired, husky-voiced former smoker, was a longtime conservative activist who worked in the Reagan administration as an assistant secretary of labor. He was known for his speeches urging business unity and comparing business engagement in politics with the noblest intentions of the nation's founders. In the 1990s, Baroody authored an article distributed to National Association of Manufacturers members called "De Tocqueville and De Manufacturers," urging member companies to join the political fray. "Corporate America holds a higher moral ground than it is accustomed to claiming of late," he wrote.[9]

The election of Bill Clinton in 1992 was a temporary setback for conservative visionaries who wanted to make business a more active arm of the Republican Party. Clinton, a centrist Democrat, had succeeded in Arkansas and nationally by building alliances with business and industry leaders. He consistently displayed a willingness to play ball on bottom-line concerns in exchange for business engagement on big issues that many executives cared about, such as health care and education policy. In Arkansas, Clinton built his power by aligning with business groups to upgrade the state's education system. His gains in funding for education—and state test scores—won him plaudits from business leaders and broad support across the political spectrum. Clinton hoped to do the same nationally by focusing on economic issues, including health-care costs, a concern that had long galvanized the left but that increasingly drew the attention of business leaders as well.

The Clinton health proposal did, in fact, mark a turning point for corporate involvement in politics—but not in the way the first-term president had hoped. The issue ultimately galvanized and united businesses with conservatives as never before.

That wasn't the case at first. Conservatives watched with unease verging on horror as some business leaders—from Chrysler's Lee Iacocca to the chamber of commerce's Richard Lesher—gave a warm reception to Clinton's early economic and health-care proposals.

Unnerved House Republican leaders fired off a letter to Lesher in 1993 warning him of "a rapidly spreading frustration and anger" with the chamber's failure to challenge the Clinton program."[10] Lesher ignored the early complaints, dispatching his chief lobbyist, William Archey, to meet with Clinton aides to hammer out differences in the initial health reform proposal. The chamber's continued interaction with Clinton riled conservatives like Norquist and DeLay, who increasingly railed against the chamber, at one point even threatening to form a competing business organization. Norquist found a conservative philanthropist to donate funds to produce and mail a video to every chamber of commerce affiliate in the United States, warning them of the "betrayal" by the national chamber on the health-care issue.[11]

Conservatives saw the proposal as an enormous threat, not only because of its massive scale but because of its popularity and the possibility that it could provide Clinton and the Democrats with a lasting legacy comparable to that of Social Security. In 1994, the *National Review* quoted the Republican Policy Committee's Eric Ueland—who years later became chief of staff to Senate Majority Leader Bill Frist—as saying that Democrats had "created a theology around health care which insists that St. Bill and St. Hillary will deliver to the middle class an entitlement from which the middle class will never be able to unwrap itself. And as a consequence, Democrats will be the governing majority in this country for generations to come."

Norquist said he and fellow conservatives were terrified by the Clintons' proposal, and its early popularity. "Our fear was that if they got health care they would turn the United States into a social democracy where a majority of people viewed the state as central to their lives the way they do in Europe," he said. "It would make more people dependent on government and the more people are dependent on government the more likely they are to be Democrats."[12]

Even as chamber executives were meeting with Clinton aides at the White House, Senator Paul Coverdell, a conservative Georgia Republican who had once been an insurance executive, was organizing a coalition to counter the Clinton plan.[13] Conservatives like Norquist and Dirk Van Dongen of the National Association of Wholesaler-Distributors joined immediately with two better-known business groups that had opposed the Clinton approach from the outset: the National Federation of Independent Business and the Health Insurance Association of America. The opposition reached critical mass on August 12, 1993. On that day, Coverdell's weekly coalition meeting in the Dirksen Senate Office Building swelled to more than 250 people. Oregon senator Bob Packwood opened the session, referring to the Clinton legislation as a "lethal weapon" that would torpedo the nation's economy. Packwood introduced Alabama senator Richard Shelby, a Democrat who later switched parties, to declare that he intended to filibuster the plan. The audience rose and applauded. "I've never seen this type of unity, this type of enthusiasm and strength of purpose," one Senate staffer told the *National Review*, "especially not in the business community."[14]

Not long after the Senate meeting, the chamber switched sides. Archey was fired to be replaced by R. Bruce Josten, who immediately made up with Republican representative John Boehner and other Capitol Hill conservatives who had complained about the chamber's coziness with the Clintons.[15] Josten ultimately rose to become the organization's second-ranking officer. The chamber had thrown out the compromisers, but the conservatives wanted more.

Meantime, the Health Insurance Association of America, which had been part of Coverdell's group, launched its own campaign against the Clinton plan, including the famous ads featuring middle-class couple "Harry and Louise" worrying that the proposal would cost them a chance to pick their own doctor. The ads were misleading. Americans may have had reason to worry about losing their ability to choose their doctors, but the threat did not begin with the Clinton plan. It was already happening through the spread of managed care medicine. Studies at the time showed that Europeans, Canadians, and the Japanese all had more choice of providers than Americans did. But the ad campaign took hold and the Clinton plan tanked. Public support declined from 59 percent to 46 percent, according to Gallup, between September 1993 and February 1994.[16]

Nothing did more to drive business into retail politics on behalf of the Republican Party than the 1994 elections. After forty years, Republicans won control of both the Senate and the House of Representatives. In one day, the Republicans ascended and longtime Democratic leaders in the House saw their traditional base of power in Washington severely crippled if not completely obliterated. Replacing the Democratic leaders was a cadre of self-described backbench radicals: Newt Gingrich, Dick Armey, and DeLay, along with advisers such as Norquist and Ed Gillespie. They quickly turned to a goal that even Lewis Powell and William Buckley might have deemed impossible: transforming the Washington lobbyist establishment—long reviled by conservatives as lacking backbone and remaining cozy with Democrats—into a Republican Party asset.

The new Republicans in the House offered a dream agenda for business built around the much-vaunted Gingrich-designed Contract with America: deregulation, tax cuts, and shrinking government. They insisted, though, that corporate America provide the financial support they thought their effort deserved while also changing hiring patterns and the management of Washington trade associations to reflect their true GOP leanings. In other words, firms and trade associations were told to hire Republicans.

No one was more aggressive in relaying those instructions to business brass than DeLay, the new majority whip. A former insect exterminator, DeLay had come to Washington from Texas to push a moral-values agenda, carry forward the Reagan revolution, and above all reduce the weight of government regulations. The Environmental Protection Agency was a particular target for DeLay's ire. Like other pest control companies in the South, DeLay's old firm had used the pesticide Mirex to kill fire ants, aggressive South American insects that were resistant to other pesticides.[17] The Environmental Protection Agency found that Mirex was also a possible carcinogen and, in 1978, banned the substance, infuriating DeLay and inspiring him, in part, to run for Congress. As a candidate, DeLay had vowed to vote against every spending bill and pledged to cast a particularly skeptical eye on the environmental agency, which he called the "Gestapo of government."

DeLay believed that businessmen shared his desire to eviscerate costly regulations and should join his party's effort to make it happen. One former DeLay congressional aide, Stuart Roy, said that his former boss's goal was to make business as pro-Republican as labor was pro-Democratic. "Labor unions were a lot more effective than the size of their membership" because they gave overwhelmingly and unfailingly to Democrats, Roy said.[18] Labor leaders were also trusted political advisers to Democrats. But business, DeLay believed, was less effective because its attempts to appease both parties only frustrated its natural Republican allies while never winning unequivocal support from Democrats. "That's something DeLay pointed out," Roy said. "When you try to play both sides the way the business community always has, and whether that's in hiring people, political giving, or other kinds of support like grassroots activities, you don't end up with double the amount of friends. You wind up with half as many. But when you pick your friends like the labor unions do, you have friends for life."[19]

For trade groups to match labor's marriage to Democrats, DeLay believed strongly that the associations needed to prove their bona fides by placing Republicans in top jobs. The idea, he said, was never simply to find good jobs for GOP friends but to build a cycle in which powerful, well-heeled organizations could help push conservative ideology in a government that had long been dominated by

Democratic thinking.[20] DeLay pushed the cycle by placing his top aides in key lobbying positions all over Washington. And he pushed individual corporations and their Washington lobbyists to contribute more to the GOP. DeLay's hectoring of the business community may have served the GOP and the movement in the short term. But the deals made by some business lobbyists with DeLay's friends, family, and former staffers would eventually become fodder for congressional hearings and investigative reporters and would lead, in part, to DeLay's fall from the political heights. And the shock waves from that fall would continue to damage party leaders and their plan to build a durable GOP majority.

To keep pressure on businesses, DeLay and his allies began to compile lists, starting in 1995, of business-affiliated political action committees, along with their patterns of campaign donations. Lobbyists were told their ranking, and DeLay personally pressed those low on the list to raise their standing.

The accounting profession, for example, gave more than half of its campaign donations to Democrats in 1994. A decade later, 65 percent had gone to Republicans. Other industries followed suit.[21] To monitor business hiring in Washington, Gingrich and Norquist used the K Street Project to track job openings among the city's big downtown lobbying firms and whether Republicans filled them.

"We got grid sheets listing every lobbying position and the party affiliation of the lobbyist," Norquist recalled. He presented an updated list to Gingrich and DeLay and others. DeLay was not the project's leader, but he was its most effective advocate. His in-your-face style was not easily brushed aside by business executives and trade association chiefs, many of whom were Democrats themselves and had long operated in a close-knit bipartisan fraternity that gathered in upscale restaurants and private clubs in the district. DeLay's brass-knuckled ferocity was new and peculiar. Some businesses continued to hire Democrats for top positions. DeLay pressed harder. The electronics industry felt the whip's sting in the fall of 1998, when one of its leading trade associations hired a Democrat as its top lobbyist, former representative Dave McCurdy of Oklahoma. DeLay and his staff got mad and then got even, temporarily blocking one of the industry's priority measures from coming to a vote. DeLay's slap at the Electronics Industry Alliance led to a private reprimand from the House Ethics Committee in 1999, and even some Republicans called the tactic heavy-handed. That did not deter DeLay or his allies in the K Street Project.

When the National Association of Securities Dealers hired a former Clinton administration official, John Hilley, as a vice president in 1998, DeLay told the industry publication *Traders* magazine that the hiring was a "very big mistake," adding that hiring "a highly-partisan Democrat gives me great concern, because I won't deal with such organizations."

Although such outbursts were not particularly effective in the short term (both Hilley and McCurdy kept their jobs), the pressure eventually ushered in a new era on K Street. Lobbying organizations got the message: if they wanted to have good relations, or even get appointments to see the leaders of Congress, they needed to have Republicans in top positions.

In 1997, the U.S. Chamber of Commerce tapped Thomas J. Donohue to replace Lesher as its president. Donohue was not the preferred pick of Norquist and other conservatives. But he was a savvy political player and longtime Washingtonian who had been deputy assistant postmaster general and chief executive officer of the American Trucking Association. He quickly distinguished himself from Lesher by distancing the chamber from the Clinton White House and turning around the financial fortunes of the organization, which had been losing money. Donohue turned his energies to marketing the chamber and turning the organization into a more aggressive force in the capital.

Within three years, Donohue tripled the chamber's annual budget to $150 million, allied himself more closely with Republican candidates, and increased the lobbying staff from two to eighteen.[22] Donohue had effectively turned the chamber into Washington's premier lobbying shop, and he linked it increasingly with the party that was on the rise. At the same time, Donohue's chamber expanded its political reach far outside the Beltway, into state capitals and cities across the nation. It opened phone banks and launched direct mail and advertising campaigns, pushing for pro-business legislation and electing business-friendly candidates as state legislators, attorneys general, and state Supreme Court judges.

The chamber was not alone in intensifying its involvement in electoral politics. In 2000, the National Association of Manufacturers and the Business Industry Political Action Committee (BIPAC) joined together to pursue the so-called Prosperity Project, an initiative designed to teach companies how to turn their workers into activists. The goal was to enlist employees in a political army to rival that deployed every election cycle by the pro-Democratic labor unions. All of the business groups insist that they are nonpartisan and point out that they endorse moderate Democrats with pro-business records from time to time. Nonetheless, the vast majority of their campaign contributions and endorsements go to Republicans, and the tilt has only increased during the past decade.

When the 2000 campaign was heating up, BIPAC named a new chairman, Gregory S. Casey, who previously worked as chief of staff to Republican senator Larry Craig of Idaho and then as Senate sergeant at arms. Casey also had managed congressional and Senate campaigns. He found an ally in a new and aggressive member of BIPAC's board, David Gribben, then the soft-spoken executive vice president of Halliburton Corporation and a loyal former aide to Dick Cheney at Halliburton, on Capitol Hill, and at the Pentagon.

Early in 2000, well before Cheney had been selected as Bush's running mate, Gribben became intrigued with the idea of encouraging more employee activism. He and Casey and a few other business executives together helped push BIPAC into its new role that year. Gribben's boss felt so comfortable with this new approach that when Cheney was asked by then governor Bush to find a vice presidential candidate, the campaign secretly hired BIPAC to vet the contenders.[23] BIPAC staff scrubbed potential candidates, using its database to study and contrast voting records, policy positions, and campaign contributions. Eventually, Cheney himself became the nominee. BIPAC's close coordination with the Bush campaign and its vice presidential search effort is not generally known, but the collaboration undermines its oft-professed claim to be an independent nonpartisan organization. To the contrary, it suggests that BIPAC, at least on this occasion, operated as an affiliate of the Republican Party.

At about the same time that the vice presidential search was going on, BIPAC officially launched its Prosperity Project, though modestly. The project began with just one full-time field staffer, Darrell Shull, a clean-cut political activist in his forties who had worked as a union shop steward at a paper company, as a political consultant in California, and as a district office manager specializing in voter outreach for an embattled California Republican congressman, Frank Riggs.

Armed with a "business tool kit" that included a careful explanation of how corporate managers could legally talk politics with their underlings, Shull traveled the country explaining to wary business owners in battleground states the basic facts of federal election law. Much to the surprise of many business owners, Shull explained that companies were in fact permitted to participate in campaigns. Federal law blocked them from using corporate dollars to influence federal elections directly, but executives were told they could talk about issues and candidates and inform their employees about how those candidates stood on the issues. BIPAC and other groups offered ideas to get around the corporate money ban, like inviting candidates to meet with workers, tour a plant, or receive an award. Others distributed voter guides, as Vermeer did in Iowa a few years later for Bush's reelection.

The more aggressive tactics underwent a major test in 2000 in the battle for a traditionally Democratic U.S. House seat in Lexington, Kentucky. Democrats thought they had the upper hand. Their candidate, Scotty Baesler, was a popular former congressman seeking to reclaim his seat from a first-term Republican who had opposed popular legislation designed to ease lawsuits against health maintenance organizations that were proliferating in Kentucky and across the nation. The incumbent, Ernie Fletcher, was a physician who had won his first race narrowly with support from health-care companies. His HMO vote angered many of his fellow doctors, who teamed up with labor unions and the Democratic Congressional Campaign Committee to try to unseat him.

Smelling victory, Democrats poured money and organizers into the race. But business owners large and small came together to back Fletcher, his conservative values, and his opposition to the patient's rights legislation that they viewed as a threat to the bottom line. Two weeks before the election, Fletcher confidently strode into the unionized Wild Turkey bourbon plant near Lexington, where he defended his opposition to the HMO bill as a bid to save workers' health benefits. He chatted enthusiastically with mash-tub operators and women on the bottling line, explaining that he was fighting to make sure their medical benefits weren't threatened by greedy lawyers suing employers over decisions made by company health plans.[24] It was just one of dozens of plants the Republican congressman toured during his campaign, often at the invitation of business owners determined to keep Congress in friendly hands. Fletcher's opponent seemed stunned by his rival's entrée into factories and offices across the district. Baesler said at the time that he, too, had been visiting work sites, "but we are always on the outside working the gate" during shift changes, not inside accepting praise from company executives. The same day Fletcher visited the Wild Turkey distillery, he gained access to nearby plants operated by Toyota Motor Corporation and Minnesota Mining & Manufacturing Company, thanks again to invitations from executives. A film crew hired by the National Association of Manufacturers recorded his tour for a twelve-minute documentary that was later distributed by the manufacturers' organization as an example of how corporations could help friendly lawmakers. Fletcher won reelection, and Baroody later described Kentucky's Sixth District as "our national model." "We have decided that we are not going to cede the grassroots to labor anymore," he said.[25]

The business groups' success in that Kentucky contest—and a handful of others—caught the attention of trade associations, corporate executives, and Ken Mehlman, who would later go on to chair the Republican National Committee. Mehlman said that victory was part of an evolution in business activism in the past decade. After 1994, Mehlman said, business leaders "changed their giving patterns. That was phase one. Then part two began, and they started changing their hiring, bringing aboard more Republican staff." Phase three, he said, "is encouraging employees to understand the stakes of the election. . . . Without saying vote Republican or vote Democrat, the more information the employees get, the better they get."[26]

With interest from high places, Shull's modest project grew dramatically after the 2000 elections. So did other fledgling efforts that linked Republican officeholders and business. The K Street Project made huge advances now that Bush occupied the White House and Republicans had firmer control of Capitol Hill. For example, within weeks of the 2000 election, retiring members of Congress lined up jobs for themselves in the K Street lobbying corps. Most of the former members who got lucrative positions were Republicans. Twenty-three of thirty-seven departing Republicans became lobbyists, while just two of the thirteen departing Democrats followed suit.[27]

That new atmosphere contributed to a helpful cycle that Gingrich, Norquist, and DeLay had envisioned five years earlier. Job openings helped draw new, young talent to work in the lobbying shops and campaigns. But the shift also cleared a career path. "We can now go to students at Harvard, and say, 'There is now a secure retirement plan for Republican operatives. There's a pot of gold at the end of the rainbow,'" Norquist said.[28]

As it pursued an often-controversial agenda, the Bush White House increasingly called on the business community for help. The drug industry helped build grassroots support for Bush's controversial Medicare prescription drug proposal. When the White House was looking for help in its quest to cut dividend taxes, Norquist teamed up with Dirk Van Dongen of the National Association of Wholesaler-Distributors, which represents forty thousand companies from pharmaceutical wholesalers to beer distributors. All told, nearly a thousand companies and organizations joined the Tax Relief Coalition that Van Dongen chaired to press Congress to pass Bush's plan.

The 2001 tax campaign illustrated how far the business world had come from the early days when just a handful of companies and trade associations joined to beat back the Clinton health-care proposals, and how accustomed executives had become to engaging in political warfare. The tax breaks in that package were not business priorities but business organizations helped the White House lobby for passage. The reason, according to the National Association of Manufacturers' Baroody: "We're adults. We understand the meaning of delayed gratification."[29]

In 2003, the dividend tax-cut package offered by the White House was of great interest to many business leaders. Encouraged by Van Dongen, Norquist, and others, corporations pushed hard for the idea. Several companies included a pitch for the tax cuts when they mailed out dividend checks. General Motors shareholders received a printed message from CEO G. Richard Wagoner saying there would be "more money for you" if the Bush plan became law. He called the tax cuts "good for our shareholders and General Motors" and urged stockholders to contact their senators and representatives. Verizon mailed a similar message to its 1 million shareholders.[30]

During this period, BIPAC expanded dramatically, adding staff and securing participation from 184 companies in 2002, up from just 50 the previous cycle. By 2004, BIPAC was a force in every region of the country, connecting with millions of workers from more than 900 companies. By then the organization had 80 field organizers concentrated in 14 battleground states. Scores of small and mid-size firms like Vermeer had joined, along with half of the top 50 multinational firms in the country, names such as Exxon Mobil Corporation, International Paper Company, and 3M Company. The chamber, meantime, contracted with an unprecedented 287 field organizers in 2004, placing them in competitive states and closely contested congressional districts.

Months before the 2004 election, the National Association of Manufacturers hired as its new president John Engler, the former Republican governor of Michigan and one of the president's closest political allies. Engler's arrival put him in command of the organization's thirteen thousand-company network in the final months of the election. As governor from 1990 to 2002, Engler had harnessed the political clout of Lansing's business lobby, partnering with executives to enact limits on jury awards and make state courtrooms more hostile toward injured consumers and the trial lawyers who helped them sue corporations. Building on Ronald Reagan's success in courting union members in Michigan, Engler helped strengthen the GOP in a state long dominated by organized labor, though he had failed to deliver Michigan's electoral votes for his friend Governor Bush in 2000.

As a high-profile Republican politician heading a major trade association, Engler had entrée to the White House and to the increasingly powerful K Street machine. No industry group was more powerful than the so-called Gang of Six, a nickname used to describe a tightly knit pack of executives from the city's biggest trade groups who had grown close personally and professionally and were aligned with the White House. The manufacturer's organization was represented in the "gang" by Baroody. The list also included R. Bruce Josten from the chamber; Dan Danner at the National Federation of Independent Business, which had experienced a surge in growth during the Clinton health-care fight from small firms worried about the plan's costs; Lee Culpepper of the National Restaurant Association, who went on to become Wal-Mart's lead lobbyist; Dirk Van Dongen of the National Association of Wholesaler-Distributors; and John Castellani, president of the Business Roundtable, which represents the CEOs of top American corporations employing more than 10 million workers.

Most of the gang members had known one another since the early wars against the Clinton health proposal. They formed Team Coverdell, which raised money from K Street to help get the Georgia Republican reelected, then used the same mechanism to help other Republicans win elections, including Senators Norm Coleman from Minnesota and Jim Talent from Missouri.

The 2004 campaign was a high-water mark for business activism in politics. Besides the presidential race, the newly muscular Wall Street–K Street–White House coalition took aim at the Democrats' top gun, Senator Tom Daschle of South Dakota. Van Dongen led the early formation of Team Thune, which raised $455,000 from Washington lobbyists for John Thune's campaign early in the cycle. The U.S. Chamber of Commerce hired fifty-five activists to work on the ground in that tiny state, with instructions to reach every business owner with entreaties to support the Republican challenger. Rove himself had handpicked Thune to challenge Daschle. A dashing former college basketball player and three-term congressman, Thune had narrowly lost a Senate bid in 2002. In 2004, the White House and the business community were united in their determination to oust Daschle, who had proven an effective spoiler for many of their legislative goals such as tax cuts and jury award limits.

Boosting the chamber's effort were other Washington-based lobbying groups, which dispatched some two hundred additional activists to help build an overwhelming grassroots network. Labor and Democrats also flocked to South Dakota, but they were outmaneuvered in the tactical arena they once dominated. The impact of this business investment was visible on Election Day. In Iowa, Bush squeaked by with a margin of 13,216 votes. BIPAC had directly registered more than 16,000 voters and recorded 334,000 hits on employer election Internet sites. In all-important Ohio, Bush won by 136,000 votes; BIPAC had assisted 119,000 people to register and cast votes before Election Day, using new early voting rules and absentee balloting. Postelection reports by BIPAC, the Republican National Committee, and even the liberal America Coming Together organization credited business with helping put Republicans over the top. Mehlman personally thanked Gregory Casey, the CEO of BIPAC, and later told reporters that the business group made a dramatic impact on the results in Ohio, Iowa, and other states.

On election night, Bush and three dozen family members and friends stayed up late waiting for networks to declare the winner. Hundreds of anxious Republicans crammed into the main hall of the massive Ronald Reagan building in downtown Washington, waiting for Bush to be named the undisputed winner. Frustrated by what he saw as unnecessary caution, Rove personally called network executives encouraging them—without success—to call the election for Bush. Victory was not certain until the next day, when Kerry conceded, concluding that the margin in Ohio was wide enough to make the scattered allegations of voter irregularities inconsequential.

In the next days and weeks, business executives added up their gains. The 2004 strategy had been far more aggressive and expensive than anything tried before. But the dividends were substantial, too. "What was the return on this investment?" the chamber's Thomas

Donohue asked his board in a letter sent out after the election. He answered his own question: the chamber's favored candidates won twenty of twenty-eight targeted House races. The group found similar success in the Senate, bagging seven of nine targets, including the grand prize: Daschle.[31] Though Donohue didn't say so in his letter, the congressional success would mean clearer sailing for business priorities: passing long-sought legislation that would make it more difficult for consumers to avoid debts by declaring bankruptcy, giving energy companies greater access to oil and gas deposits, and shielding large corporations from class-action lawsuits.

Election 2004 was a sweet victory for the Republicans and their allies. Not only had Bush secured the second term that eluded his father, but the GOP expanded its majorities in the House and the Senate. Daschle was history, his party in disarray, devoid of leadership and a clear agenda, staring into the abyss. What's more, business had emerged as an active factor of this success, while key components of the Democrats' coalition — labor, left-leaning minority voter organizations, and trial lawyers — had seen their effectiveness diminish.

Karl Rove was pleased. But he was not ready to rest.

CHAPTER 8

Put to the Test:
Social Security

For the first time in six decades, the Social Security battle is one we can win—and in doing so, we can help transform the political and philosophical landscape of the country.

—PETER WEHNER, WHITE HOUSE DIRECTOR OF STRATEGIC INITIATIVES, JANUARY 3, 2005

The day after the election, tired but ebullient, President Bush and Vice President Cheney stepped before a cheering and relieved crowd of supporters, White House aides, campaign staff, and family members gathered at the Ronald Reagan Building. Finally, with that morning's concession call from John Kerry, the GOP and the broader conservative movement could celebrate an unequivocal victory. They had won in the Electoral College. They had won in the popular vote. And, most important to some, they seemed to have won a signal victory in their quest for an enduring majority.

"Thanks to you, we have gained seats in the House of Representatives," Cheney told the crowd. "Thanks to you, I will be presiding over a larger Republican majority in the United States Senate. Thanks to you, President George W. Bush won the greatest number of popular votes of any presidential candidate in history." As Bush himself stepped to the microphone with his wife and two daughters on his left and Cheney on his right, the crowd began to chant, "Four more years!" Bush quieted the crowd and declared, "The voters turned out in record numbers and delivered an historic victory."

The president singled out key players on his campaign team: "the architect," Karl Rove; campaign manager Ken Mehlman; campaign chairman Marc Racicot; Republican National Committee chairman Ed Gillespie. Beaming from the sidelines was Don Evans, Bush's old friend and secretary of commerce. John Engler, the former governor of Michigan and an old Bush family friend, was up front, too.

From the beginning, Bush's drive for the presidency and the conservatives' drive for political dominance had depended on the power of two engines. One was the social, religious, and ideological conservatives who comprised the traditional wing of the movement. The other was American business. And a crucial element in the president's success to that point was the fact that he had avoided major issues that might force him to choose between the two. Indeed, Bush had managed to give the impression that he was equally devoted to both, though a clue to where the president's heart really lay might have been discerned from those clustered around him on that celebratory morning.

Beyond the Bush and Cheney families and professional operatives such as Rove and Mehlman, those who stood out were Engler, Evans, Racicot, and Gillespie. Engler headed the National Association of Manufacturers. The silver-haired Evans would soon become chief executive officer of the Financial Services Forum, a lobbying group representing the CEOs of eighteen of the country's largest financial service companies, including Citigroup, Goldman Sachs, J.P. Morgan Chase & Company, and American Express. Before joining the Bush campaign in 2000, Evans had been CEO of Tom Brown Incorporated, a large independent energy company. He and the president had described themselves as "best friends" since Bush's early days in the oil business.

Racicot, the former Montana governor and party chairman following Bush's 2000 victory, had been a lobbyist representing Enron, the American Forest and Paper Association, and the National Energy Coordinating Council. During the early days of Bush's first term, Racicot had lobbied Cheney to weaken the Environmental Protection Agency's regulations on older power plants. Racicot did not withdraw his equity stake in his lobbying practice during his two years as RNC chairman, a time that he was helping to craft administration strategy.

As for Gillespie, a New Jersey native who worked as a parking lot attendant when he first arrived in Washington in the 1980s, he had long since established himself as one of the capital's most skilled and highly compensated business advocates. His lobbying firm, Quinn Gillespie, founded in 2000 with former Clinton White House counsel Jack Quinn, had quickly become one of Washington's most profitable. It reported $27.4 million in lobbying-related income in its first two years of existence. The firm's clients, most of whom paid annual fees of $200,000 and up, included Tyson Foods Incorporated, Microsoft Corp., the U.S. Chamber of Commerce, the National Association of Realtors, Metropolitan Life Insurance Company, and DaimlerChrysler.[1]

When Gillespie took over the RNC in 2003, he, too, retained his stake in his old firm, drawing fire from consumer advocates and watchdog groups that accused him of peddling power between his friends in the West Wing and Wall Street. "This is just one more step in the merger of the Republican Party and corporate America," said Joan Claybrook, president of Public Citizen.[2]

If business conservatives seemed exceptionally prominent as Bush celebrated his reelection, movement conservatives were not forgotten. At the inaugural a few weeks later, Christian conservatives partied at their own alcohol-free evangelical ball at Washington's Ritz-Carlton hotel. Rove, Mehlman, outgoing attorney general John Ashcroft, and other party stalwarts showed up to embrace the Reverend Louis P. Sheldon, chairman of the Traditional Values Coalition, and other icons of the religious right. Never before had there been such a seamless link between the White House, party leadership, church groups, and corporate America. The holy grail of one-party rule appeared tantalizingly close.

All that was required, it seemed, was for the new, more muscular alliance to remain intact. That, however, could not be taken as a given. The coalition that performed so well during the presidential election would have a harder time in the second term of George W. Bush.

To begin with, Bush's presidency was not immune to the ills and scandals that had beset many reelected chief executives. House Majority Leader Tom DeLay, the muscle behind the K Street Project and a commanding force in the one-party movement, would later be indicted in Texas for activities relating directly to his aggressive dealings with corporate contributors. Meanwhile, Jack Abramoff, an über-lobbyist closely aligned with DeLay, Rove, Norquist, Ralph Reed, and other movement leaders, came under investigation for an almost unimaginable array of crimes and ethical lapses, ranging from possible connections to the murder of a gambling cruise line owner to misusing millions of dollars provided to him by Indian tribes hoping to increase their gambling revenues. As Abramoff and his associates began to plead guilty in exchange for helping federal prosecutors cast a wider net, the scandal would threaten to besmirch the Bush administration and the GOP as a whole.

Rove himself would emerge in 2005 at the center of the investigation into the outing of covert CIA officer Valerie Plame as part of an effort to undermine her husband, Joe Wilson, an administration critic. Through much of the year, the inquiry swirled around the West Wing staff of a president who had pledged to restore "honor and dignity" to the White House. When one of the vice president's closest aides, Scooter Libby, was indicted, Washington insiders began to wonder aloud whether Cheney himself might ultimately be implicated. These scandals took the moral shine off an administration that wore its piety on its sleeve and depended on the enthusiastic support of religious leaders and churchgoing Americans.

Equally challenging, the conservative coalition—like the New Deal coalition and other such amalgamations of varied goals and interests—was subject to centrifugal forces that became harder to control as time went on. Gillespie understood more than most that maintaining unity among the business interests, the social conservatives, and the White House could get tricky. During Bush's first term, Gillespie had been tapped by the domestic steel industry to persuade the administration to protect U.S. companies by imposing tariffs on imports, an apostasy to free-market traditionalists. The White House accepted the idea, in part because the steel industry was influential in Minnesota, West Virginia, Ohio, and Pennsylvania, all of which were likely reelection battleground states. But Gillespie, in his capacity as head of the RNC, had to hustle to soothe the party's infuriated free marketeers. Steel tariffs had not been a big enough controversy to split a coalition, but the dispute suggested what strains a bigger issue might bring. And one such issue was coming, whether the White House was ready or not: immigration.

Finally, as almost every president learns at some point, unforeseen and uncontrollable events can overwhelm the best-laid plans and spoil the most cunning of political stratagems. In the second term, intractable reality was going to take a hand, and this time it would not always deal aces to the president and his allies. The most obvious example was the Iraq war. Instead of a quick and easy triumph, it had turned into a protracted and thorny mess. With casualties mounting and American troops unable to suppress a brutal insurgency, Iraq during the Bush second term was sliding into a bloodbath of sectarian violence.

Politically, the problem was not really the war itself. For one thing, Democrats seemed incapable of making an issue of it; most of them had supported the invasion and the politics of war had twisted presidential nominee John Kerry in knots. Bad as the situation in Iraq had become, Bush had turned it to his advantage during the 2004 campaign, appealing to voters' patriotism and reviving old fears that Democrats were unreliable on national security. Bush and Rove understood the larger political realities of war as well. Contrary to conventional wisdom, Americans throughout their history have shown a remarkable tolerance for casualties and an enduring reluctance to pull back from wars. Some, most recently Vietnam, have given rise to large antiwar movements. Perceived inequities have provoked sometimes violent protests, as with New York's deadly draft riots during the Civil War. But in none of these cases has a majority of American voters turned a wartime president out of office in favor of a candidate who advocated withdrawal. Faced with antiwar challenges within his party, Lyndon B. Johnson decided not to seek reelection in 1968, but the eventual Democratic nominee, Vice President Hubert H. Humphrey, nearly won the election despite the divisions. And the winner that year, Richard M. Nixon not only supported the war but kept it going and in 1972 won reelection in a landslide over an antiwar Democrat. It was Watergate, not Vietnam, that drove Nixon from office.

What gradually turned Iraq into a problem for Bush was not the fact of the war itself. It was what it revealed about the president's leadership and the way his administration functioned—or failed to function in critical situations. First of all, the administration's judgment and its commitment to the truth were called into question when its case for going to war in the first place began to unravel. Saddam Hussein, it became increasingly clear, never had the close, operational relationship with al Qaeda that Bush and Cheney had sometimes implied. Nor could evidence be found to support Bush's assertion that the Iraqi regime possessed weapons of mass destruction. And pre-invasion predictions that Iraqis would welcome American troops as liberators and unite to make their country a beacon of peace and democracy in the Middle East turned out to rest on Neocon fantasies, not hard evidence or sound intelligence.

Perhaps more damaging was the accumulating evidence of sheer ineptness and inattention to the job. For instance, when it developed that American troops in Iraq were spending their own money to buy cobbled-up armor for themselves and their vehicles because the Pentagon could not get them what they needed, Bush risked sounding hollow when he expressed commitment to the young men and women who wore the uniform. The Defense Department's continuing difficulty in finding solutions to the problem of improvised roadside bombs, despite repeated assurances that the problem was being addressed, called the Pentagon's competence into question. And the spectacle of U.S. forces bogged down, suffering, and dying with no visible sign of progress was making it harder for the military to attract recruits or retain some of its best young officers. So was the overuse of National Guard and reserve troops, not to mention the painful problems that extended tours of duty created for families, employers, and others on the home front.

As the second term began, Bush and Rove still counted national security as a net plus. The war on terrorism had played to the conservative coalition's strengths in the first term, combining as it did the need for heavier spending on security and appeals to patriotism and traditional values. The White House could hope the same would be true in the second term. So confident was Rove about how a majority of Americans saw the issue that he signaled early in the second term that Republicans would play the war card again in the 2006 midterm elections, using a speech to the Republican National Committee to accuse Democrats opposed to warrantless domestic spying on terror suspects as operating with a "pre-9/11 worldview."

Still, there was widespread agreement that more was needed for the second-term agenda, if only to give Congress and the news media something to focus on besides the war and scandals. What was needed was a major domestic issue that reached out and touched Americans by the millions.

The Bush team had several priority domestic initiatives it intended to roll out in the second term: remaking the Supreme Court, along with the rest of the federal judiciary, and revamping the country's immigration system in ways that would appeal to both Hispanics and the business community. But first on the list was Social Security.

And the Rove team had the issue ready. Bush had been talking about Social Security reform for years and had, as early as the 2000 campaign, touted a rough proposal to encourage private investment accounts.

Going back to the first gubernatorial campaign, Bush and Rove had shown considerable shrewdness in identifying issues and positions that had political breadth but also harmonized the two elements in their political base. The perfect example of that had been education: business wanted workers who were better prepared; minorities wanted help for their children in dilapidated schools; conservatives liked choice and accountability; and everyone wanted better education. Bush had ridden the issue successfully in Texas. And the No Child Left Behind Act had become the crowning domestic achievement of his early years in the White House. The plan to create private investment accounts within Social Security was judged to fit the one-party playbook equally well.

For voters outside the conservative coalition, the Social Security proposal showed Bush stepping out front on a looming domestic crisis. Moreover, his plan did not affect the benefits of older Americans already receiving Social Security checks or baby boomers nearing retirement—a concession designed to diffuse a potentially powerful political base of opposition. And it offered encouragement to younger workers who doubted that Social Security would be there for them but might be eager to join an "investor class" viewed as a new and growing GOP constituency. Meanwhile, private accounts would appeal to ideological conservatives as a private-sector alternative to big government. And for many in the business community, a turn toward private investment of Social Security funds was a welcome signal of a shift away from corporate obligations to provide for employee retirement. Some, but not all, of the leading financial services companies saw the initiative as providing a bonanza of new business. Looking further ahead, Bush and Rove saw private accounts in Social Security as a core piece of the Ownership Society they were counting on to draw voters away from the government-oriented policies of New Deal liberalism and into the new conservative majority.

Designed by Franklin Delano Roosevelt as the lynchpin of the New Deal, Social Security was intended as a social compact between the generations to guarantee the health and well-being of senior citizens, the disabled, and the poor. The social welfare ideal inherent to Social Security ran through other New Deal initiatives, such as cash relief for the poor and job-training programs. To Democrats, these programs came to be seen as a safety net that symbolized precisely the mutual obligations that members of a free society owed to one another—the duty to assure at least a minimally decent standard of living for all. And they believed government should be the instrument for meeting these collective responsibilities.

Conservatives and corporate chieftains opposed Social Security from the outset, arguing that it was socialistic and would weaken the moral fiber of workers. They also viewed Social Security as being, in part, a safety net for the Democratic Party, creating generations of Americans dependent on the government and thus inclined to vote for the party they perceived as supplying and protecting their benefits. To get the plan through Congress, Roosevelt stipulated that it be financed through a payroll tax and that benefits go to all workers, regardless of how much they had contributed. Roosevelt also insisted that all workers who were covered by the program be given Social Security cards, tangible symbols of what they were entitled to. The idea was to make the program indispensable for everyone and politically devastating to repeal. As Roosevelt himself put it, "No damn politician can ever scrap my Social Security program."[3]

Social Security became the most popular federal program in history. Not only did it benefit the elderly, but it also lifted a burden from their adult children, enabling those younger generations to enjoy a higher standard of living than would have been possible had they been forced to support aging parents as had previous generations. Thus Roosevelt's remark proved prescient. So devoted was the public to the program that by the late twentieth century, Social Security had become known as the "third rail" of American politics: touch it and you die.

For Democrats, the political benefits of Social Security and other government assistance programs were reinforced by another New Deal law, the Wagner Act of 1935. It extended the legal rights of labor unions, enshrining as federal statute their right to organize and bargain collectively with employers. It also explicitly outlawed a range of practices that corporations had used to block or weaken unions. The Wagner Act facilitated the development of a rich and powerful union movement that would play a central role in Democratic election campaigns for decades.

Republican attacks on the labor law began relatively quickly after passage, with conservatives arguing that it took away individual workers' rights. But on Social Security, the conservatives were stuck. The Depression had destroyed the public's trust in business leaders and conservative politicians, at least for a time. While they might fulminate against the "socialistic" idea of big government that was inherent in Social Security, the program was too popular to attack directly. As *Newsweek* columnist Jonathan Alter has noted, Republican leaders fell into line. The next five Republican nominees for president—Alf Landon, Wendell Wilkie, Thomas Dewey, Dwight D. Eisenhower, and Richard Nixon—all pledged to maintain it.[4] Even Barry Goldwater cried foul when Democrats depicted him as planning to destroy Social Security. Not until the 1980s did the climate begin to change.

Ronald Reagan believed Social Security was a "Ponzi scheme."[5] He said as much as a candidate for president in 1975, suggesting it be turned into a voluntary program. But Reagan learned the hard way that Social Security was a political untouchable. To a significant degree, his criticism of the program cost him the chance to run for president in 1976. Reagan challenged President Gerald R. Ford, who had entered the Oval Office after Nixon's resignation, for the GOP nomination. But Ford turned back Reagan's challenge by winning several key primaries, including Florida with its huge population of elderly voters. Ford, who had carefully avoided any suggestions that he might tamper with Social Security, got 53 percent of the overall GOP vote—and 60 percent of voters over sixty-five.[6] Reagan was not totally deterred. Years later, as president, he proposed that benefits be cut. The idea drew such strong opposition, however, that he backtracked and ultimately supported bipartisan legislation to strengthen the program.[7]

Even though politicians who talked about changing Social Security got nowhere, conservative theorists continued to generate ideas for revamping it. In 1980, Edward Crane, founder of the libertarian Cato Institute, read a paper by a Harvard Law School student that proposed a system of private investments to replace the government program, which was essentially financed with general revenues.[8] The student was Peter Ferrara, who would later become one of Washington's leading advocates for the privatization of Social

Security and other conservative causes. Cato pushed the idea with the help of like-minded organizations and activists including Norquist, Ferrara's friend and associate from Americans for Tax Reform.

Advocates of private investments in Social Security were pragmatic—and patient. They were confident that if they developed the ideas and the arguments necessary to enhance its political appeal, a climate for enacting the proposal would eventually develop. Two Heritage Foundation analysts, Stuart Butler and Peter Germanis, predicted in 1983 that it would take "many years before the conditions are such that a radical reform of Social Security is possible." But, writing in the Cato journal, they concluded, "As Lenin well knew, to be a successful revolutionary, one must also be patient and consistently plan for real reform."

Fourteen years later, Crane, Cato's president, traveled to Austin, Texas, for a dinner with the governor. To Crane's surprise, George W. Bush was already talking up the idea of private accounts. Also dining with Crane and Bush that night was José Piñera, an architect of the program that transformed Chile's equivalent of Social Security into private retirement accounts in 1981. Privatization backers in Texas had arranged the dinner. And Bush seemed to have a good grasp of the concept. "I was pleasantly surprised by the kind of intelligent questions he asked," Crane said. He recalled that Bush was worried at the time about the political sensitivity of the issue. "I think he wanted to support the idea but needed to be convinced," Crane told the *Los Angeles Times*.[9]

A 1999 Cato report proved key as Bush and his political team mapped the 2000 presidential campaign. The report concluded that private accounts would be more popular among Americans who owned stock than among those who did not. Given the fact that more Americans owned stock than ever—six out of ten in 2000, up from two in ten in 1980—Bush strategists reasoned that the climate might finally be right for privatizing Social Security. Correctly or not, Bush strategists interpreted the data as confirmation that advocating Social Security privatization would not be politically fatal.

To the contrary, they thought it could boost Republicans' long-

and short-term prospects. Polls showed that private accounts were popular among younger voters, some of whom were believed to resent shelling over a chunk of their paychecks to a retirement system that might not survive long enough for them to benefit. The polls suggested that advocating privatization might give the GOP a toehold with the investor class eyed closely by Republican strategists. Eventually, if private accounts were approved and worked out as predicted, they would become as important to contemporary workers as those Social Security cards had been to earlier generations. And the GOP, as the creator and protector of private accounts, would command the same kind of unswerving loyalty that had been FDR's legacy to the Democrats. As the RNC's Mehlman told party activists on the eve of Bush's second inaugural, simply proposing the private accounts sent a clear message to people under thirty worried about retirement savings: "The Republican Party has a plan for you."

Democrats were convinced that the broader public would not back privatization and eagerly anticipated a second-term brawl on the issue. What Mehlman, Rove, and Norquist thought the Democrats failed to grasp was this stunning political theory: even if Democrats defeated the Bush plan in the second term, Republicans could win the long-term war for an important class of voters—upwardly mobile Americans. Thus long-term Republican gains might be achieved merely by making the case for private investment accounts, even if the proposal itself flamed out.

This was a central strategic concept behind Bush's continual references to the Ownership Society during the 2004 election. Social Security was a social compact built on the New Deal–era idea of shared responsibility. The Ownership Society, by contrast, emphasized the individual—self-empowerment and maximizing opportunities to get rich. GOP strategists, focusing on likely voters instead of on total population, believed their approach would pay political dividends not only among upwardly mobile whites but also among blacks, Latinos, and new immigrants with high aspirations. Norquist argued that the Democrats' opposition to changing the system would help Republicans—much as Republicans' opposition to civil rights laws in the 1950s and 1960s had helped Democrats. "The Democrats cannot survive the fact that they are making the mistake with people under forty that the Republicans made [with African American voters] when they voted against the Civil Rights Act," Norquist said.[10] "They are sending a signal to a generation that will be around for a long time that, 'We don't respect you.' The Republican Party message is that, 'We'll make you more rich.' Which party do you want to belong to?"

"This has the potential to do for the Republican Party what the New Deal did for the Democratic Party," said Greg Strimple, a New York–based Republican pollster. "The Ownership Society could become the ownership realignment."[11]

In 2005, Rove and Bush believed the time had come. With the president's reelection, they had secured the political capital, and conservative scholars at Cato, Heritage, and elsewhere had provided the necessary economic and philosophical rationale. So early in his second term, Bush embarked on a national campaign to make private accounts happen.

From the start, Bush sought to reassure older workers and retirees that his plan was neither radical nor a threat to their benefits. "Social Security was a great moral success of the twentieth century, and we must honor its great purposes in this new century," Bush said in his 2005 State of the Union address, which served as the official kickoff of a multistate swing promoting his overhaul ideas. "The system, however, on its current path, is headed toward bankruptcy. And so we must join together to strengthen and save Social Security." Bush, as he had in numerous appearances before and as he would in dozens of speeches later, then sought to draw a clear dividing line between the generations. His goal was to simultaneously mollify senior citizens while enticing younger voters.

As Bush traveled the country, he hosted events billed by the White House as "conversations" on Social Security. In reality, they were highly orchestrated and carefully scripted. The conversations featured Republican-friendly "experts" and "average citizens," who responded to rehearsed questions from Bush. In many cases, audiences were screened to keep opponents of the president's Social Security ideas from disrupting the flow. But the events received generally positive coverage from local television stations, and White House strategists believed they were effective.

At the same time, the White House was using some of its campaign-tested techniques to reach beyond the typical conservative base. Rove and other administration strategists believed that the investor class could include the same younger, middle-class minorities that had been courted during the reelection campaign. Polls found an opening for the GOP, for example, with a new class of African American voters who cared more about gaining wealth than fighting over such issues as segregation. Blacks under thirty, after all, did not necessarily identify with the civil rights movement and its political ties to Democrats as much as their parents did. Instead, "African Americans in their twenties and thirties experienced the power of the market during the Clinton years, and they viewed the idea of private accounts favorably," said David Bositis, an expert on African American public opinion. A 2002 survey found that 67 percent of blacks favored the idea of private Social Security accounts. Support was even higher—about 79 percent—among blacks aged eighteen to twenty-five, the very group Republicans believed would be attracted by policies promoting wealth, ownership, and self-empowerment. Bositis said younger African Americans showed a "consistent attraction to private accounts, and we have seen it for some time."

Bush administration officials seized on this opening early in 2005, inviting black clergy and business leaders to a White House meeting at which aides made the case that the existing Social Security system cheated blacks. Bush and other officials argued that African Americans benefited less because, on average, they lived shorter lives than whites, and thus received less money. The argument was hugely controversial. Critics noted that blacks relied disproportionately more than whites on other parts of Social Security, such as survivor benefits, which might be placed at risk under the Bush plan. Still, White House supporters organized town hall meetings in black neighborhoods from Los Angeles to Memphis to press their case. Similar outreach on Social Security was targeted at Latinos, but with a seemingly contradictory argument to the one offered to African Americans: that Latinos, with their fast-growing presence in the workforce, relied more than others on Social Security and therefore should support Bush's plan.

These arguments were rooted in the strategy for long-lasting political realignment. Some senior White House staffers spoke about Social Security reform as an epoch-making step. "For the first time in six decades, the Social Security battle is one we can win — and in doing so, we can help transform the political and philosophical landscape of the country," wrote Peter Wehner, a White House strategist working under Rove, in an internal memo that was leaked to the press. "We have it within our grasp to move away from dependency on government and toward giving greater power and responsibility to individuals. . . . Democrats and liberals are in a precarious position; they are attempting to block reform to a system that almost every serious-minded person concedes needs it. They are in a position of arguing against modernizing a system created almost four generations ago. Increasingly the Democrat Party is the party of obstruction and opposition. It is the Party of the Past."

White House officials understood that they were engaging in a marketing and public education campaign. So, as Bush embarked on his town hall meetings, the White House maintained constant contact with its corporate allies to make sure of their support. The effort produced unprecedented cooperation between the White House and its base, but not without exposing the fault lines running through a fragile coalition consisting of players with varied and competing interests.

The administration's new point man on Social Security privatization, Charles P. Blahous III, had been the director of the business coalition formed in the late 1990s to push private accounts. That group, called the Coalition for the Modernization and Protection of America's Social Security, or COMPASS, emerged as a central player in the campaign, recruiting industry associations and individual corporations to the cause. At the Republican National Committee, Chairman Mehlman and his top lieutenants turned the party apparatus into a full-time Social Security campaign operation. Each Friday during the first months of Bush's second term, the RNC hosted representatives from the Business Roundtable, COMPASS, and allied organizations, along with staff from Rove's office. At these meetings, RNC staff tallied efforts to build support for the president's plan in key congressional districts. COMPASS's director, Derrick Max, said his organization had generated 300,000 telephone calls to voters in key states, organized 150 town hall meetings on the topic, and was active in 70 congressional districts. The group planned to spend $18 million backing the president's initiative, with a special emphasis on placing ads in states with competitive races in 2006.

In effect, the nation's biggest corporations—using trade associations and ad hoc organizations—were pouring millions of dollars into political campaigns engineered by the RNC and the White House. The practice was legal, but to some critics it violated the spirit of the 2003 campaign finance reform legislation that specifically banned corporate and union "soft money" from influencing federal elections. Of course, this was no election. It was a policy debate. But critics charged that organizations such as COMPASS operated as arms of the Republican Party, meaning that contributions to the coalitions were the same as campaign contributions. "This is the new soft money," said Bruce F. Freed, codirector of the Center for Political Accountability, an organization advocating greater corporate transparency. "Donations made by corporations through trade associations are becoming a very serious problem. This spending can have a profound effect on political outcomes—and sometimes on a company's bottom line and reputation. Yet trade associations and their corporate members don't have to disclose where the money comes from or how it is spent."

The Social Security effort was always a gamble. And problems arose quickly, many of them the result of savvy agitating by leaders of the AFL-CIO, senior citizen organizations, and a left-leaning activist group, the Campaign for America's Future, whose codirector, Roger Hickey, made a compelling case for rallying the fractured and discouraged Democrats in opposition to Bush's proposal.

"For progressives, the battle for Social Security represents a rare opportunity to stop the newly reelected president dead in his tracks, to demonstrate the bankruptcy of his extreme conservative agenda, and to point to a new politics of 'shared security' around which we can build a new majority for change," Hickey wrote in an early 2005 essay in *American Prospect* magazine titled "A Battle Progressives Can Win." He and others organized a public education and political campaign to counter the Bush effort. And the campaigns found soft targets in squeamish corporate supporters and nervous Capitol Hill Republicans.

Starting in February 2005, the same month that Bush kicked off his Social Security road show, officials from the AFL-CIO threatened to picket corporations that openly backed the Bush plan. The fact that labor officials controlled billions of dollars in union pension investments gave them clout in the business community, especially with the brokerage houses that were supporting the White House. Advocates for senior citizens threatened to join the pickets, causing many corporate boards to worry that openly backing the Bush privatization plan might turn into a public relations fiasco. Two investment firms that initially agreed to support Bush, Edward Jones Investments and Waddell & Reed, became the subject of union demonstrations and pulled their support.

But other corporations attempted an awkward dance, endeavoring to appease consumer and labor groups while heeding the desires of a White House that was not afraid to punish its enemies. Executives at Pfizer Corporation told labor leaders early in 2005 that the company would remain neutral on Social Security, even though Pfizer had long been listed as a member of the alliance backing private accounts. A corporate spokeswoman reiterated that stance in a statement released to the *Los Angeles Times*, saying in February 2005, "We do not have a position on the current Social Security debate."

Pfizer, whose products cater largely to senior citizens, was viewed as vulnerable to mass protests by the retiree activists and by labor shareholders. But the company also could not afford to alienate the Bush administration, particularly given the federal scrutiny at the time of two Pfizer products, the painkillers Celebrex and

Bextra. Further complicating matters for the drugmaker, CEO Hank McKinnell was chairman of the Business Roundtable, which was firmly in Bush's camp on Social Security private accounts despite Pfizer's attempts to declare neutrality.

The White House was beginning to worry. Weeks had elapsed since Bush began jetting around the nation leading town hall meetings like an itinerant talk show host. Even though he was using hand-picked participants as human props to convince senior citizens that their checks would not be in jeopardy and that young workers would be better off, the broader public's response was as chilly as the Washington winter. Polls showed the public unmoved. Republicans were balking on Capitol Hill. And the business alliance was looking shaky.

Rove sought stability. In late February, he summoned major Washington lobbyists and trade association representatives to the White House complex. In Room 450 of the majestic Old Executive Office Building, Rove, his aide Barry Jackson, and economic adviser Allan Hubbard addressed a crowd of 150. Rove spoke first, reminding the lobbyists that Social Security was the president's top domestic priority. The request for help was not at all subtle, according to one Washington lobbyist in the audience. Rove made clear that the White House expected financial and grassroots support. Jackson then took the podium to explain that COMPASS needed to raise $20 million or so for a national advertising campaign.

As an added incentive, Rove let participants know that the White House was paying attention to which firms contributed. It was clear "from folks who looked you right in the face that . . . anything business can do to help on this journey will be important. And it will be noted," recalled Dirk Van Dongen, one of the trade association leaders charged with lining up support from the business community.

The private talking-to had an effect. Pfizer halted its tap dance and backed private accounts openly rather than remaining neutral. Within days, nearly one hundred state and national trade associations—representing bankers and bakers, restaurateurs and road builders—signed up with COMPASS. Still, the Rove meeting was not a cure-all. While the business associations voiced support to the White House—and funneled money to the Social Security campaign—many individual companies held back from taking public positions. A *Los Angeles Times* telephone survey of the twenty largest U.S. companies found only two willing to voice on-the-record support for the private accounts plan.[12]

One trade association representing securities firms experienced a near-mutiny over the issue. The chief executive of Sanford C. Bernstein & Company penned a letter in April demanding that the Securities Industry Association board "formally issue a statement of complete neutrality" on private accounts. "Given the divergence of views among the member firms and the complete lack of unanimity that we have, it seems inadvisable to maintain our recent posture," wrote the CEO, Lisa Shalett, who represented the company's parent firm, Alliance Capital Management, on the association board. The letter went on to say that Alliance Capital officials believed they served their clients "by devoting our energies to reacting to and interpreting public policy, and not by aggressively attempting to shape the course of public debate."

At the same time, another securities trade association—the Financial Services Forum—opted to pull out of COMPASS. The forum, then headed by former New York representative Rick Lazio, had been a founding member of the coalition, but the board could not agree on private accounts. "I couldn't in good conscience sign our guys up for this," said Ken Trepeta, the forum's then vice president said at the time. "It's all over the news, and people are debating and rebutting and hedging, and I guess in a way we are too."[13]

The pullout was a major blow for the White House and for the efforts to further entwine business and Republican Party ambitions. But within weeks Lazio and his executive director were replaced by White House comrades. Don Evans, the former commerce secretary who stood with Bush at the reelection celebration just a few months earlier, became the new chairman of the investment group. Evans quickly rejected the suggestion that his organization's withdrawal from the broader Social Security coalition represented a drop-off in support for Bush's proposal. In his new role, Evans said, "I will be out there applauding the president and his leadership and talking about how important it is that our entitlement plans be reformed."[14]

The arm-twisting and upbeat statements had little effect. By the fall of 2005, prospects for congressional action on private accounts were almost completely extinguished. Dozens of speeches by Bush, Cheney, and other administration officials had failed to move opinion polls; in fact, the president's ideas had grown less popular over time. Bush's summer vacation in August had been dominated by anti-Iraq war protests outside his home near Crawford, Texas. Negative reports from Iraq were fast eating into the president's political capital. The swagger that marked Bush's demeanor after reelection began to disappear.

Then Hurricane Katrina struck, driving Social Security reform out of the news and replacing it with horrific images of suffering, destruction, and government paralysis. For the White House, it was one fiasco after another. The president had no sooner praised the director of the Federal Emergency Management Agency, Michael Brown, than Brown had to be forced out because of the manifest incompetence of the government's performance. Bush's praise, "You're doing a heckuva job, Brownie," not only betrayed his ignorance of what was happening inside his own administration, but the casual, almost flippant tone suggested a profound failure to understand the tragedy that had befallen the Gulf Coast and thousands of its people. And this time, instead of forming a protective ring around their president, congressional Republicans—especially in the Senate—launched investigations that would reveal in stupefying detail how completely the Bush White House had failed in the country's biggest crisis since 9/11. As weeks turned into months and the administration continued to falter, public opinion about Bush's performance in office plunged ever lower.

Katrina also exposed another fissure in the Republican coalition. Spending hawks, already grumbling over the return of big deficits, balked at the multibillion-dollar price of reconstruction. That made it even harder for the White House to show that it was getting on top of the problem: without massive infusions of federal aid—including a major increase in spending for flood control—New Orleans and the Gulf Coast were stymied, unlikely to recover for years, if ever. And it was lost on nobody in the one-party movement that the vast majority of the victims in this case were black—seemingly undermining every recent GOP effort to cast the party as a comfortable home for African Americans in the twenty-first century.

Amid all this, the campaign to create private investment accounts in Social Security was quietly laid to rest. Democrats portrayed it as a major defeat for one of the most cherished ideas of the conservative coalition. Americans, they said, were not ready to abandon six decades of social progress after all. Conservatives insisted privatization was not dead but only deferred. They had made the case for private accounts and strategists insisted the investor class had heard it. What's more, they claimed, the West Wing alliance with corporate America remained very much intact, well heeled, and ready to soldier on.

Meanwhile, another trial was under way on the plan for long-term conservative dominance, this one involving the Supreme Court.

CHAPTER 9

Put to the Test: The Bench

One of George W. Bush's greatest contributions as president will be the changes he's brought about in our courts and our legal culture.

—KARL ROVE, SPEECH TO THE FEDERALIST SOCIETY, WASHINGTON, D.C., NOVEMBER 10, 2005

I t's not always easy, but almost any law or executive branch regulation can be overturned when a new party takes power. What cannot be reversed is the appointment of a federal judge. With lifetime tenure on the bench, strong-willed federal judges may have decades to shape the law to suit their ideological leanings, no matter which party controls Congress and the White House. Over time, a cadre of like-minded and determined judges can reconfigure the landscape in which policy makers work, advancing the interests of one party and point of view over those of its rivals. It was a recognition of this reality of the American Constitutional system that led a frustrated Franklin Roosevelt to launch his ill-fated court-packing scheme, hoping to dilute the power of conservative Supreme Court justices who were striking down New Deal initiatives. This same understanding of the long-term impact of the judicial branch led George W. Bush and his political allies to make shaking up the courts one of their top priorities.

As Bush and others described it, their goal was to end the reign of "activist" judges, by which they meant jurists who supported abortion rights, gay marriage, affirmative action, and other liberal policies. What conservatives said they wanted instead were judges who would show "judicial restraint," jurists who would not "legislate" from the bench. Some advocated a theory called "original intent"—interpreting the law and the Constitution to mean what the Founding Fathers intended it to mean.

In practical terms, such phrases are primarily political buzzwords. The Constitution is literally silent on the question of abortion rights, for instance, just as it is on the question of whether homosexuals may marry. Similarly, the Constitution does not directly address the question of whether a state Supreme Court justice may erect a monument inscribed with the Ten Commandments in his courthouse, or under exactly what circumstances the state of Florida may recount the ballots in a cliff-hanger presidential election. Nor is there any evidence that the Founding Fathers discussed these issues when they met in Philadelphia in 1787 to draft the Constitution. Affirmative action apparently did not come up either, though on this as on other questions the evidence is somewhat sketchy because the Constitutional Convention met behind closed doors and no systematic record of its deliberations was kept. Over the years, federal judges, conservative and liberal, have steered by whatever moral, legal, or political compasses they chose to employ. And both liberal and conservative jurists have struck down laws approved by Congress and signed by the president with great regularity; some Republicans have complained that the Supreme Court was especially vigorous in overturning legislation during the years that William H. Rehnquist, a Nixon appointee, was chief justice.

Indeed, it is precisely the absence of clear-cut, universally accepted rules for making decisions that gives federal judicial appointments their particular importance—especially to political groups with long-term agendas. The kind of fundamental ideological and political change sought by conservatives at the beginning of the twenty-first century could not be complete without remaking the nation's legal system along lines that groups such as the Federalist Society and the Heritage Foundation advocated. Gaining control of the federal bench—especially the Supreme Court—would not only enable them to put their stamp on law and policy, but also help them achieve permanent majority status in national politics. Business corporations, for instance, wanted protection from trial lawyers and their costly civil liability lawsuits. Evangelicals wanted to overturn *Roe v. Wade*, the 1973 Supreme Court ruling that legalized abortion. By enacting so-called lawsuit reform, Republican strategists could suck resources away from trial lawyers, who, along with labor unions, formed the financial backbone of the Democratic Party. In pushing a business agenda, they could also ensure ample financing for the costly political operations that were required in order to build a permanent majority. By appointing antiabortion justices to the high court, they could ensure that the energy, moral fervor, and votes of antiabortion religious groups remained in the service of the GOP. This is not to question the moral and ideological commitment of George W. Bush or Republican strategists such as Rove and Mehlman to limiting civil lawsuits or striking down abortion rights. It is just to note that the issues they pursued had a practical political dimension, too.

In the case of lawsuit reform, the Federalist Society and other such groups had provided the policy rationale and Bush had embraced the issue going back to his gubernatorial campaigns in Texas. He presented the case against tort litigation not as a boon for big business or for the Republican Party. Rather, he pushed it as a benefit for working people and consumers. Trial lawyers, he and other Republicans argued, took advantage of sympathetic juries and liberal judges to win multimillion-dollar judgments against companies and medical practitioners. Ultimately, ordinary people paid for those judgments in the form of higher prices and reduced service. Bush repeatedly argued that medical malpractice suits, particularly against gynecologists, made practicing medicine so costly that many doctors gave up and left their communities, while the rising cost of malpractice insurance forced the remaining doctors to raise their fees.

Jeb Bush pressed the same agenda in Florida, winning lawsuit limits and passage of new laws that gave him greater power to appoint conservative judges to the state bench. And immediately after his 2004 reelection, President Bush made clear that such changes would be a second-term priority in the White House.

"To accelerate the momentum of this economy and to keep creating jobs, we must take practical measures to help our job creators, the entrepreneurs and the small business owners," Bush said on November 4, at his first press conference following the election. "We must confront the frivolous lawsuits that are driving up the cost of health care and hurting doctors and patients."

Since their days together in Texas, Rove and Bush viewed trial lawyers as tribal enemies. They believed that these lawyers reaped millions in contingency fees at the expense of GOP business allies, and then invested the money in liberal causes and campaigns. Lawyers and their allied organizations pumped at least $30 million into Democratic causes during the 2004 election cycle.[1] Diminishing the influence of that key Democratic special interest was a stepping-stone to ensuring GOP dominance.

As one of the Republican Party's own new stars, South Dakota senator John Thune, put it shortly after he ousted Senate Democratic leader Tom Daschle: "If we could succeed in getting some form of litigation reform passed—medical malpractice reform or any of part of that—it would go a long ways toward . . . taking away the muscle, the financial muscle that they have."[2]

For the U.S. Chamber of Commerce, this was not a new insight. For decades, chamber officials had recognized the power of courts and juries to hit corporations with large judgments and attendant bad publicity. Since 2000, the chamber had poured nearly $100 million from its Institute for Legal Reform into political campaigns for state judges and attorneys general. The chamber took credit for making the legal climate more business-friendly in Michigan, Ohio, West Virginia, Texas, and other states, thus reducing the number of lawsuits filed and shrinking damage awards levied against corporations. The man in charge of this effort, a former Nixon White House aide named Stanton Anderson, readily acknowledged the potential political benefits. "I want to de-fund the trial lawyers—that's a primary goal," Anderson said in an interview.[3] The chamber's legal reform operations were well funded, thanks to the help of some of the nation's biggest insurance carriers, the retailer Wal-Mart, and other firms willing to pay $1 million each to defeat judges viewed as likely to favor large judgments against corporate defendants.[4]

In 2004, Anderson went so far as to establish a newspaper in Madison County, Illinois, just to fight the issue. Over the years, Madison County had become famous for granting large awards in liability lawsuits. As a result, trial lawyers looked there for favorable judgments, while corporate groups came to regard it as a symbol of a legal system run amok. The new paper, the *Madison County Record*, featured commentary advocating limits on damage awards and rebuking judges deemed overly sympathetic to plaintiffs. The paper's Web site displayed slogans such as "Land of Lincoln has become the land of lawsuit abuse." One article, headlined "Public Nuisance," profiled a local lawyer suing a major corporation. The piece branded the lawyer "perhaps the Metro East's most aggravating plaintiff's attorney." In late 2005, the chamber bankrolled a second, similar newspaper in West Virginia. The chamber tended to invest its funds in battleground states and its efforts were often helpful to Republican campaigns.

In public at least, Bush's intense focus on issues important to business came at the expense of some of the social issues that dominated his campaign, such as his commitment to a "culture of life" and his support for a constitutional ban on gay marriage. He did not talk about those issues during his first postelection press conference, which was dominated by discussion of jobs and the economy. Still, social conservatives and evangelical leaders believed that Bush would reward their campaign efforts. That payback, they believed, would come when the president filled the first of as many as three anticipated Supreme Court vacancies. They counted on Bush to use judicial appointments both to achieve their policy goals and—by provoking a high-profile battle with Democrats and liberal interest groups—to motivate the evangelical base and to keep donations flowing to antiabortion groups and other conservative organizations.

Evangelical leaders received their much-awaited signal within weeks of the election. It came in a written White House statement issued during the typically quiet Christmas break. The administration announced that Bush would soon renominate twenty jurists to the federal bench whose Senate confirmations had been blocked by Democrats who branded them as right-wing ideologues with extreme views on race, abortion, and the environment. Liberal groups such as People for the American Way and their Democratic friends in the Senate fumed. But the numbers favored Bush. The 2004 election had boosted the number of Republican senators to fifty-five, just five short of the supermajority required to stop Democratic filibusters. Moreover, Majority Leader Bill Frist was openly suggesting that the GOP might use its majority to change Senate rules to prohibit filibusters on judicial nominations.

The suggestion was cheered by Christian conservatives. But in the Senate, it was considered so drastic that it became known as the nuclear option. Such a rule change might have been unthinkable in the gentlemanly Senate of the past, but it reflected the modern-day Republican tactic of turning a small advantage in one area into a lasting structural advantage in another. Eliminating the filibuster required using the Republicans' bare majority to change the rules so that, in the future, a bare majority was all that would be needed to confirm even the most conservative judge. Moreover, leaders of a slim Senate majority in the past would have feared such a rule change coming back to haunt them if they should later wind up back in the minority. But by even considering the nuclear option, Frist and the GOP were demonstrating confidence in the one-party strategy. Each side knew the standoff was a preview of events to come—when one of several anticipated Supreme Court vacancies would arise.

Into that fractious environment jumped John Engler, the long-time Bush friend who had recently taken the reins at the National Association of Manufacturers. Engler had already emerged as a power player who helped mobilize his organization on behalf of the White House and the GOP during the election. Now he was proclaiming himself united with the White House to transform the federal courts. The U.S. Chamber of Commerce had already made an aggressive push to change the third branch of government in the states, drawing large corporate donations into the once tranquil world of judicial elections. Engler was going to use the manufacturers' lobby to do the chamber one better. He not only promised future funding and grassroots action in state races, but he offered help for the White House in upcoming confirmation battles for federal nominees.

In the past, business groups had tended to stay on the sidelines when it came to Supreme Court nominations, and they had ignored most other federal judicial nominations.[5] There were few parallels for applying the kind of muscle that Engler had in mind. His new project, called the American Justice Partnership, would build on the business lobby's 2004 campaign achievements, using its grassroots network to influence the only branch of the government not yet entirely under GOP control. Unlike the chamber, the manufacturers' association would mobilize at the grassroots, Engler said. In interviews, he expressed hope that the Business-Industry Political Action Committee—an organization the manufacturers had helped establish decades earlier to engage businesses in legislative races—could now help in judicial confirmation battles. Engler's announcement and his pugnacious response to liberal critics reflected his determination to push the manufacturers further into the political arena. Under his direction, the group representing the nation's biggest manufacturers would effectively become an arm of the GOP, quick to fall in line behind the White House to mobilize on behalf of the party and its priorities. Rather than lobbying for the manufacturers' narrow interests, the National Association of Manufacturers under Engler would lobby the American public on behalf of a Republican president. But Engler would argue that advocating for the judicial nominees of a Republican president would ultimately serve the interests of the association's members.

The involvement of lobbies such as the National Association of Manufacturers could be a powerful force in a closely fought legislative battle. The association's ten thousand members included such behemoths as General Motors, Boeing, and Caterpillar. Its broad reach could put a squeeze on moderate senators whose votes had helped block confirmation of ten appellate nominees during Bush's first term. Several of those senators faced reelection in 2006 and were already hearing threats from religious conservative leaders. As one stunned senior Democratic staffer cautioned at the time of Engler's announcement, "It's certainly going to up the ante and increase the pressure on vulnerable Democratic senators. I can't think of a similar situation where a group so little identified with such a debate is getting involved at this level in this way."[6]

Engler's plan was praised by White House officials and conservative activists who had already been working with businessmen to promote changes in the courts. It also offered one of the first post-2004 examples of how Republicans intended to apply their massive vote gathering and public relations apparatus to struggles over issues.

Engler's declaration was immediately greeted with concern from the left. "I believe that a sizable percentage of NAM's membership would be stunned to learn that NAM's leadership has decided to join the right wing's effort to eliminate a constitutional right to privacy, to strong civil rights protection and a woman's right to reproductive freedom," said People for the American Way president Ralph Neas.[7] Engler argued that the effort to "cast this in terms of a few social issues that Neas and his supporters deem important ignores the fact that much of the work of the courts has to do with America's ability to compete internationally."[8]

In effect, Engler was making the case for why social conservatives and business advocates were on the same team when it came to the federal courts. In truth, he argued, businesses might have more at stake than antiabortion activists. "There has been too much of a tendency in the past to cast these judgeship battles as a social debate about abortion or gay rights," he said. "In fact, there are very few of those cases in contrast to those dealing with the tort system and the rights of individuals and companies."[9]

But just as some in the business world were uneasy about jumping into the Social Security fight, Engler ran into some opposition over getting into the battle over judicial nominations. Some CEOs feared putting their companies' names, reputations, and share prices on the line to join a team that included some of the country's most controversial evangelical leaders and social conservatives. Some privately groused at National Association of Manufacturers board meetings, complaining that Engler was asking them to join fights that were effectively about abortion, affirmative action, school prayer, flag desecration, and other social issues that had nothing to do with their fiduciary responsibilities to shareholders and customers. Two members of the association, General Electric Company and the Southern Company, a multistate electric utility, opted out of the project.[10] Even a comrade in the Gang of Six—the informal group of lobbyists who knit the business community to the conservative movement—Dirk Van Dongen, of the wholesaler distributors group, said his organization was reluctant to play in the court debates. "Supreme Court nomination fights tend to be about abortion in the public mind, and our members are not interested in our getting involved in social issues," he said.[11]

While individual firms opted out, the nation's two leading business associations had committed themselves to be political players in judicial issues in ways they had not been previously. Corporate America was, at least on paper, engaged with social conservatives in a unified effort.

The ability of these groups to work together on this issue faced its first difficult test in the spring of 2005. Democrats had been blocking the confirmation of several Bush nominees to the federal bench whom they described as "extreme." Their opposition focused on two in particular: Janice Rogers Brown, a California Supreme Court judge who once referred to the New Deal as a "socialist revolution," and Priscilla Owen, a member of the Texas Supreme Court who sided with corporations in high-profile cases and authored a series of decisions that effectively weakened state civil rights statutes. The Democrats had blocked Brown and Owen and eight other nominees the previous year using the filibuster. Ending that longtime practice in judicial confirmations became a rallying cry for conservatives during 2005. Senate majority leader Frist, eyeing the 2008 presidential nomination and eager to court the conservative coalition, began speaking out about the need to change Senate rules. "One way or another, the filibuster of judicial nominees must end," he said in a speech to the Federalist Society in December 2004, labeling the use of filibusters against judicial nominees a "formula for tyranny by the minority."[12]

As the year wore on, wealthy businessmen and evangelical Christians poured millions of dollars into ad campaigns backing Bush's nominees. Progress for America, a group that had dumped tens of millions of dollars into ads promoting Bush's reelection, aired television commercials calling for up or down votes on the president's judicial choices. The Family Research Council and another powerful evangelical group, Focus on the Family, founded by James C. Dobson, a child psychologist turned evangelical activist, sponsored "Justice Sunday," a Christian call-to-arms broadcast nationally from a church in Louisville, Kentucky. It urged support for God-fearing, conservative judges. Frist appeared by videotape, while others appeared in person at the six-thousand-member Highview Baptist Church to speak from a stage adorned with massive pictures of some of Bush's most conservative judicial nominees. Dobson, whose radio show and ministry reached several million people, railed against the "out-of-control" Supreme Court.

Although their support was sought, business groups had not initially joined in the fight over the filibuster rule. To bring them in, the White House deputized a group of outside activists known as the "four horsemen": C. Boyden Gray, tobacco heir and White House counsel for the first President Bush who had formed the business-backed Committee for Justice to push conservative court nominees; former attorney general Edwin Meese, who maintained close ties to social conservatives and wealthy philanthropies; Jay Sekulow, a Jew-turned-evangelical-Christian who was chief counsel for the Reverend Pat Robertson's American Center for Law and Justice; and Leonard Leo, a vice president of the Federalist Society.

The horsemen conferred weekly by telephone and often huddled with top Republican National Committee officials and the White House's chief liaison to the conservative movement, Tim Goeglein.[13] Despite lashes from the horsemen, leading business groups continued to stay out of the filibuster fight, fearing it would slow or halt Senate progress on other business priorities. U.S. Chamber of Commerce CEO Tom Donohue told reporters that he opted out of the filibuster fight out of concern that "all else is going to stop," in the Senate.[14] Democrats had threatened as much and, in the early months of 2005, Donohue and other business leaders believed they were on a roll with the issues that mattered most to business. They had already won passage of long-sought measures to shield large businesses from class-action lawsuits. They were on the verge of winning an eight-year battle for legislation making it more difficult for consumers to declare bankruptcy and avoid debts to credit card companies and automobile dealers. The business leaders also believed, correctly, they could soon secure passage of energy legislation sought by oil and gas companies as well as limits on lawsuits against the many firms that had used asbestos.

The last thing business wanted was to shut down Congress. But that's exactly what their party partners, religious conservatives, hoped would happen. The disagreement was troubling for those who believed the coalition that reelected Bush could morph into a durable alliance to reshape government and its place in American life.

Tony Perkins, the president of the Family Research Council, the group sponsoring "Justice Sunday," highlighted this divide during a closed-door meeting with activists in March. He drew applause by mentioning the potential for a Senate shutdown. "That might be the best thing," said Perkins, according to an audio recording of the March meeting that had been captured by the advocacy group Americans United for Separation of Church and State and disclosed to the Los Angeles Times. "As I've sat in this city, been here in this city, you know, gridlock is not a bad thing," he said. "Rarely do they do things for us. Usually it's against us."

The comments by Perkins, who was joined by his comrade Dobson, illustrated exactly how feelings on the religious side of the GOP contrasted with the more practical impulses of the business wing. Dobson predicted that the war over judges would be the "mother of all battles." He and Perkins strongly implied that they had been working with like-minded members of Congress on a plan to abolish courts they considered too liberal, specifically citing the California-based Ninth U.S. Circuit Court of Appeals. The Ninth Circuit had enraged conservatives by holding that the words "Under God" in the Pledge of Allegiance were unconstitutional. "There's more than one way to skin a cat, and there's more than one way to take a black robe off the bench," Perkins said, according to the tape provided to the *Times*. Dobson added: "Very few people know this, that the Congress can simply disenfranchise a court. They don't have to fire anybody or impeach them or go through that battle. All they have to do is say the Ninth Circuit doesn't exist anymore, and it's gone." It was an extreme notion by any standard, but the comments that day by Dobson and Perkins showed just how much the one-party mentality had seeped into the everyday thinking of the movement's leaders—how far they were prepared to go, not only to win a particular battle but to gain permanent, structural advantages.

Some Republicans distanced themselves from such talk. A spokesman for Senate majority leader Frist said the senator did not agree with the strategy of de-funding courts. But for Frist, the contrasting approaches of business and religious leaders presented a dilemma. Rather than building friendships all across the Republican Party, he was being pressed to take sides against one or the other of the two pillars of conservative politics: evangelicals, with their proven ability to marshal millions of voters; and business, the source for millions of dollars in campaign contributions and a newly proven weapon in delivering political messages to workers.

The tension between business leaders and social conservatives over the filibuster fight foreshadowed potential problems for the GOP in the 2006 and 2008 elections and in the one-party coalition's ability to keep its varied interests unified and focused over the longer term. Republicans continued to rely on an energized and unified base to win closely fought contests, but in giving too high a priority to the agenda of business interests, GOP leaders risked deflating a crucial segment of that base. Eventually, the Senate confirmed several of Bush's appellate nominees after a bipartisan group of moderates struck an agreement to let some judges through in order to avoid the dreaded nuclear option.

If the battle over the appellate nominees was a warm-up, the real show opened in early July, when Justice Sandra Day O'Connor, the longtime moderate swing vote on abortion and affirmative action and other hot-button topics, told Bush in a teary conversation that she would retire. Days of frenzied speculation over what constituency Bush might seek to satisfy for his first high-court appointment ended when Bush tapped John Roberts, a brilliant and politically agile judge from the District of Columbia U.S. Circuit Court of Appeals.

Although Roberts's views on hot social issues were unclear—he had once provided advice to lawyers asserting gay rights but his wife was an ardent antiabortion activist—he boasted a long record of representing corporate clients before the Supreme Court. He was also rich, thanks to his investments. And he turned out to be a relaxed, reassuring, and utterly unflappable witness on his own behalf when he appeared before the Senate Judiciary Committee. He was clearly conservative, but he was graceful and good-humored in turning aside questions designed to draw him into ideological controversy. The death of Chief Justice Rehnquist—coming as the administration struggled to cope with the devastation and political fallout wrought by Hurricane Katrina's destructive collision with New Orleans and the Gulf Coast—prompted Bush to nominate Roberts for that slot rather than O'Connor's. Roberts was the business community's kind of candidate and it quickly offered support for the nominee. Both the chamber and the National Association of Manufacturers formally endorsed his confirmation. During September, when the nomination was pending, the judge's photo dominated the manufacturers' association Web site along with a headline: "The Business Case for Supreme Court Chief Justice Nominee John Roberts."

Other pillars of the conservative movement joined the push, with the Family Research Council and Sekulow's American Center for Law and Justice distributing mass e-mails to their growing grassroots networks. If the reelection of President Bush had been a culmination of sorts for the conservative movement's one-party electoral ambitions, the Roberts nomination emerged as a bright spot for what the network could achieve in governance. With social and economic conservatives united behind Roberts, he went on to win easy Senate confirmation, securing votes from every Republican and half the Democrats in the Senate. In the wake of Katrina and the mounting scandals that continued to ensnare some of the movement's most pivotal players, the Roberts confirmation provided a sweet victory for the White House and its allies.

Despite the smooth appearance of the coalition's support for Roberts, there were signs of strain behind the scenes. Engler had pressed BIPAC to make its resources available to companies wanting to support the nominee through election-style grassroots efforts such as e-mails, corporate meetings, and phone calls. But the group's steering committee—made up of a dozen executives—voted not to jump completely into the fight. Instead, the group offered limited access to its network: making available pro-Roberts Web pages and downloadable form letters to Capitol Hill. Only a few companies took BIPAC up on its offers, and only about one thousand letters were downloaded. By contrast, when BIPAC members were invited to write on asbestos lawsuits, nearly forty thousand letters were downloaded, showing that many businesses remained more comfortable engaging with issues that directly affected their bottom line.

With the Roberts victory behind them, conservatives looked forward to another Supreme Court victory, filling the vacant O'Connor seat. It was to be the revenge they had waited for, ever since the defeat of Supreme Court nominee and conservative hero Robert Bork in the 1980s. For many social conservatives, changing the court was the motivating force behind their enthusiasm for Bush's reelection. And nothing was more important than replacing O'Connor's shifting views with a reliably conservative vote. Republican activists in Washington expected Bush to consult the GOP durable majority playbook as he made his choice. Would he make history by naming the first Hispanic justice, fostering a legacy with the nation's fastest-growing constituency? Would he go with a woman to boost GOP chances with a gender that still leaned Democratic? Surely, conservatives felt, Bush would at a minimum find a rock-solid conservative to finally transform the court.

But on the very day that John Roberts took his seat as Chief Justice, the movement was stunned by the president's announcement that he was nominating his longtime friend and White House counsel, Harriet Miers, to replace O'Connor. Miers was an unknown. She had never been a judge. She had no experience outside a limited role representing business clients for a Texas firm. Only scattered, sometimes contradictory clues existed about her views and judicial philosophy. And there was nothing apparent in her career to distinguish her from literally thousands of other capable but undistinguished members of her profession—unless you counted her history of writing embarrassingly idolatrous notes to and about Bush. Overnight, the Miers nomination plunged the conservative movement into crisis. For many activists, the nomination was an offensive back-of-the-hand to the years of work and millions of dollars that the movement had devoted to recruiting and training conservative jurists qualified to sit on the high court. Decades of research, fellowships, internships, expansion of the Federalist Society into liberal-bastion law schools—all were part of the effort to purge the legal system of liberal toxins—and in the process further the plan for a one-party country. For conservative intellectuals, the Miers nomination was a waste of what the movement had built. And it was insulting at a deeper level as well. As best anyone could determine, the reason Miers had been chosen was because the White House thought her limited résumé and lack of a record would make her hard to attack: liberals would be forced to reveal that they actually opposed any nominee who was not one of them—to admit that it was liberals, not conservatives, who had a litmus test for judges. There were two problems with that line of reasoning, as conservative intellectuals saw it. First, it implied that conservative legal values openly expressed might not prove acceptable, that they had to be advanced by stealth—a proposition that mocked the conservatives' belief that they represented the nation's deepest and truest values. The second problem was that conservative intellectuals yearned for a high-profile advocate of their ideas. They wanted a judicial giant who would not merely vote right but articulate the conservative credo in such dazzling terms that it would eclipse the long-dominant dogma of liberalism. For these conservatives, Harriet Miers was an embarrassment.

A long and rapidly growing list of conservative icons publicly criticized her selection. Paul Weyrich of the Free Congress Foundation; William Kristol, editor of the *Weekly Standard*; columnists George Will and Charles Krauthammer; American Conservative Union president David Keene; and former presidential contender Patrick

Buchanan all expressed dismay. Even reliable administration defenders like radio talk show host Rush Limbaugh and Senator Trent Lott ridiculed the appointment. Formerly loyal White House allies, including Judge Robert Bork and speechwriter Peggy Noonan, called Miers unqualified. Her nomination was pure cronyism, they said, and a lost opportunity. Core elements in the coalition that had proven so effective in pushing the White House agenda were erupting in full rebellion.

Emotions boiled over at Grover Norquist's Wednesday meeting two days after she was named. The White House had dispatched one of its ablest advocates, Ed Gillespie, to reassure the troops. But Gillespie's face reddened as speaker after speaker condemned the nomination. One longtime movement heavyweight stared the former Republican National Committee chairman in the eye and said, "This is just like the 'read my lips' blunder that cost the first president Bush his support from the right." The audience of one hundred burst into applause. These were the captains and the lieutenants in the fight against the old Democratic coalition. Yet here they were clapping at accusations that the Bush White House had betrayed them. Bush "acceded to the left, because he has said that a jurist with established conservative credentials cannot be confirmed for the Supreme Court," said Richard Lessner, former director of the American Conservative Union. "He has capitulated to that view and that's why this is a major loss for the conservative movement."[15]

The White House tried to rally by seeking public support from influential conservatives outside Washington. Rove called Dobson four times to convince him to publicly back Miers. Dobson did so, telling fellow members of an evangelical coalition called the Arlington Group that he was not at liberty to explain why he had decided to support her. Dobson did influence some evangelicals. But many of his conservative allies remained unconvinced. Weyrich, for example, said he could not help but compare Bush's "trust me" promises to those of previous Republican presidents from Nixon to Reagan who had appointed Sandra Day O'Connor, Anthony Kennedy, John Paul Stevens, Harry Blackmun, and David Souter with similar assurances. Weyrich recalled that the Reagan White House had actually put him and other conservatives on a conference call with Kennedy's priest. "He told us Kennedy was pro-life," Weyrich said, noting that Kennedy later joined the majority in upholding abortion rights.[16]

Norquist defended the White House against its strongest critics, saying that the nomination was "not a betrayal because we don't know how she will vote." But, he said, "it was a huge disappointment. We were promised a Bo Derek 'ten.' What we got was a fuzzy, fixed portrait of Anne of Cleaves," a reference to a flattering painting that convinced England's King Henry VIII to marry Anne. When the king saw her in person, he said he had been misled and had the marriage annulled.

The Miers nomination exposed deep fissures within the conservative movement, underscoring again the fragility of the plan to build a twenty-first-century Republican replacement for the Democrats' New Deal coalition. The uproar also underscored Rove's continuing importance in pushing the Bush agenda and coaxing the conservative coalition to move forward in unity. Bush had nominated Miers in September 2005, just as Rove was preparing for his fourth appearance before the grand jury investigating the Valerie Plame CIA leak case. His legal problems had distracted Rove, some friends suggested, and had blurred his usually penetrating political vision. In October, with the grand jury appearance behind him, Rove and others in the White House recognized the destructive power of the Miers nomination. Rather than a fight with liberals that would excite the conservative base, it had provoked conservatives to attack one another. So Miers withdrew her name, giving up the chance for a lifetime appointment to save the Republican coalition from imploding.

With that, the one-party coalition did a swift pivot and worked in unison to turn an apparent setback into a major achievement. Miers was replaced by a New Jersey federal appeals judge named Samuel Alito, a well-known conservative with years of written opinions to prove it. "The disappointment disappeared as soon as the announcement was made," said Norquist. "It was like lifting a fog." Alito's nomination, like Roberts's before him, illustrated the power of the one-party movement. Both men were relatively young. Both had served legal apprenticeships under previous Republican presidents.

And both gave their supporters every reason to suppose that they had the intellectual gravitas to bring about the kind of permanent change conservatives sought. At least where the courts were concerned, the machinery that Rove, Mehlman, and Norquist had put together seemed to be working once again.

But those strategists knew that elections were won with more than just machinery and a favorable legal climate. Parties succeeded first and foremost by presenting good candidates and coherent messages. Even if all else were stacked in the GOP's favor, poor candidate recruitment and a sour message would overpower the most sophisticated political strategy. And in the fall of 2005, things were turning sour. President Bush's popularity sank. So did that of the Republican congressional leadership. In addition to Rove's entanglement with the CIA leak case, Tom DeLay continued to fight his own indictments, had been stripped of his leadership post, and would later announce that he would not seek reelection to the House. Bill Frist, the Senate leader who had tried so hard to thread the needle with Christian conservatives and business lobbyists in anticipation of his presidential bid, faced an investigation into his stock dealings by the Securities and Exchange Commission. The wide-ranging Abramoff investigation continued to threaten prominent Republicans; a senior White House budget aide was arrested in September 2005 for making repeated false statements to government officials and investigators about the case.

The White House that autumn was inundated with other problems as well: the public relations wreckage over its response to the Gulf Coast hurricanes and an increasingly deadly, unpopular, and costly war. Democrats during the first Bush term were famously limp in their attempts to mount a case against the Republican majority. But by early 2006, it seemed, the Republicans were making the case themselves. Would the Democrats develop a coherent message to seize on the GOP's apparent weaknesses? Or would the machine that Rove, Mehlman, and Bush put into place survive these immediate woes and go on to earn more long-term gains?

Epilogue

I n the preceding pages, we have told the story of how the Republican Party gained a remarkable series of strategic, structural,
and organizational advantages over a period of several decades.
The 2004 election, in which George W. Bush scored an unequivocal
victory only four years after entering the White House with the support of less than half the voters, was a milestone in the GOP's quest
for one-party dominance. And its continued success in state and local
contests reflected both the depth and breadth of the movement's
strength. The 2006 midterm elections would be a first test of the
durability of that achievement.

For its part, the GOP entered the 2006 cycle with unusually
serious problems. There was the Iraq war, of course, along with the
scandals that enmeshed former House leader Tom DeLay and
the Republican congressmen who had dealings with lobbyist Jack
Abramoff. And the president seemed to have lost his way with the
public. Neither his governing philosophy nor his agenda had changed
materially, yet his approval rating had gone into a free fall, hitting
just 38 percent by the spring of 2006. So dramatic was the slide that

Bush could only joke about it. At the annual Gridiron Club dinner, he cracked that when he broke the news of his laggard rating to Dick Cheney, whose own approval rating stood at 18 percent, the vice president responded, "What's your secret?"

Karl Rove, whose own legal fate remained in question, seemed to have lost his almost magical ability to pick candidates ideally suited to win key races. In state after state, prospective Senate candidates were telling Rove no thanks. A prime example was Florida, where the GOP controlled every statewide office except Democrat Bill Nelson's Senate seat. In 2004, Rove had personally lured Cuban-born Mel Martinez onto the ballot, in part to rev up Latino voters for the president's reelection. But in 2006, every prospect that Rove and the national leadership approached said no, leaving the GOP without a credible challenger. In Ohio, the Republican grip on the state that put President Bush over the top in 2004 was threatened by the Abramoff affair and by a state corruption scandal that tainted the governor and many prominent GOP leaders.

Beyond such immediate—and potentially ephemeral—problems, the Republicans faced a largely unforeseen crisis within their base. The battle over immigration, which divided congressional Republicans and sent tens of thousands of angry Hispanics into the streets, pitted the party's business wing against many social conservatives and split the evangelicals as well. Moreover, the virtual stagnation of middle-class incomes, coupled with rising health-care costs and gas prices, were eating away at public confidence in the GOP's economic stewardship. Considered as a whole, the U.S. economy seemed to be growing nicely with relatively little inflation. But middle-class voters expressed increasing dissatisfaction, in part because the gains did not seem to trickle down and also because of an alarming stream of news reports about corporations abandoning pensions and other commitments to their workers. At the very least, rising concern about bread-and-butter issues threatened to reduce the effectiveness of once-powerful appeals based on moral or social values. Even Daniel Bartlett, the always optimistic White House spinmeister, had to acknowledge on the morning of Bush's 2006 State of the Union address that the public felt a palpable "level of angst."

Moreover, for the first time in thirty years, the conservative movement had to begin searching for a new standard-bearer. There was no clear heir to take the mantle of the Republican Party, and by all indications, the process shaped up as a bloodbath. One early front-runner was Senator John McCain of Arizona. But McCain had been Bush's rival, a critic of evangelical leaders who was distrusted by movement conservatives, including Grover Norquist, who opposed McCain's presidential candidacy in 2000. Subsequently, McCain's Senate committee investigation highlighted connections between Abramoff, Norquist, and other conservative movement leaders.

In 2006, McCain moved to the right with almost embarrassing élan. Norquist suggested that the Arizona Republican faced enormous hurdles to winning the affection of the right. "McCain's challenge is that he walked out of the conservative coalition and betrayed it on several occasions—on gun rights, on judicial confirmations, and on tax cuts," Norquist said. "Now he has got to explain to people why they should trust him in the future. That's going to be very difficult."[1]

All of this led the RNC's Ken Mehlman to make this characteristically antiseptic understatement: "This is a challenging environment."

As for the Democrats, they at last seemed to awaken to the seriousness of their plight. And their response included a large measure of that sincerest of all forms of flattery: imitation. In January 2006, for example, some of the party's highest congressional leaders gathered at the Library of Congress for a highly choreographed attack on what they called a Republican "culture of corruption." With a snare drum laying down a Revolutionary War beat in the background, members queued up to sign a new charter: the Declaration of Honest Leadership and Open Government.[2] The symbolism was not subtle. Democrats were hoping to create their own version of the Contract with America, Newt Gingrich's 1994 manifesto that helped galvanize the GOP takeover of the House for the first time in forty years.

Some of Washington's liberal activists knew that such theatrics would get the Democratic Party only so far. Acknowledging the structural differences that separated their party from the GOP, these activists organized a "Tuesday meeting," modeled directly on the success of Norquist's Wednesday gatherings of conservatives. And just as

Norquist convened his meeting every week at the offices of an organization representing the heart of the conservative movement—his own antitax activist group—the liberals met in the conference room of one of their own critical constituencies: the AFL-CIO. On the morning of the 2006 State of the Union address, the Tuesday Group was chaired by Bob Borosage, a longtime liberal strategist and codirector of the Campaign for America's Future. The group had helped lead grassroots opposition to Bush's plan to privatize Social Security. The meeting drew fifty or so attendees, far fewer than Norquist's gatherings. Still, the organizations represented that day in the AFL-CIO's comfortable first-floor conference room just a block from the White House suggested the potential for a new cohesiveness on the left.

The group included representatives from the Democratic National Committee, the labor unions, and People for the American Way, an organization bankrolled initially by Hollywood director Norman Lear that took a leading role in battling Bush's court nominees. They were joined by civil rights and environmental activists, along with leaders from the National Women's Law Center and the antipoverty Coalition for Human Needs. Equally significant was the presence of representatives from several new organizations that had formed to soothe tensions between wings of the liberal movement—tensions that had caused the movement to fray in the years since Republicans took control. The Apollo Alliance, for example, was created to link environmental groups such as the Sierra Club with labor unions whose members—in pursuit of jobs—had joined with Republicans on matters like expanding oil exploration in the Arctic National Wildlife Refuge. Republicans had successfully exploited those tensions, wooing steelworkers and coal miners in the traditionally Democratic battlegrounds of West Virginia and Pennsylvania by arguing for jobs over environmental restrictions. Liberals hoped the Apollo Alliance would highlight common ground and help halt the growing union member support for Republican candidates.

Another new addition, the Center for American Values in Public Life, was designed to rebuild Democrats' relationships with churches, an attempt to compensate for the GOP's success in mobilizing evangelicals and other religious conservatives of all ethnicities. This particular Tuesday meeting centered around a presentation from Cornell Belcher, a Democratic National Committee pollster who argued that the party was losing support from God-fearing voters. One survey showed that 70 percent of "frequent" churchgoers sided with the Republicans in 2004. "We can't hope to win if we continue to lose this group," Belcher said.

The most upbeat news for the alliance of the left came from the group America Coming Together, which was created in 2004 with help from billionaire George Soros to lead get-out-the-vote efforts in the presidential campaign. This group had successfully tested new outreach techniques in the 2005 Virginia governor's race and hoped to apply its findings to congressional, Senate, and governor's races nationwide.

Still, the activists gathered in that room were not delusional. They knew that despite the polls, the growing enthusiasm among liberal activists, and the efforts to strengthen the Democratic coalition, the party of the left remained behind the GOP as an effective political force.

Steve Rosenthal, the former union organizer who ran America Coming Together, conceded as much in interviews: come what may, the GOP had built a more sophisticated machine. The centerpiece of that machine, he said, was Voter Vault, which surpassed anything currently in the liberal movement's arsenal.

Logic would hold that the Democrats would rush to build their database, to catch up with Voter Vault, and return to an era in which liberals—not conservatives—reigned supreme in grassroots politics. Instead, more party infighting broke out, pitting Democratic National Committee chairman Howard Dean against tacticians who believed he was not devoting enough time or money to strengthening the party's voter file.

By the spring of 2006, a former Bill Clinton aide, Harold Ickes, was laying plans with Democratic Party veteran Laura Quinn for an expanded but privately financed voter database. Ickes and his allies believed that Dean was undervaluing the practice of microtargeting that was credited with so much of the GOP success. Rosenthal and Quinn, along with Donna Brazile, were among the Democrats' most seasoned experts on voter mobilization. But in early 2006 they had yet to discuss the matter in detail with Dean. The Democratic chairman insisted he understood the importance of building a state-of-the-art voter database and in 2006 said he had dedicated $6 million to doing that. But a Republican National Committee spokeswoman, Tracey Schmitt, said the Republicans were spending a considerably higher amount enhancing an already more sophisticated data set.[3] Dean, meanwhile, had other priorities: he was investing millions in staff and salaries to place organizers on the ground in the states rather than fully investing in the tools that had proven effective for the GOP.

There were more fundamental problems for the Democrats: they continually failed to articulate an overarching sense of purpose. Republicans, for all their problems, still easily identified their core principles: lower taxes, smaller government, reliance on market forces, promoting traditional values, and personal responsibility. Even the Bush foreign policy of spreading freedom was clear-cut and simple. What did Democrats stand for at the start of the twenty-first century? They rallied to defend Social Security and other progressive programs of the past, but they offered no coherent answer to the hottest issues of the moment: rapid globalization, growing economic disparities, and the soaring cost of health care.

The Democrats' deficiencies were laid completely bare over the issue of Iraq. Although solid majorities of Americans had concluded that the war was not worth the price and believed the Bush adminis-tration had mishandled it, Democrats had not agreed on an alterna-tive. Indeed, they seemed no closer to solving the riddle of wartime politics than John Kerry had been in 2004. Senator Hillary Clinton, the apparent Democratic front-runner for 2008, was triangulating as a hawk, but the liberal, antiwar base that elected Dean chairman was divided. Democrats bashed Bush for incompetence in waging the war, but the polls showed that the public remained skeptical that Democrats could offer a viable alternative. Democrats could not even agree how to respond when one of their own heroes, Representative John Murtha, a decorated former Marine and noted war hawk, called for a withdrawal of troops.

And all but three Senate Democrats scattered like startled mice when Senator Russ Feingold of Wisconsin offered a censure proposal against the president for his use of the National Security Agency to eaves-drop without warrants on certain domestic telephone conversations.

And while Republicans were divided over solutions to illegal immigration, the Democratic message was muted and largely irrele-vant. The party's congressional leaders were inclined to back liberal laws, but some Democrats feared they would be accused of being soft on crime if they opposed strict border enforcement. And labor unions were not fully supportive of loose immigration laws that many believed resulted in fewer jobs for Americans.

With the president's popularity sagging and a cloud of anxiety gathering over the GOP, Republicans hoped for a typical midterm election in which congressional results would be decided not by a national plebiscite but on local issues and personalities that tend to favor incumbents.

But by late spring, GOP hopes for a survivable storm were being threatened by the tsunami of scandals, screwups, and sinking poll rat-ings. Even some gerrymandered Republican House districts were shifting to the competitive column, and the fifteen seats the Democ-rats needed to seize control seemed attainable, and the Senate was in their sights as well.

But if Democrats are successful in 2006, there are few signs that their party will be prepared to turn those victories into a winning move-ment. As the preceding chapters illustrated, the structural foundations built by the Republicans are so firmly planted that one dismal election cycle alone will not be enough to shake them loose.[4] The tools of the one-party coalition—the business alliance, the voter database, the GOP tilt in redistricting, the money, and the control of the executive branch—will remain after the 2006 elections are over. Then, unless Democrats find a way to build firm foundations of their own, they will confront the same disadvantages that doomed them to the minority.

Nevertheless, Republican strategists had to face a tough reality in 2006: the one-party dream, decades in the making, faced a huge test.[5]

As GOP chairman Mehlman surveyed the situation, he acknowl-edged that conservatives had not locked up the electorate. Referring to the 2004 presidential balloting, he said, "We had a fifty-one percent election last time. We have a healthy, two-party system."

That did not mean he was writing off the dream of a durable conservative majority. The Republicans of the twenty-first century had not sought to duplicate the New Deal realignment, he said; the country was polarized in a way it was not back then. Now, the people would always be closely divided on major issues. "I never said to you I think we're going to be FDR," Mehlman said in an interview heading into the 2006 campaign. "The country's in a different place."

But so is the Republican Party. Rather than the Southern strategy, for instance, the GOP in 2006 had the potential to field four black candidates in major state races: for governor in Ohio and Pennsylvania and for the U.S. Senate in Michigan and Maryland. Republicans were competitive among Latinos across the country. And even in the aftermath of Hurricane Katrina, Mehlman was jetting from city to city making pitches to potentially sympathetic minority voters just as he had done on that night in February 2005 in Prince George's County, Maryland.

Still, when we asked him to consider the state of the one-party dream, Mehlman posed a question: "If you get fifty-one percent, fifty-one percent, fifty-one percent, is that a durable majority?"

Mehlman insisted he didn't know. And it would take more than one midterm election to provide even the beginnings of a historical answer. But given the winner-take-all realities of national politics, "51 percent, 51 percent, 51 percent" was something any Democratic strategist in the land would cheerfully settle for. And even with all the GOP's problems heading into 2006, few conservative strategists would have traded places with the Democrats.

NOTES

INTRODUCTION

1. Deans's remarks to the party's black caucus were reported widely in early February 2005. See, for example, Mark Lebovich, "Special Interest Group Hug," *Washington Post*, February 12, 2005, p. C1.
2. Authors' interview with David Bositis, Washington, D.C. If Bush had received the same proportion of black votes in Ohio as he did in 2000, the president's margin of victory could have narrowed from the actual 118,000 to about 25,000—close enough, says David Bositis, senior analyst at the Washington-based Joint Center for Political and Economic Studies, that Kerry could have reversed the results in court. Given the high number of provisional ballots filed in Ohio, said Bositis, "Ohio would have become Florida, the legal battleground of 2004." And Bush, like his father, would have returned to Texas as a one-term president.

1. THE REAL CENTER OF POWER

1. New York's conservative gathering, modeled after the Wednesday meeting in Washington, meets Monday evenings in Manhattan, chaired by Public Relations firm owner and GOP financial benefactor Mallory Factor.
2. Authors' interview with Grover Norquist, Washington, D.C., November 12, 2005.
3. Norquist permits only selected journalists to attend his Wednesday meetings and only on the condition that they consider comments made in the session off the record unless approved later by the individual speakers. The authors of this book attended more than a dozen meetings in 2004 and 2005 and obtained information about other meetings from attendees.
4. Chris Suellentrop, "Grover Norquist, the Republican Party's Prophet of Permanence," *Slate*, www.slate.com, posted July 7, 2003. See also Thomas B. Edsall, "Right in the Middle of the Revolution," *Washington Post*, September 4, 1995, p. A1.
5. Authors' interview with Grover Norquist, Washington, D.C., November 12, 2005. For further discussion of Norquist's coalition building, see John Maggs, "Grover at the Gate," *National Journal*, October 11, 2003. See also, Robert Dreyfuss, "Grover Norquist: Field Marshal of the Bush Tax Plan," *Nation*, May 14, 2001.

6. Gaffney has charged that Norquist has opened "important doors for pro-Islamist organizations" that he says are creating "the makings of a Saudi-funded Fifth Column in America." For a detailed look at Gaffney's charge, see Frank J. Gaffney, "A Troubling Influence," *Front Page*, www.frontpagemag.com/articles/readarticle.asp?ID=11210, posted December 9, 2003.

7. Tom Hamburger and Glenn Simpson, "Reaching Out: In Difficult Times, Muslims Count on Unlikely Advocate," *Wall Street Journal*, June 11, 2003.

8. Tom Hamburger interview with Hilary Rosen, Washington, D.C., September 2005.

9. Tom Hamburger interview with Donna Brazile, Washington, D.C., September 2005.

10. Wittman's views were first publicly reported by Peter Stone, "Jack and Grover's Long Adventure," *National Journal*, October 3, 2005. Wittman was interviewed during the summer of 2005 by researcher Benjamin Weyl. Wittman's thoughts on this topic are also discussed in an article by Michael Isikoff, Holly Bailey, and Evan Thomas, "Washington Tidal Wave, *Newsweek*, January 16, 2006.

11. Grover Norquist interview with "Frontline," Public Broadcasting Service, September 2, 2004, transcript available at www.pbs.org/wgbh/pages/frontline/shows/choice2004/interviews/norquist.html, posted October 12, 2004.

12. Grover Norquist, "The Democratic Party Is Toast," *Washington Monthly*, September 2004.

13. Norquist has mentioned "drowning government in the bathtub" to numerous journalists, including the authors, though he may have first uttered it in an interview with Mara Liasson on National Public Radio's *Morning Edition*, May 25, 2001.

2. Stacking the Electoral Deck

1. Barbara Bush, *Barbara Bush: A Memoir* (New York: Charles Scribner's Sons, 1994), p. 63.

2. George Bush, *All the Best, George Bush: My Life and Other Writings* (New York: Charles Scribner's Sons, 1999), p. 88.

3. Ibid.

4. Ibid.

5. David Robb, "Bush Covenants: George Bush's Record on Civil Rights and Racism Is Inconsistent with His Stated Beliefs," *Nation*, November 28, 1987, p. 616.

6. Bob Herbert, "Impossible, Ridiculous, Repugnant," *New York Times*, October 6, 2005.

7. Jake Tapper, "The Willie Horton Alumni Association," www.salon.com, posted August 25, 2000.

8. John Joseph Brady, *Bad Boy: The Life and Politics of Lee Atwater* (Reading, Mass.: Addison-Wesley, 1996).
9. This comes from researcher Benjamin Weyl's analysis of the Georgia secretary of state's office voter data.
10. The Justice Department had jurisdiction over states with a proven history of diluting minority voting strength; from authors' interviews with Benjamin Ginsberg during the spring of 2005.
11. Authors' interviews with Benjamin Ginsberg, Washington, D.C., spring 2005.
12. Ibid.
13. Tom Hamburger interview with Donna Brazile, Washington, D.C., September 2005.
14. Authors' interview with Benjamin Ginsberg, Washington, D.C., spring 2005.
15. "For the Republic or for the Republicans?," *National Journal*, December 9, 1989, p. 2986.
16. Ibid.
17. Karen Branch, "Two Candidates Wage Surprise Senate Battle," *Miami Herald*, October 29, 1998.
18. Guy Gugliotta, "Blacks Join Forces with GOP on Remap," *Washington Post*, May 11, 1992.
19. Ibid.
20. Bill Moss, "Redrawn Districts Help GOP, Minorities," *St. Petersburg Times*, November 15, 1992.
21. Ibid.
22. Twelve African Americans entered Congress as a result of redistricting changes. An additional African American, J. C. Watts, a Republican, was elected from Oklahoma, but his election is not attributable to redistricting. Research on redistricting from interviews with secretaries of state in several states by researcher Benjamin Weyl.
23. Kevin A. Hill, "Congressional Redistricting: Does the Creation of Majority Black Districts Aid Republicans?" *Journal of Politics* 57 (2): 384–401, May 1995.
24. Peter Wallsten interview with Miguel de Grandy, Miami, Florida, fall 2005.
25. Gugliotta, "Blacks Join Forces."
26. Peter Wallsten interview with Mark Gersh, Washington, D.C., spring 2005.
27. Texas redistricting efforts were stalled at this time by Democrats. But Texas congressman Tom DeLay would later harness his power in Washington to force changes in that state to add Republican seats and further enhance the GOP majority. Those actions helped spark a criminal probe into DeLay's political action committees and led to indictments of the House majority leader.
28. Larry Martz, "Biting the Bullet," *Newsweek*, July 9, 1990, p. 16.

29. Richard L. Berke, "G.O.P., in Revolt on Taxes, Steps Up Criticism of Bush," *New York Times*, June 28, 1990.
30. Election night atmospherics and detail drawn from the following accounts: Henry Allen, "The Republicans and the Faces of Defeat," *Washington Post*, November 4, 1992; Kathy Lewis, "The End of the Trail: Longtime Bush Supporters Emotional During Final Gathering with President," *Dallas Morning News*, November 4, 1992; Matthew Engel, "George Bush Bows Out with Grace," *Guardian*, November 5, 1992; and *Reuters News Service*, "Bush Concedes Election to Clinton," November 4, 1992.
31. John King, "Departing GOP Chief Delivers Abortion Warning," *Associated Press Wire*, January 29, 1993.

3. The End of the Southern Strategy

1. Lois Romano and George Lardner Jr., "Bush's Move Up to the Majors," *Washington Post*, July 31, 1999, p. A1.
2. Peter Schweitzer and Rochelle Schweitzer, *The Bushes: Portrait of a Dynasty* (New York: Doubleday, 2004).
3. Ibid., p. 414.
4. Ibid.
5. Lois Romano and George Lardner Jr., "Bush Earned Profit, Rangers Deal Insiders Say," *Washington Post*, July 31, 1999, p. 12A.
6. Romano and Lardner, "Bush's Move Up."
7. Ibid.
8. Ibid.
9. "Hispanics in the State of Texas: Highlights from the 2000 Census," Hispanic Research Center, University of Texas-San Antonio, April 8, 2002; see also U.S. Census Department, "2000 State and County QuikFacts."
10. Jorge Ramos, *Latino Wave* (New York: HarperCollins, 2004).
11. Authors' interview with Grover Norquist, Washington, D.C., summer 2005.
12. Ibid.
13. Ellen Debenport, "GOP Candidates Glibly Hold Court," *St. Petersburg Times*, July 28, 1994.
14. Ibid.
15. Brian E. Crowley and Larry Kaplow, "For Chiles and Bush, This Is Living on the Edge," *Palm Beach Post*, November 6, 1994, p. 1a.
16. Patrick Cockburn, "Bush Campaign Ad Sparks Backlash," *Independent*, November 5, 1994.
17. Brian E. Crowley, "Missteps Tripped Up Bush Campaign," *Palm Beach Post*, November 10, 1994.
18. Kathy Lewis, "Former First Family Feels Joy, Sadness," *Dallas Morning News*, November 10, 1994, p. 40a.
19. William Schneider, "Immigration Furor," *National Journal*, August 7, 1999.

20. Ibid.
21. David Elliott, "Bush Says He'll Attend Mexico's Swearing-in," *Austin American-Statesman*, November 29, 1994.
22. Ibid.
23. Peter Wallsten telephone interview with Pete Wilson, February 2006.
24. Ibid.
25. Authors' interview with John Engler, Washington, D.C., September 2005.
26. "Bush Assails GOP Candidate for Isolationism," *Austin American-Statesman*, August 15, 1995.
27. Peter Wallsten interview with T. Willard Fair, Miami, Florida, fall 2005.
28. Ibid.
29. Margaret Talev, "New Jeb Bush Aims for Blacks, Women; in His Second Run for Governor, Jeb Bush Will Try to Woo Blacks and Women," *Tampa Tribune*, November 16, 1997.
30. Peter Wallsten, "Bush, GOP Try to Bridge Racial Divide," *St. Petersburg Times*, November 23, 1997.
31. Ibid.
32. Jodi Wilgoren, "Softening Republican Immigration Stand," *Los Angeles Times*, November 23, 1997, p. A1.
33. Authors' interview with Ken Mehlman, Portland, Oregon, September 14, 2005.
34. Authors' interview with Grover Norquist, Washington, D.C., spring 2005. There is also a description of the meeting in an article by Robert Dreyfuss, "Grover Norquist: 'Field Marshal' of the Bush Tax Plan," *Nation*, May 14, 2001.
35. Authors' interview with Grover Norquist, Washington, D.C., summer 2005.
36. Matthew Dowd, "Doing the Latino Swing," *Weekly Standard*, December 3, 2001.
37. William Yardley, "Bush Details Anti-Bias Plan," *St. Petersburg Times*, November 10, 1999.
38. Ibid.
39. William Yardley, "Two Legislators Stage Sit-in in Bush's Office," *St. Petersburg Times*, January 19, 2000.
40. Ibid.
41. Peter Wallsten interviews with eyewitnesses.
42. Peter Wallsten interviews with meeting participants.
43. Ibid.
44. Peter Wallsten interview with Chris Henick, Washington, D.C., November 2005.
45. G. Robert Hillman and Wayne Slater, "Bush Stumps in Minnesota While Gore Courts Floridians," *Dallas Morning News*, November 2, 2000.
46. Ibid.

47. Authors' interview with Ken Mehlman, Washington, D.C., September 2005.

4. THE ROVE DOCTRINE

1. Donald Lambro, "Bush's Signals to the Right," *Washington Times*, January 18, 2001.
2. Ibid.
3. David E. Sanger, "Transition in Washington: The GOP Begins a Party 8 Years in the Making," *New York Times*, January 18, 2001.
4. Ibid.
5. Ibid.
6. James Carney and John F. Dickerson, "W. and the Boy Genius," *Time*, November 10, 2002.
7. A turd blossom is a Texas flower that sprouts from cow manure, an apt metaphor for Rove's pattern of surviving unpleasant situations and sometimes even thriving in them.
8. Tom Hamburger interview with Deborah Burstion-Donbraye, Columbus, Ohio, June 16, 2005.
9. Nicholas Lemann, "The Controller: Karl Rove Is Working to Get George Bush Reelected, But He Has Bigger Plans," *New Yorker*, May 12, 2003.
10. Lemann, ibid; see also Public Broadcasting Service, "Karl Rove's Life and Political Career," online chronology available at www.pbs.org/wgbh/pages/frontline/shows/architect/rove/cron.html, downloaded June, 12, 2005.
11. Lemann, "The Controller."
12. Ibid.
13. This conclusion was reached after a survey of nearly a dozen presidential historians by the authors and researcher Benjamin Weyl.
14. Dana Milbank, "Serious 'Strategery': As Rove Launches Elaborate Political Effort, Some See a Nascent Clintonian 'War Room,'" *Washington Post*, April 22, 2001.
15. Ronald Suskind, "Why Are These Men Laughing?" *Esquire*, January 2003.
16. Dan Balz and Mike Allen, "Four More Years Attributed to Rove's Strategy; Despite Moments of Doubt, Adviser's Planning Paid Off," *Washington Post*, November 7, 2004.
17. Lemann, "The Controller."
18. Ibid.
19. American Enterprise Institute, conference on "The Bush Presidency: Transition and Transformation," posted December 11, 2001; transcript available at www.aei.org/events/filter.,eventID.14/transcript.asp.
20. Tom Hamburger, Laurie McGinley, and David S. Cloud, "Influence Market: Industries that Backed Bush Now Seek Return on Investment," *Wall Street Journal*, March 6, 2001.
21. Jeanne Cummings and Tom Hamburger, "Bush Could Move to Wipe Out Clinton's Final Act," *Wall Street Journal*, January 19, 2001, p. A16.

22. Authors' interview with Ken Mehlman, Washington, D.C., October 2005.
23. Ernest Gellhorn, Wendy L. Gramm, and Susan E. Dudley, "President Expands Oversight of Federal Agency Rulemaking," *Washington Legal Foundation Legal Backgrounder*, Vol. 16, No. 51, November 16, 2001.
24. Return letters are posted by the Office of Management and Budget at www.whitehouse.gov/omb/inforeg/return_letter.html.
25. John Graham, "Memorandum for the President's Management Council," Office of Management and Budget, September 20, 2001. Memo is available online at: www.whitehouse.gov/OMB/inforeg/oira_review-process.html.
26. Authors' interview with Ken Mehlman, Portland, Oregon, September 14, 2005.
27. Tom Hamburger interview with Wayne Smith, Washington, D.C., August 2005.
28. Tom Hamburger, "Oregon Water Saga Illuminates Rove's Methods with Agencies, *Wall Street Journal*, July 30, 2003.
29. Tom Hamburger, "A Coal-Fired Crusade Helped Bring a Crucial Victory to Candidate Bush," *Wall Street Journal*, June 13, 2001.
30. Jennifer Hattan, "Dethroning King Coal," *Sierra Magazine*, November 2003.
31. Frances Williams, "WTO Tries to Break Deadlock on Medicines Access," *Financial Times*, January 28, 2003.
32. Tom Hamburger, "U.S. Flip on Patents Shows Drug Industry's Growing Clout," *Wall Street Journal*, February 6, 2003.
33. Jeffrey H. Birnbaum, "The Road to Riches Is Called K Street; Lobbying Firms Hire More, Pay More, Charge More to Influence Government," *Washington Post*, June 22, 2005.
34. Tom Hamburger interview with Stanton Anderson, Washington, D.C., August 2005.
35. Alan C. Miller, Tom Hamburger, and Julie Cart, "White House Puts the West on Fast Track for Oil, Gas Drilling," *Los Angeles Times*, August 25, 2004.
36. Tim Johnson and Curtis Morgan, "Deals Block Gulf, Glades Drilling," *Miami Herald*, May 30, 2002.
37. Larry Lippman, "President Bush Announces Deal Blocking Florida Drilling," *Palm Beach Post*, May 30, 2002.
38. Richard Simon and Edwin Chen, "Bush Curbs Oil Drilling in Florida Coast Tract," *Los Angeles Times*, May 30, 2002.
39. Sara Fritz and Lucy Morgan, "The Power of Family Politics," *St. Petersburg Times*, October 22, 2002.
40. Ibid.
41. Matt Bai, "Rove's Way," *New York Times Magazine*, October 22, 2002.
42. Ibid. This account was confirmed by Tom Hamburger interviews with Pawlenty staff, summer 2005.

43. Ibid.
44. James Carney and John F. Dickerson, "W. and the Boy Genius," *Time*, November 10, 2002.

5. THE ORGANIZED SHALL INHERIT THE EARTH
1. Peter Wallsten telephone interview with Matthew Dowd, January 2005.
2. The Southern Poverty Law Center and some national newspapers revealed that Lott had spoken on multiple occasions to a group promoting racist views, the Council of Conservative Citizens. The council called blacks genetically inferior, but in one appearance Lott lauded the group for "standing for the right principles." See Judy Pasternak, "Lott Campaigns to Segregate Himself from Extremist Group," *Los Angeles Times*, January 26, 1999.
3. Trent Lott, *Herding Cats* (New York: HarperCollins, 2005), p. 259.
4. Ibid., p. 271.
5. Associated Press, "Reaction to Bush's Announcement on Faith-Based Initiative," December 13, 2002.
6. Representative Chet Edwards, speech at a forum on the faith-based initiative sponsored by the Roundtable on Religion and Social Policy, Washington, D.C., December 14, 2004.
7. Anne Farris, newsletter of the Roundtable on Religion and Social Welfare Policy, June 24, 2003; and Tom Hamburger interview with Representative Chet Edwards, Washington, D.C., spring 2005.
8. Tom Hamburger interview with Grover Norquist, Washington, D.C., November 12, 2005.
9. "Pat Gets Paid," newsletter of Americans United for Separation of Church and State, November 2002. Separately, conservative Cal Thomas said that he was concerned about the faith-based grant program.
10. Amy Sullivan, "Faith Without Works," *Washington Monthly*, October 2004.
11. Suskind, "Why Are These Men Laughing?"
12. David Grann, "Where W. Got Compassion," *New York Times*, September 12, 1999.
13. Suskind, "Why Are These Men Laughing?"
14. Authors' interview with James Towey, Washington, D.C., February 2005.
15. White House transcript, February 1, 2002.
16. David Kuo, "Please Keep Faith," Web column, posted February 14, 2005, www.beliefnet.com/story/160/story_16092_1.html.
17. Thomas B. Edsall and Alan Cooperman, "GOP Using Faith Initiative to Woo Voters," *Washington Post*, September 15, 2002, p. A5.
18. Ibid.
19. Peter Wallsten, Tom Hamburger, and Nicholas Riccardi, "Bush Rewarded by Black Pastors' Faith," *Los Angeles Times*, January 18, 2005.
20. Kuo, "Please Keep Faith."

21. Tom Hamburger interview with Robert Wineburg, Washington, D.C., spring 2005.
22. Lin's case was accepted for investigation in late 2005 and was pending at the time of publication.
23. Tom Hamburger interview with Eugene Lin, Gaithersburg, Maryland, July 2005.
24. Tom Hamburger e-mail interview with Eugene Lin, February 26, 2006.
25. Anne Farris, "Florida Site of 16th White House Training," newsletter of the Roundtable on Religion and Social Policy, October 25, 2004.
26. Tom Hamburger telephone interview with Reverend Timothy McDonald, January 2005.
27. President George W. Bush, "President Speaks with Faith-Based and Community Leaders," New Orleans, Louisiana, January 15, 2004; official White House transcript available at www.whitehouse.gov/news/releases/2004/01/20040115-7.html.
28. Peter Wallsten, "Abortion Foes Call Bush's Dred Scott Reference Perfectly Clear," Los Angeles Times, October 13, 2004, p. A23.
29. Richard B. Schmitt, "Justice Unit Puts Its Focus on Faith," Los Angeles Times, March 7, 2005, p. A1.
30. Wallsten, Hamburger, and Riccardi, "Bush Rewarded by Black Pastors' Faith."
31. Peter Wallsten interview with Lieutenant Governor Michael Steele, Washington, D.C., January 2005.

6. DEATH BY A THOUSAND CUTS

1. Authors' interview with Ken Mehlman, Portland, Oregon, September 14, 2005.
2. Peter Wallsten interviews with rally participants and organizers, winter 2005.
3. Ibid.
4. Steve Lipman, "Values War Splitting Jews," Jewish Week, November 12, 2004.
5. Jews backed Dwight Eisenhower in large numbers because of his role in defeating the Nazis, while Nixon was credited with helping Israel defeat the Arabs in the 1973 war. Reagan was more popular among Jews in 1980 after Carter was viewed as more pro-Palestinian and weak on Iran.
6. Peter Wallsten telephone interview with David Heller, fall 2005
7. Jay Lefkowitz, "The Election and the Jewish Vote," Commentary Vol. 119, No. 2, February 1, 2005, p. 61.
8. Ibid.
9. Ibid.
10. Ralph Reed interview with PBS's Charlie Rose, The Charlie Rose Show, December 13, 2004.

11. Tom Hamburger interview with Lawrence Jacobs, Minneapolis, Minnesota, summer 2005.
12. Authors' interview with Ken Mehlman, Portland, Oregon, September 14, 2005.
13. Tom Hamburger interview with Michael Erlandson, Washington, D.C., June 2005
14. Tom Hamburger interview with Dennis White, Columbus, Ohio, June 2005.
15. Tom Hamburger and Peter Wallsten, "Parties Are Tracking Your Habits," *Los Angeles Times*, July 24, 2005. See also Jon Gertner, "The Very Personall is the Political," *New York Times*, February 15, 2004; and Matt Bai, "Who Lost Ohio," *New York Times*, November 21, 2004.
16. Peter Wallsten, "Bush Sees Fertile Soil in 'Exurbia,'" *Los Angeles Times*, June 28, 2004.
17. Ibid.
18. Ibid.
19. Ibid.
20. Ibid.
21. Ibid.
22. Tom Hamburger interview with John Perez, Columbus, Ohio, June 2005.
23. Peter Wallsten telephone interview with Sergio Bendixen, fall 2005.
24. Peter Wallsten telephone interview with Lionel Sosa, fall 2005.
25. Peter Wallsten interview with Stanley Greenberg, Washington, D.C., January 2006.

7. THE BUSINESS OF AMERICA IS BUSINESS—AND LOBBYING

1. The Powell memo is available online at www.mediatransparency.com; for a discussion of the memo's import, see also Jerry Landay, "The Powell Manifesto," a paper posted at www.mediatransparency.com; and John B. Judis, *The Paradox of American Democracy* (New York: Routledge, 2000), pp. 117–118. Academics continue to debate the significance of the Powell memo. For a summary, see Mark Schmitt, "The Legend of the Powell Memo," *American Prospect Online*, April 27, 2005, www.prospect.org/web/page.ww?section=root&name=ViewWeb&articleId=9606.
2. Coors recalls that the Powell memorandum "stirred" him up and convinced him that American business was "ignoring" a crisis. This is described in Lee Edwards, *The Power of Ideas: The Heritage Foundation at 25 Years* (Ottawa, Ill.: Jameson Books, 1998). The relevant pages are available online at www.nytimes.com/books/first/e/edwards-ideas.htm?_r=1&oref=slogin. See also John Micklethwait and Adrian Wooldridge, *The Right Nation: Conservative Power in America* (New York: Penguin Press), 2004, pp. 77–78.

3. "Buying a Movement: A Special Report by People for the American Way," 1996, available online at www.pfaw.org/pfaw/general/default.aspx?oid=2061.
4. Ibid.
5. Lee Edwards, *The Power of Ideas: The Heritage Foundation at 25 Years* (Ottawa, Ill.: Jameson Books, 1998).
6. James A. Smith, *The Idea Brokers: Think Tanks and the Rise of the New Policy Elite* (New York: Free Press, 1991), pp. 197–198.
7. "Buying a Movement."
8. Fred Barnes, "The Impresario," *Weekly Standard*, August 20, 2001.
9. Michael Baroody, "De Tocqueville and De Manufacturers," *National Association of Manufacturers Quarterly*, winter 1998.
10. Clay Risen, "Business Weak," *New Republic Online*, August 16, 2004, www.tnr.com/doc.mhtml?i=business&s=risen081604.
11. Tom Hamburger interview with Grover Norquist, Washington, D.C., November 12, 2005.
12. Ibid.
13. Tom Hamburger interview with Dirk Van Dongen, Washington, D.C., October 22, 2005.
14. Rich Lowry, "The Lost Crusade: Health Care," *National Review*, September 12, 1994.
15. John Judis, "Business and the Failure of Health Reform," *American Prospect*, March 21, 1995; see also Clay Risen, "Business Weak," *New Republic Online*.
16. Tom Hamburger, Theodore Marmor, and Jon Meacham, *Washington Monthly*, November 1994; and Lawrence Jacobs and Robert Shapiro, "Don't Blame the Public for the Failure of Health Care Reform," *Journal of Health Politics, Policy and Law*, summer 1995. See also John Judis, *The Paradox of American Democracy*, pp. 212–216.
17. Michael Weisskopf and David Maraniss, "Forging an Alliance for Deregulation; Rep. DeLay Makes Companies Full Partners in the Movement," *Washington Post*, March 12, 1995, p. A01.
18. Peter Wallsten interview with Stuart Roy, Washington, D.C., September 29, 2005.
19. Ibid.
20. Ibid.
21. The Center for Responsive Politics provides detailed reviews of partisan contribution patterns over time. The center's searchable database is available at www.crp.org.
22. Jeffrey H. Birnbaum, "A Quiet Revolution in Business Lobbying," *Washington Post*, February 5, 2005, p. 1a.
23. Tom Hamburger interviews with BIPAC staff, Washington, D.C., October 2005.

24. Tom Hamburger, "Betting to Win: In Kentucky, Business Makes Bold Bid to Play a Grass-Roots Game," *Wall Street Journal*, November 2, 2000, p. A1.

25. Tom Hamburger interview with Michael Baroody, Washington, D.C., October 2002.

26. Authors' interview with Ken Mehlman, Portland, Oregon, September 14, 2005.

27. Public Citizen's Congress Watch: *Congressional Revolving Doors: The Journey from Congress to K Street*, released July 2005; available online at www.LobbyingInfo.org.

28. Tom Hamburger interview with Grover Norquist, Washington, D.C., November 12, 2005.

29. Tom Hamburger interview with Michael Baroody, Washington, D.C., fall 2005.

30. Laurence McQuillan, "White House Lobbies for Tax Cut Plan," *USA Today*, March 5, 2003. See also Nicholas Confessore, "Welcome to the Machine: How the GOP Disciplined K Street and Made Bush Supreme," *Washington Monthly*, July/August, 2003.

31. Letter from U.S. Chamber president and CEO Tom Donohue to U.S. Chamber Board of Directors, "President's Update–Elections 2004," December 6, 2004.

8. PUT TO THE TEST: SOCIAL SECURITY

1. Congress Watch, *Ed Gillespie: The Embedded Lobbyist* (Washington, D.C.: Public Citizen, 2003), available at www.citizen.org/documents/Gillespie_June.pdf.

2. Press release from Congress Watch division of Public Citizen announcing report on Ed Gillespie, available at www.citizen.org/pressroom/release.cfm?ID=1457.

3. Jonathan Alter, "Roll over FDR," *Newsweek*, February 14, 2005.

4. Jonathan Alter, "The Bush Deal," *Newsweek* online, February 20, 2005. See also presidential papers of Dwight Eisenhower, president's personal letter to his brother, Edgar Newton Eisenhower, November 8, 1954. Eisenhower appears to accept the New Deal as part of the political firmament, writing in 1954 that if any political party attempted to abolish Social Security, unemployment insurance, labor laws, or farm programs, "You would not hear of that party again in our political history. There is a tiny splinter group, of course, that believes you can do these things. . . . Their number is negligible and they are stupid." Eisenhower letter available online at www.eisenhowermemorial.org/presidential-papers/first-term/documents/1147.cfm.

5. Alter, "The Bush Deal."

6. Lou Cannon, *Ronald Reagan: The Role of a Lifetime* (New York: Simon & Schuster, 1991) p. 206.

7. Alter, "The Bush Deal."
8. Jeffrey H. Birnbaum, "Proposal Grew from Obscure Roots," *Washington Post*, February 22, 2005.
9. Janet Hook, "Years Invested in Social Security Plan," *Los Angeles Times*, January 30, 2005.
10. Peter Wallsten interview with Grover Norquist, Washington, D.C., January 2005.
11. Peter Wallsten telephone interview with Greg Strimple, spring 2005.
12. Tom Hamburger, "Trade Groups Join Bush on Social Security; Though Individual Firms Are Wary, Nearly 100 Associations Answer a White House Battle Cry," *Los Angeles Times*, April 11, 2005, p. A1.
13. Peter Wallsten, "Group Leaves Social Security Overhaul Bloc," *Los Angeles Times*, March 15, 2005.
14. Martin Crutsinger, "Evans New CEO of Lobbying Firm," Associated Press, May 3, 2005, available online at http://news.yahoo.com/s/ap/20050503/ap_on_go_ca_st_pe/evanshttp://news.yahoo.com/s/ap/2005050/ap_on_go_ca_st_pe/evans.

9. PUT TO THE TEST: THE BENCH

1. Data from Dwight L. Morris & Associates, a firm that analyzes campaign finance data, as reported by Peter Wallsten and Warren Vieth, "Dominance on GOP Agenda," *Los Angeles Times*, February 2, 2005.
2. Wallsten and Vieth, "Dominance on GOP Agenda."
3. Tom Hamburger interview with Stanton Anderson, Washington, D.C., August 2005.
4. Jim VandeHei, "Major Business Lobby Wins Back Its Clout by Dispensing Favors," *Wall Street Journal*, September 11, 2001, p. A1.
5. The U.S. Chamber of Commerce had officially endorsed some previous Supreme Court nominees but had never trumpeted the endorsement or engaged its powerful lobbying operation on behalf of a federal judicial nominee.
6. Tom Hamburger and Peter Wallsten, "Business Lobby to Get Behind Judicial Bids," *Los Angeles Times*, January 6, 2005, p. A1.
7. Ibid.
8. Ibid.
9. Ibid.
10. Letters sent to the Center for Political Accountability by executives of the two firms in response to a center survey. The letters' content was reported in a draft Center for Political Accountability report, "The Hidden River: The Role of Trade Associations in Corporate Political Spending and Risks for Shareholders," to be released mid-2006.
11. Tom Hamburger interview with Dirk Van Dongen, Washington, D.C., September 2005.

12. Mike Allen and Helen Dewar, "GOP May Target Use of Filibuster," *Washington Post*, December 13, 2004.
13. Jeanne Cummings, "In Judge Battle Mr. Sekulow Plays a Delicate Role," *Wall Street Journal*, May 17, 2005, p. A1.
14. Donohue made the comment at a breakfast meeting with reporters sponsored by the *Christian Science Monitor*, Washington, D.C., April 25, 2005.
15. Maura Reynolds and Tom Hamburger, "Bush's Supreme Court Nominee; GOP Doubts Build Over Court Choice," *Los Angeles Times*, October 6, 2005.
16. Peter Wallsten telephone interview with Paul Weyrich, fall 2005.

Epilogue

1. Tom Hamburger interview with Grover Norquist, Washington, D.C., April 18, 2006.
2. James Traub, "Party Like It's 1994," *New York Times*, March 12, 2006.
3. See Thomas B. Edsall, "Democrats' Data Mining Stirs an Intraparty Battle," *The Washington Post*, March 8, 2006. Dean made these comments at a breakfast meeting with reporters at the Ritz-Carlton Hotel in Washington, D.C., on April 19, 2006; Tracey Schmitt's comments were made to Tom Hamburger in a telephone interview on the same date.
4. Michael Barone, "The Lessons of 1994," *U.S. News and World Report*, March 20, 2006.
5. Larry Sabato, "The Senate and Governors: The Constant is Change," Larry J. Sabato's Crystal Ball Web site, www.centerofpolitics.org/crystalball, posted March 30, 2006. See also Karen Tumulty and Mike Allen, "Republicans on the Run," *Time*, April 3, 2006.

BIBLIOGRAPHY

Barone, Michael, and Richard E. Cohen. *The Almanac of American Politics.* Washington, D.C.: The National Journal Group, 2005.

Brady, John Joseph. *Bad Boy: The Life and Politics of Lee Atwater.* Reading, Massachusetts: Addison-Wesley, 1996.

Brown, Peter. *Minority Party.* Washington, D.C.: Regnery, 1991.

Bruni, Frank. *Ambling into History: The Unlikely Odyssey of George Bush,* New York: HarperCollins, 2002.

Bush, Barbara. *A Memoir.* New York: Charles Scribner's Sons, 1994.

Bush, George H.W. *All the Best, George Bush: My Life and Other Writings.* New York: Scribner, 1999.

Bush, George W. *A Charge to Keep: My Journey to the White House.* New York: William Morrow, 1999.

Cannon, Lou. *Ronald Reagan: The Role of a Lifetime.* New York. Simon & Schuster, 1991.

Dubose, Lou, Jan Reid, and Carl Cannon. *Boy Genius: Karl Rove, The Brains Behind the Remarkable Political Triumph of George W. Bush.* New York: Public Affairs, 2003.

Easton, Nina J. *Gang of Five: Leaders at the Center of the Conservative Crusade.* New York: Simon & Schuster, 2000.

Edsall, Thomas Byrne, and Mary D. Edsall. *Chain Reaction: The Impact of Race, Rights and Taxes on American Politics.* New York: W.W. Norton, 1991.

Frank, Thomas. *What's the Matter with Kansas?* New York: Henry Holt, 2004.

Frum, David. *The Right Man: The Surprise Presidency of George W. Bush.* New York: Random House, 2003.

Hill, Steven. *Fixing Elections: The Failure of America's Winner Take All Politics.* New York: Routledge, 2002.

Hughes, Karen. *Ten Minutes from Normal.* New York: Viking, 2004.

Judis, John B. *The Paradox of American Democracy: Elites, Special Interests and the Betrayal of Public Trust.* New York: Routledge, 2001.

Judis, John, and Ruy Texeira. *The Emerging Democratic Majority.* New York: Charles Scribner's Sons, 2002.

Kessler, Ronald. *A Matter of Character: Inside the White House of George W. Bush.* New York: Penguin, 2004.

Micklethwait, John, and Adrian Wooldridge. *The Right Nation: Conservative Power in America*. New York: Penguin, 2004.

Minutaglio, Bill. *First Son: George W. Bush and the Bush Family Dynasty*. New York: Crown, 1999.

Moore, James, and Wayne Slater. *Bush's Brain: How Karl Rove Made George W. Bush Presidential*. Hoboken, N.J.: John Wiley & Sons, 2003.

Norquist, Grover G. *Rock the House: History of the New American Revolution*, Fort Lauderdale, Fla.: VYTS Press, 1995.

Phillips, Kevin. *American Dynasty: Aristocracy, Fortune and the Politics of Deceit in the House of Bush*. New York: Viking, 2004.

——. *The Emerging Republican Majority*. New Rochelle, N.Y.: Arlington House, 1969.

Rakove, Jack N. (ed.). *The Unfinished Election of 2000*. New York: Basic Books, 2001.

Schier, Steven E. *By Invitation Only: The Rise of Exclusive Politics in the United States*. Pittsburgh: University of Pittsburgh Press, 2000.

Schweitzer, Peter, and Rochelle Schweitzer. *The Bushes: Portrait of a Dynasty*. New York: Doubleday, 2004.

Smith, James A. *The Idea Brokers*. New York: Free Press, 1991.

Suskind, Ron. *The Price of Loyalty: George W. Bush, the White House and the Education of Paul O'Neil*. New York: Simon & Schuster, 2004.

Woodward, Bob. *Bush at War*. New York: Simon & Schuster, 2002.

INDEX